# The Challenge of Economic Development

# The Challenge of Economic Development

## *A Survey of Issues and Constraints Facing Developing Countries*

Norman L. Hicks

*AuthorHouse™*
*1663 Liberty Drive*
*Bloomington, IN 47403*
*www.authorhouse.com*
*Phone: 1-800-839-8640*



*First published by AuthorHouse 05/23/2011*

*ISBN: 978-1-4567-6633-7 (sc)*
*ISBN: 978-1-4567-6632-0 (dj)*
*ISBN: 978-1-4567-6631-3 (ebk)*

*Library of Congress Control Number: 2011908037*

*Cover photo by Matthew Marek*

*Printed in the United States of America*



*This book is printed on acid-free paper.*

# CONTENTS

# List of Acronyms and Abbreviations

C—Consumption
CBR—crude birth rate
CDR—crude death rate
d—discount rate (or depreciation)
D—demand
DAC—Development Assistance Committee (OECD)
DC—Developed Country
EU—European Union
FAO—Food and Agriculture Organization (UN)
FX—foreign exchange
GDP—Gross Domestic Product
GNP—Gross National Product
GNI (or GNY)—Gross National Income
HDI—Human Development Index (UN)
ICOR—Incremental Capital-Output Ratio
i—interest
I—Investment
IMF—International Monetary Fund
K—Capital stock
L—Labor force
LDC—Less Developed Country
n—population growth rate
NGO—Non-Government Organization (= non-profit)
NPV—net present value
p—price
PCY—Per Capita Income
PPP—Purchasing Power Parity
QR—quantitative restriction
S—Savings (or Supply)
SME—small and medium enterprises
t—time (in years)
TFP—Total Factor Productivity
USAID—United States Agency for International Development
UNDP—United Nations Development Program
WC—Washington Consensus
WDI—World Development Indicators (World Bank)
WDR—World Development Report (World Bank)
XR—exchange rate
YPC—per capita income
Y—income or GDP

# Introduction

We live in world where 2.6 billion people live on less than two dollars per day. Five billion people live in developing countries, over 80 percent of the world's population. Yet they produce only 40 percent of the world's output. Large parts of the world still lack access to such basic needs as clean water, adequate sanitation, and basic health care. Over nine million children die every year before they reach the age of five.

Thinking on economic development has shifted over time. Early theories stressed rapid industrialization and a heavy reliance on the public sector, but those ideas proved inadequate. Gradually, economists saw that development was a complex, multifaceted problem that combined economic issues with problems of poverty and income distribution, institution building and governance. Still, there is much we do not know and the learning process goes on.

While there have been many failures, there have also been many successes. Countries such as China, Chile, Ghana, and Korea demonstrate that good policies and strong institutions can result in remarkable progress. However, many poor countries, particularly those in Africa, continue to lag behind. The gap between the richest and the poorest countries continues to grow. Closing this gap remains a major challenge for our world, particularly as the growing population and output of developing countries accelerate tensions in trade, immigration and financial flows.

This book provides a general overview of the challenges of economic development and world poverty. It grows out of my over 40 years of experience and research in development, including experience from a long career in the World Bank, as well as an international consultant and with USAID. This experience includes extensive travel and discussion of development concerns and policy issues in developing countries, with government officials, academics, NGOs, and private businessmen. This book also reflects my lectures in economic development at George Washington University, where I teach masters degree students in international development and international relations.

While the book provides an overview of current thinking on development issues, it also reflects my personal biases and insights, which in some places differ from the standard textbooks on the subject. Rather than attempt a totally comprehensive treatment of a complex subject, I have endeavored to keep this book short, to provide the reader with an overview of the basic issues. This can provide a basic framework to which supplemental readings from the economic literature can and should be added. The book limits discussions of economic theory to only those areas that are important for economic development. It expects, however, that the reader has some understanding of basic economics, such as would be obtained from an undergraduate course.

The book makes extensive use of the World Bank, World Development Indicators data bank, which is available on line at: http://data.worldbank.org/data-catalog.

I would like to thank my various students at George Washington University who have commented on drafts and corrected errors. I would also like to thank my wife, Ann Marie, for her encouragement and insights on teaching and learning, as well as to thank several colleagues who have read and commented on drafts, particularly Lee Bettis, Maria Donoso Clark and Sander Hicks.

Norman Hicks<br>Falls Church Va.<br>December, 2010

# CHAPTER I

# THE CHALLENGE OF ECONOMIC DEVELOPMENT

"We hold these truths to be self-evident, that all men are created equal, that they are endowed by their Creator with certain unalienable Rights, that among these are Life, Liberty and the pursuit of Happiness".—T. Jefferson

"Poverty is the worst form of violence"—Gandhi

## Introduction

In 1980, Ecuador and Korea had about the same level of development, as measured by per capita income. In 2008, Korea's income was about four times that of Ecuador. Korea's income was half that of Argentina in 1980; twice that of Argentina in 2008. In Haiti, per capita income has fallen by one-half over the same period (see Table 1.1), while in China, per capita income has increased 10 fold. While countries like Mozambique and Philippines have grown, their growth has not been as fast as that of the United States, so that the gap between them has widened. Why can one country do so well, and others, equally endowed with natural resources, do so badly? This is a great mystery which we will examine in this book, but not fully resolve. We will look at the evidence, the theories, the ideas of economic development to see what works, and what doesn't, and why. But in the end, we will have to admit, there is much that economists cannot explain about economic development, and the quest for understanding still goes on.

**Table 1.1 Gross National Income (PPP $) in 1975 prices, selected countries**

| Country Name | YR1980 | YR1985 | YR1990 | YR1995 | YR2000 | YR2005 | YR2008 |
|---|---|---|---|---|---|---|---|
| China | 523 | 813 | 1099 | 1847 | 2664 | 4076 | 5511 |
| Haiti | 2133 | 1807 | 1638 | 1156 | 1190 | 1068 | 1088 |
| Korea, Rep. | 5544 | 7547 | 11383 | 15761 | 18730 | 22783 | 25498 |
| Mozambique | 440 | 312 | 400 | 403 | 506 | 677 | 791 |
| Argentina | 10089 | 8225 | 7472 | 9599 | 10292 | 10815 | 13248 |
| Philippines | 2618 | 2147 | 2385 | 2368 | 2587 | 2927 | 3244 |
| Ecuador | 5794 | 5427 | 5501 | 5658 | 5491 | 6737 | 7402 |
| United States | 25506 | 28553 | 31942 | 33839 | 39111 | 41873 | 43179 |

Source: World Bank, WDI data bank

## The State of the World

Despite progress, the world's economic output is dominated by a few rich countries. In 2007, there were about 7 billion people in the world, but only 16% lived in what we call a high income or rich country (mostly Europe, Japan, North America). These 16% produce about 58% of total world production (see Table 1.2). The poorest of the developing countries, or low income countries, account for 20% of world population but produce only 3% of world output.

**Table 1.2 World Population and GDP**

| | Population | | GDP, 2007, $ trillion | |
|---|---|---|---|---|
| | 2007, billions | Growth 1990-2007 | X-rate conversion | PPP conversion |
| World | 6.6 | 1.5 | 54.6 | 66.0 |
| High income | 1.1(16%) | .3 | 40.3 | 38.3(58%) |
| Developing | 5.6(84%) | .6 | 14.3 | 27.9(42%) |
| Middle Income | 4.3 | .6 | 13.4 | 26.0 |
| Low Income | 1.3(20%) | 1.6 | .8 | 2.0(3%) |

Source World Bank, WDI data, rev 8/2009. Totals may not add due to rounding. Shares are calculated from the unrounded data.

On average, world per capita income is about $9400, but this ranges from $34,000 in the rich countries to $1400 in the poorest (see Table 1.2)[1]. Furthermore, growth has been uneven, as noticed above. The high income countries grew at an average rate of 1.8% per annum during 1990-2007,

1 All per capita income figures quoted here are in US dollars, converted to reflect purchasing power parity (PPP). For explanation of the PPP conversion approach, and why it is important, see box.

while the developing countries grew at 3.0%. However, within this group, there were disparities. The middle income developing countries average 3.3%, indicating significant progress in closing the gap between themselves and the rich or high income countries. However, the low income countries averaged only 1.9%, indicating that they were merely keeping the same relative distance and not closing the gap (in absolute terms, of course, the gap increases). In terms of regions, the largest growth took place during this period in South Asia, led by China and India, and in East Asia/ Pacific. Sadly, the slowest growth happened in Sub-Saharan Africa, one of the poorest regions of the world. Per capita income here had an average growth of only .9% per annum over the period (see Table 1.3).

The real question is not whether there are gaps between countries and/or regions, but whether or not the gap between people is widening or narrowing. The rapid growth of South and East Asia comes from two of the world's largest countries, China (1.3 billion people) and India (1.1 billion). These two countries alone represent over one-third of the world's people. Thus, while the disparity in income between *countries* may be widening, it is not necessary true that the disparity between *people* is widening. In fact, it may even be narrowing. Milanovic in his study in 2005 called this the "mother of all inequality disputes"[2]. Income inequality can change both between countries and within countries, and between country inequality needs to be weighted by the population size of the country. His conclusion, as of 2000, was that there was about a 10% improvement in income distribution in twenty years, but most of this was caused by China. Continued rapid growth by China and India during the present decade probably means that this trend has continued.

## Measuring Welfare

The preceding section has measured "development" by the use of per capita income, or per capita Gross Domestic Product. The development of national income accounts during the 1930s allowed economists to measure total output of an economy's goods and services. Divided by total population, the resulting measure of GDP per capita produces a way of comparing countries level of output. However, the GDP concept was never meant to

2 Branko Milanovic, *Worlds Apart* (Princeton University Press, 2005).

measure "welfare" or the well being of the population. The problem is the interpretation of per capita GDP figures as a measure of relative welfare. Thus, many people criticize the World Bank and other institutions for improperly focusing on per capita income and using it as a welfare measure. But the problem is, what is "welfare"? And how is it measured?

Intrinsically, every single person has some "welfare function" which is the value she/he places on various items that are important in making her/him better off, or more simply "happier". These may range from the pure economic to include many non-economic and difficult to measure aspects of life, such as personal freedom, having good health, being able to participate in a democratic political system, freedom from arbitrary arrest, being able to attain a full education and make use of one's "capabilities". Thus, a person's welfare function might be expressed, where W is total welfare, as:

$$W = a_1 YP + a_2 Health + a_3 Educ + a_4 Freedom + a_5\ Vote \ldots.$$

Where YP is personal income, Health is a measure of a person's health, Educ is a measure of education, Freedom is a measure of political freedom, and Vote is a measure of political participation, and so on with the total number of elements in the function not yet fully defined. In fact, the total number could be close to infinite. The problem is the "a" coefficients, which if we had them, would tell how to get a weighted average of all these components and produce an estimate of W, total personal welfare. In theory, we could then add individual welfare functions and measure total national welfare.

In fact, we know that income itself does not make a person happy. Income allows us to purchase the things we think will make us happier, clothes, food, housing, even education and better health. As Paul Streeten has pointed out, focusing on income confuses "ends" with "means". Income is the means to an end, which is better welfare, or perhaps the elimination of poverty.

Striving for a better measure of welfare, economists have suggested various alternatives. One, put forward by economists William Nordhaus and James Tobin[3], would be to adjust GDP to take out the "bads" from the

---

3 See Norman Hicks and Paul Streeten, "The Search for a Basic Needs Yardstick", *World Development* 7 (June, 1979) pp.567-580, for a fuller discussion and the citation for Nordhaus and Tobin.

"goods" and services. Thus, one would eliminate from GDP the "regrettable necessities" of life, but particularly those things which do not directly raise welfare. For instance, if crime is high in country A, there are high costs for private and public police protection. Country B, without crime, does not have to undertake these expenditures. If GDP per capita is the same in A and B, welfare is definitely higher in B, since they are not spending money on crime protection (and thus have more for something else). The same argument could be made for defense expenditures, pollution abatement, time lost commuting to work, cost of heating in temperate climates, etc. The problem with this concept is that there is no end of possible adjustments. Would one take out food expenditures as a "regrettable necessity"? In the end, all one would be left with is luxury goods. Several attempts have been made to construct adjusted GDPs, subtracting economic and social costs, and adding in non-market activities, such as housework. These have not been accepted as improved measures of GDP or welfare because of the arbitrariness of the adjustments. Adjustments to GDP that measure the depletion of natural resources, particularly oil and other mineral resources, have been easier to construct although rarely used.

However, in recent years there has been growing interest in calculating a GDP figure that reduces GDP by the amount of environmental destruction, including the use of natural resources and the cost of pollution abatement. Since the use of natural resources is a transformation of an existing natural asset into a financial stream, it is not an addition to national wealth, so it is wrong to count resource use as a net income. These "Green GDP" calculations, however, face serious problems assigning values to ecological destruction, and consequently have not gone much beyond the methodology stage.

An alternative focus on measuring development is to focus more on meeting "basic needs", such has health care, nutrition, education, water, etc. Many people find that social indicators of development give a better view of progress, and can give different insights as to the stage of development. Table 1.4 shows some social indicators for selected countries. One can easily see that while social indicators are somewhat correlated with the level of per capita income, there are significant divergences. Sri Lanka and Angola have about the same level of per capita income but infant mortality in Agnola is 116, while in Sri Lanka it is 17. In fact, the level of infant mortality in Sri Lanka is lower than that of Brazil, despite Brazil having a per capita income twice as high.

| Table 1.4 Selected Social Indicators | | | | | |
|---|---|---|---|---|---|
| | Gross National Income (PPP) 2007, per capita | Infant Mortality per 1000 births (2006) | Adult Literacy (% ) | Physicians per 100,000 pop. | Access to Improved Water Source (% of pop.) |
| United States | 45890 | 7 | 99 | 256 | 99 |
| Brazil | 9510 | 20 | 89 | 115 | 91 |
| China | 5430 | 19 | 91 | 151 | 88 |
| Angola | 4400 | 116 | 67 | 8 | 51 |
| Sri Lanka | 4200 | 17 | 91 | 55 | 82 |
| Note: data from World Bank, WDI, or UN HDR; data for 2007 or latest available year | | | | | |

Disparities in meeting basic needs, or human development, have led people to suggest that some sort of composite index of social indicators would serve as a better measure of "development" than just GDP or GNI per capita. Several authors have put forward synthetic composite indicies, but they all have the same problem; how do we know what combination of social indicators is better than just per capita income (PCY)? The most popular composite index is the UN's Human Development Index, published every year since 1993 in their Human Development Report. This index combines three variables: a measure of education achievement, life expectancy (being a measure of health), and per capita income. Each is given one-third weight in the total index. Rankings of countries by the HDI are different than rankings by per capita income (see Table 1.4 below). For instance, the U.S. is ranked 9$^{th}$ in the world on the basis of PCY, but 13th on the basis of HDI, indicating that the US underperforms relative to its income. Likewise, Sri Lanka and Korea rank somewhat higher on HDI compared to their PCY rankings, while Brazil ranks somewhat lower. However, the rankings are not that much different from each other, in part because per capita income is part of the HDI, and in part because education and health indicators are correlated with PCY.

| Table 1.5 Countries Ranted by GDP per capita and the UN Human Development Index, 2007 | | |
|---|---|---|
| Country | HDI rank | GDP rank |
| Norway | 1 | 5 |
| United States | 13 | 9 |
| Korea | 26 | 35 |
| Brazil | 75 | 79 |
| China | 92 | 102 |
| Sri Lanka | 102 | 116 |
| Mozambique | 172 | 169 |
| Source: UN, Human Development Report, 2009. Data are for 2007 | | |

But what does this tell us? There is little or no rationale why development or welfare should be an equally weighted index of these three variables, and so it is not clear what insights the HDI brings. It might be equally valid to have an index of five variables combined with differing weights, and include such items as political freedom and democracy. Recognizing this, the HDI has spawned a whole subset of similar indicies, that focus on such aspects as gender issues and poverty.

## Welfare as Happiness

Jefferson wrote in the Declaration of Independence that "life, liberty and the pursuit of happiness" were rights to which every man and woman was entitled. Perhaps happiness then is a general index of welfare, and we can simply ask people if they are "happy" or not, measured not by some absolute scale, but by their own intrinsic scale. This has been done periodically in various surveys, such as the World Values Surveys, which asks such questions as "How satisfied are you with your life" or "How happy are you with your life", and asks respondents to rank their happiness on a scale of one to ten. The surprising results from these surveys indicate that people in richer countries are not much happier than people in poorer countries, except at the bottom end of the income scale. This effect was first noted by Richard Easterlin, in comparisons of happiness in Japan between 1950 and 1970, when perceived happiness actually declined over the period. Similar effects of stable happiness despite rapid per capita income growth have also been found in the US and the UK.[4]

International comparisons are difficult, because different surveys ask somewhat different questions, and often use samples not representative of the entire population. Deaton reports on the results of the Gallup survey (see fig. 1.1). Here we see that at low levels of income, there is a substantial increase in happiness with increments to income, but the impact is reduced at higher levels (although still positive). Even so, there are some big anomalies. At the same levels of income, people in Denmark are signficiantly happier than people in Hong Kong, and people in Saudi

---

4 See Carol Graham and Stefano Pettinato, *Happiness and Hardship*, Washington DC: Brookings, 2002., p.3.

Arabia are much happier than people in Puerto Rico. People in Brazil are about as happy (on average) as people in the U.S., even though the U.S. has four times the per capita income.

Fig. 1.1

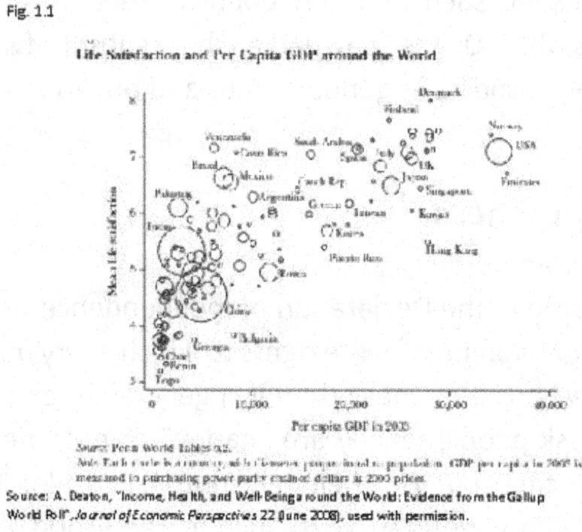


Source: A. Deaton, "Income, Health, and Well-Being around the World: Evidence from the Gallup World Poll", *Journal of Economic Perspectives* 22 (June 2008), used with permission.

Deaton also notes that people are unhappier in countries that are growing, compared to stable countries. Within countries, Graham finds that the richer groups are generally happier than the poorer, but the middle class are often the unhappiest. In the US, men are happier than women, although this is a reversal of the situation in 1970[5].

So what are we to conclude? The growth process is apt to make people unhappy, and when they finally do arrive at a situation with more income, they are likely not to be nuch happier than when they had a lower income. The only people that seem to be markedly better off, and happier, are those that move out of severe poverty. Why should we "push" development if it not going to make people happier? I give three reasons:

- Reducing severe poverty in the world clearly makes people happier and better off, and is worth concentrating on those very poor countries in order to help eliminate world poverty and human costs of deprivation, malnutrition and disease;

---

5 Angus Deaton, "Income, Health, and Well-Being around the World: Evidence from the Gallup World Poll", *Journal of Economic Perspectives* 22 (June 2008), pp. 53-72.

- As economists, we answer the question "how can we develop rapidly" to increase material wealth; we do not promise that this material wealth will make them happier; and
- The whole issue of happiness is outside the realm of economics, and best left to psychologists, sociologists and others.

## Annex: Purchasing Power Parity

Comparing countries per capita incomes requires putting estimates of national income in national currencies into a common denominator, traditionally US dollars. The traditional way is to simply convert a local currency number (e.g. Pesos per capita) to an equivalent in dollars using the current exchange rate, The problem with this approach is that it understates the purchasing power of the currency of a poor country, where typically wages are low. For instance, a haircut (man's) in Washington DC may cost $15.00, and in India 100 rupees (Rs). However, with an exchange rate of 45 Rs./ $, this works out to costing only the equivalent of $2.22, a real bargain.

India's per capita GDP in 2008 is about 48,000 rupees. If we divide by the official exchange rate for 2008 of 44, this would produce a per capita income in US dollars of about $1090. But if Rs. 100 buys a haircut worth $15, then the "haircut" exchange rate is 100/15 is 6.7, not 44. At the "haircut" exchange rate, the per capita income of India would be $7, 164. The problem arises because only a small part of India (and the US) GDP enters into trade, and thereby affects the exchange rate. The exchange rate represents and equilibrium in the demand and supply of "tradables". It is not affected by such non tradables as haircuts, government services, education and other services which are big part of GDP.

To adjust for these disparities, we use the concept of purchasing power parity. Studies are undertaken which look at the prices of comparable products across countries, and the ratio of their prices compared to the official exchange rate. In a sense, every product has its own exchange rate vis a vis the same product in another country. This allows for the construction of a Purchasing Power Parity (PPP) conversion index, and an estimate of the GDP per capita in PPP terms. For India, for instance, in 2008, the PPP per capita GDP is $2972, not $1090, roughly three times the standard exchange rate conversion figure. This gives us a much better idea of the gap between rich and poor countries, and reduces the exaggeration of the gap caused by the exchange rate conversion.

The table below gives a comparison of selected countries with the per capita incomes in standard exchange rate conversion and PPP adjusted. For the poorest countries, the adjustment is quite substantial. Countries like Kenya and Lesotho almost double their measured per capita income, although they still remain well below the level of the richer countries, such as Japan and the UK. The adjustment for middle-income countries, such as Brazil is much less, and for some of the richer countries, such as Japan and United Kingdom, the PPP conversion actually lowers their per capita income. This reflects the fact that many non-traded goods and services in these countries are relatively expensive when compared to the US, and the US remains the comparator country. Thus, there is no PPP conversion for the US, since good and services in other countries are being valued at US prices, while US output is already at US prices.

**Table 1.6. Per Capita GDP: PPP vs Exchange Rate Conversion, 2008 (US $ per capita)**

| | exchange rate conversion | PPP conversion. |
|---|---|---|
| United States | 46716 | 46716 |
| United Kingdom | 43088 | 35445 |
| Korea, Rep. | 19115 | 27939 |
| Japan | 38443 | 34099 |
| India | 1094 | 2972 |
| China | 3263 | 5962 |
| Kenya | 895 | 1590 |
| Brazil | 8400 | 10296 |
| Lesotho | 804 | 1588 |

Source: World Bank, WDI

# CHAPTER II
# GROWTH AND DEVELOPMENT

"I've been rich, and I've been poor, and believe me honey, rich is better"—Sophie Tucker

## Roots

Before World War II, there was no such thing as a "developing country." Major European powers and the United States had colonies and territories that they controlled overseas. Other countries, such as most of Latin and Central America, Liberia, Haiti, Ethiopia, and Thailand were either always independent countries, or had succeeded in escaping from colonial domination. The colonial system provided cheap raw materials for the industrialized countries and ready markets for products. Colonial territories were, in fact, prevented from industrializing.

The philosophical basis of WWII was the fight against the non-democratic domination of the Axis powers over places like Indonesia, Burma, Algeria, and Morocco. Would the UN allow the former colonial powers to resume their control over their former colonies? Wasn't the whole colonial system anachronistic if the Allied powers had been fighting for freedom from Axis domination of various peoples? Thus, the post WWII era was one in which there was growing pressure in colonies for independence, and growing awareness among industrialized countries of the legitimate demands for independence. The number of independent countries in the world grew exponentially. In 1945, the UN was formed and had only 51 members; by 1970 the number had reached 127. Today it has 192. India, which had been agitating for independence since the early 1900s, and particularly since the 1920s under the leadership of Mahatma

Gandhi, was one of the first, becoming independent in 1947, with the Moslem dominated areas being divided off into the independent country of Pakistan. In Africa and Asia, a succession of leaders of independence movements came forward. Many were jailed as "communists" or subversives by the colonial powers, and then eventually released to take part in national elections and/or eventually became major political leaders (e.g. Kwame Nkrumah in Ghana, Cheddi Jagan in Guyana, Leopold Senghor in Senegal, Gandhi in India, and more recently Nelson Mandela in South Africa).

The new group of developing countries even struggled for a proper name. Initial efforts labeled them as "poor" or "backward" countries, but those terms were considered pejorative, and was followed by "under-developed", "less-developed", and finally "developing", the latter term being seen as more optimistic and forward looking.[6] Alternatively, they became known as the "Third World", where the OECD countries were the first world, and the Soviet Union, China and their satellites were the second world, although no body called them that. The world became sharply divided into two competing groupings after 1947, the western bloc and the communist bloc. The result was competition for influence in the neutral developing countries by both blocs, which in turn led to increased interest in development assistance for these less developed countries. At the same time, the US organized the Marshall Plan to provide emergency assistance for the recovery of Europe, fearing that otherwise the communist bloc would gain preeminence, and that a strong Europe would be a defensive line against the Soviet Union and its allies. The Marshall Plan was unparalleled in history, in that it provided unrequited transfers of up to 3% of US GDP per year to European countries, and provided the financing that did indeed generate a rapid recovery. The success of the Marshall Plan, in fact, led to the assumption that the same kind of transfers to developing countries could achieve the same kind of results.

Within developing countries, there was much talk of socialism and a socialist model of development. Many African and Asia leaders were Influenced as students by left-wing teaching in European universities, as

---

6 In this volume, we will use the term LDC for less-developed county, and DC for developed country, as well as the term "developing" countries for the LDCs.

well as the apparent success of the Soviet Union in rapid industrialization, and returned to their home lands convinced of the need to adopt a form of socialism for the rapid development of their countries. This meant the creation of Five Year Plans, building state-owned industries, expansion of public infrastructure and education, limiting private enterprise, but also often limiting political opposition and discussion. Many developing countries, particularly those with strong socialist governments, tended to learn toward the Soviet bloc. However, the majority considered themselves independent and became members of the G-77, an informal grouping of "non-aligned" developing countries. Among the ex-colonies, the general thinking was that colonialism had retarded development, and it was the function of government to achieve rapid industrialization as a way of accelerating growth, and bridging the gap between themselves and the richer developed countries.

## Early Thinking on Growth

Causal empiricism of the state of developing countries led to the observation that they were abundantly endowed with labor resources, but critically short of capital. The problem was summarized in terms of a a "vicious circle" or more elegantly, a "low level equilibrium trap". The thinking was that (see diagram) the low incomes of the developing countries mean low savings, and low savings limited the amount of investment, which in turn limited the growth of the capital stock, and therefore limited the growth of output. The way out of the "trap" would be to supplement domestic savings with foreign aid, or foreign savings, leading to an increase in investment, etc.(see Fig. 2.1). Of course, this assumed that developing countries could efficiently use foreign aid to raise investment, that all foreign aid would add to the capital stock (and not be consumed), and that these investments at the margin would have the same productivity as existing investments. These turned out to be heroic assumptions.

**Fig 2.1: The Vicious Circle or Low-Level Equilibrium Trap: An Illustration**

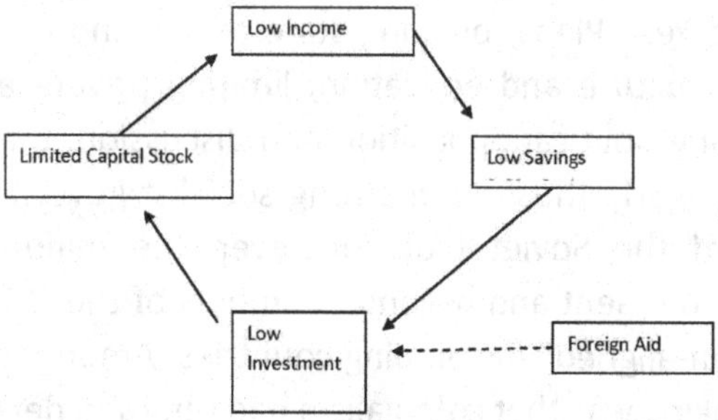

One of the most influential books of the time was Walt Rostow's "The Stages of Economic Growth: A Non-Communist Manifesto"(1960)[7]. This book developed the low level equilibrium trap theory to a higher level of sophistication, by comparing countries to an airplane which accelerates down a runway and then, once it has sufficient speed, takes off to a higher level. Rostow claimed (with little or no empirical evidence) that countries went through five stages: First "traditional society", with low savings and zero growth. Second, a stage of "Pre-Conditions for Growth" where savings and capital is increased. Third, the sudden acceleration of growth and output during A "Take Off to Self Sustaining Growth". Fourthly, a leveling off during the "Drive to Maturity", and finally the last stage (as per the US model), the stage of "High Mass Consumption." Again, the process could be accelerated by injections of foreign capital which would push countries more rapidly toward the "take-off" stage, and therefore be less likely to fall under the sway of anti-US Marxist ideologies. Furthermore, the end result would be conditions for "self-sustaining" growth,that would not require outside assistance. This was a very influential book, written by a man who was influential in foreign policy in the 1960s, and provided a very strong rational for a major increase of foreign aid by the US under the Kennedy Administration. However, researchers found little or no evidence that in fact countries go through these stages, when examining, for instance, the economic history of such now developed countries as the US, the UK or Germany. The book and the theory were soon cast onto

---

7 W.W. Rostow, *The Stages of Economic Growth: A Non-Communist Manifesto,* Cambridge:Cambridge University Press,1960, esp. Chapter 2.

the scrapheap of defunct theories, but in fact there was a strong element of truth to what Rostow said, as we shall see later.

Fig 2.2 Rostow's Stages of Growth

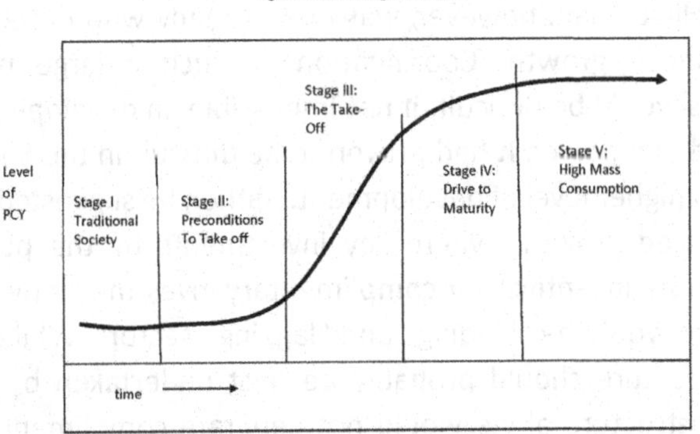


## Externalities, Balanced Growth, and the "Big Push"

Many economists realized the problem was more complicated than achieving a Rostovian "take-off". One of the most influential of these was Paul Rosenstein-Rodan (19 43), whose seminal article addressed the development needs of Southern Europe[8]. He noted that anyone making an investment generates "externalities", in that there are benefits to society that are not captured by the investor. For instance, if I invest in and establish a steel industry, a host of industries will arise that use steel, and benefit from having a secure source of steel. Society's benefit from the steel mill, or the social benefit, exceeds my private benefit, and since I cannot capture these external benefits, there is less incentive to invest. Furthermore, I will not invest in producing steel unless there is demand for steel in the economy, but without a steel industry, there is no incentive for others to invest in steel using industries. Thus, various industries are complimentary to others, and to have rapid industrialization it would be necessary to invest in a wide range of industries all at once, so that these externalities and complementarities could be realized. No private investor could undertake such a wide range of investments, so the role falls to the

[8] P. N. Rosenstein-Rodan, "Problems of Industrialization of Eastern and South-Eastern Europe" *Economic Journal* (June-Sept. 1943).

public sector. What is needed, therefore, is a "big push" where simultaneous investments are made many industries, as well as the necessary supporting infrastructure (electricity, transport, water). Ragnar Nurske[9] and others termed this "balanced growth".

Albert Hirschman, however, was one of many who raised questions about balanced growth. Coordination of such a large program of investments would be difficult, if not impossible, in developing countries with limited manpower. It had proven to be difficult in the Soviet Union, which had a higher level of development. Rather, he suggested a program of "unbalanced growth" where key investments by the public sector would generate incentives for complimentary investments by the private sector. There would be "leading" and "lagging" sectors. While he argued that infrastructure should probably be best undertaken by the public sector, infrastructure alone would not generate complimentary private sector investments. It was also necessary that the public sector take the lead in investments in "directly productive activities" (DPA).

## Industrialization as Import Substitution

The colonies had been primarily suppliers of raw materials, and even the independent developing countries were generally exporters of primary products: agricultural products—coffee, cocoa, tea, cotton, rubber, bananas, or mineral products: oil, copper, tin, bauxite. Industrialization was seen as key to "modernization", but also it was seen as important to end post-colonial ties with developed countries and become independent. Because developed countries imposed high tariffs on manufactured goods, and low tariffs on raw materials, there was reduced incentive to move from a supplier of raw materials to producer and exporter of manufacturers. Furthermore, some economists (Raul Prebisch, Hans Singer) argued that there was built in bias in the trading system: prices of raw materials were competitively determined, whereas manufactured goods prices were monopolistically determined. Manufactured goods prices would remain high, but there was a secular trend for raw material prices to decline. Thus, the terms of trade, (TOT) the prices of LDC primary

9 Ragnar Nurkse, "Some International Aspects of the Problem of Economic Development", *The American Economic Review* (May, 1952).

exports ($P_x$) compared to manufactured imports ($P_m$) would decline over time and move adversely against the LDC. Thus, the purchasing power of each unit of exports would erode over time (the so called Prebisch-Singer Hypothesis).

$$TOT = P_x / P_m$$

This theory, that the terms of trade would erode overtime, has been hotly debated, and is still not clear whether it is true or not. In addition, the simple terms of trade does not allow for productivity changes.

The discussion of terms of trade formed part of a more radical "dependency theory", which held that developing countries in the "periphery" were dependent on the rich countries of the "center". Such dependency held these countries in a permanent state of underdevelopment that could be broken only by breaking the trade and other ties between the two groups. In a way, is was a reaction against the idea that there was a natural tendency for countries to proceed through stages of growth.

The net result of these ideas was "export pessimism", the idea that LDCs could not embark on an industrialization strategy based on manufactured exports because markets in developed countries were closed or had prohibitively high tariffs. Rather, the idea was to embark on a strategy of import substitution industrialization (ISI), where high tariffs and quantitative limits on imported manufactures would encourage the investment by the private sector in industries that would provide substitutes, domestically manufactured goods to replace imported ones. Thus, the industrialization strategy for most countries focused on large public sector industries and private industries benefitting from protection from imports. The idea was that industries needed protection as a temporary measure, until they could achieve the economies that would enable them to compete directly with imports. This is the so-called "infant industry" argument. The reality was that protected industries often remained inefficient, in part because they were often serving a limited market, and lacked the technology or management expertise that would drive down costs. It was often easier and more productive to influence political leaders to keep high tariffs and other import restrictions in place.

## The Harrod-Domar model

The early formulation of a "growth model" was based on the supremacy of capital as the driving force. A standard production function assume three factors of production; land, labor and capital (for which we have their related income streams; rent, wages and profits/interest). Thus, a simple production function becomes:

$Y = f(A, L, K)$; where Y is GDP, A is land, L is labor and K is the capital stock, and f indicates some functional form that is not identified.

However, in a growth context, land is fixed and does not grow. Therefore, the growth of output y, is a function only of the growth of the labor force, l, and the growth of the capital stock, k., or

$y = f(l,k)$

Early economists considered developing countries to be highly "dualistic"; that is they consisted of a backward rural sector with low productivity and redundant workers, and a modern, urban sector based on more modern industrial techniques. The problem was seen as providing capital so that the redundant workers in the rural areas could be brought into the urban areas and made more productive. Thus, labor was not a constraint on development, and the model got further simplified into

$y = f(k)$, and even more simply:

$Y = a(K)$; implying a direct, linear relationship between capital and output, with no diminishing returns. Graphically, "a" is the slope of the line showing various levels of capital and output (see Fig. 2.3). Alternatively, we can define "v" as the incremental-capital output ratio, which is the ratio between the change in capital stock and output (the inverse of the "a" coefficient):

$v = \Delta K / \Delta Y$

**Fig. 2.3: The simple Y=aK model**

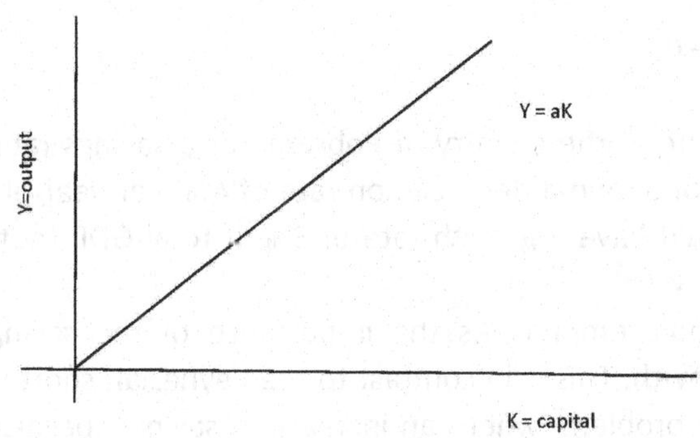


In the long run, however, we hold that output is a function of the capital stock. The capital stock, is the accumulation of past investment. Thus, the capital stock in period t is the sum of the previous period's capital stock, minus the depreciation (d) of this stock, and new investment, I. Thus:

$K_t = I_t + (1\text{-}d)\ K_{t-1}$, but since we know in equilibrium:

S = I, ; savings (S) must equal investment, so we can write this as:

$K_t = S_t + (1\text{-}d)\ K_{t-1}$,

If we subtract $K_{t-1}$ from both sides, we get the increment to the capital stock Δ K (= $K_{t-}K_{t-1}$), where Δ signifies change:

$\Delta K_t = S_t\text{-}d\ K_{t-1.}$

Thus, the size of the capital stock depends on savings and the rate of depreciation, and the size of the capital stock will determine the size of overall output. More savings, more capital. More capital, more output. With the magic of algebraic manipulation, plus some simplifying assumptions, the above can be shown to yield the famous Domar growth equation, namely:

ΔY/Y = (s/v)-d ; where s is S/Y, the savings rate, v is the ICOR and d is the depreciation rate.

Defining g as the growth rate of Y (= ΔY/Y), we have the full Harrod-Domar formula:

$$g = (s/v) - d$$

To illustrate, if the country of Pobreza has a savings rate of 21% of GDP, a ICOR of 3, and a depreciation rate of 4% (per year of the capital stock), it would have a growth rate of 3% of total GDP (not per capita income).

The formula emphasizes the importance of the savings rate for long term growth. This is in contrast to the Keynesian short term macro management problem, where an increase in savings, because it meant a commensurate decline in consumption, meant a fall in output and more unemployment. For Keynes high savings was an impediment to full employment which could only be offset by greater government (deficit) spending. Keynes was not concerned with longer term growth but rather returning to full employment in a situation where there was excess capital capacity and unemployed labor. For Harrod-Domar, savings is the key to growth, since it determines the level of capital accumulation.

If Pobreza is an open economy, the rate of savings can be supplemented by foreign capital inflows, F, so that :

$$I = S + F$$

And the growth equation has to be rewritten as:

$$g = (i/v) - d$$

Thus, Pobreza has a 21% savings rate, but receives 3% of GDP in foreign capital inflows (foreign aid, private investment), and with the same values for v and d as before, it would be able to reach a 4% growth rate. Since the ICOR is 3, every 3% of GDP added to the investment rate raises the growth rate by one percentage point.

In actual practice, the formula is often written without depreciation, since depreciation rates are difficult to estimate, particularly in developing countries. Thus, we get the simple Harrod-Domar formula, or:

$$g = i/v'$$

(but since g is $\Delta Y/Y$, and $v = I/\Delta Y$, this dissolves into a tautology). Thus a country with a 25% investment rate and an ICOR of 5, would grow at 5%. In this case, the ICOR has to be calculated without allowing for depreciation, so it is labeled v', indicating it is not the same as v in the previous equation. Using this equation gives some possible misleading results, however, since it implies with zero growth one has zero investment. In fact, even with zero growth, there will always be investment to replace the existing capital stock (the missing depreciation factor).

The beauty of the Harrod-Domar(HD) formula, and what made it so popular, was that it provides a convenient way to estimate foreign aid "requirements'. If f = F/Y (foreign inflows to GDP) then the full Harrod-Domar equation can be rewritten as:

$$g = (s + f)/ v - d \text{ ; and}$$

$$f = gv - s - dv$$

If the Government of Pobreza issues a Five Year Plan calling for a 5% growth rate, then with the same parameters as before, it can show that it "needs" a capital inflow of 6% of GDP to attain its goals. e.g.:

$$f = 5 \times 3 - 21 + 4 \times 3$$

If it is now only receiving 3%, it can make an urgent appeal for a doubling of foreign aid (although this gap could also be filled with private capital as well).

In national income accounting, the domestic resource gap always equals the foreign resource gap, so that:

$F = I - S = M - X$; where M equals imports (goods and services) and X equals exports.

Thus, there are potentially two "gaps", and the overall gap can be estimated either as S - I or M - X[10].

[10] The two-gap model was extensively developed and applied by Hollis Chenery and Alan Stout "Foreign Assistance and Economic Development" *American*

The problems with this approach center on the use of a fixed ICOR. In reality, ICORs are not a fixed coefficient that are stable over time, like the force of gravity or the expansion coefficient of copper. The reason is that investment efficiency varies widely among countries, and often substantial resources are placed by governments in projects that yield little or no return (prestige projects, Presidential planaces, steel mills, etc.), Even aside from this factor, the pay back from investments is often not immediate. It may take as long as five years to build a dam or a bridge, and the return on this investment may last 20-30 years. One way around this problem is to estimate ICORs over a long period of time, and with a lag. Even so, there are problems, as shown in Table 2.1, which shows ICORs estimated for some selected countries for the period 1990-2004. The results vary widely, from fairly reasonable rates of 3.6 and 4.1 for China and India, respectively, to absurdly high levels of 52.5 for Armenia, and even negative values (-18.7) for Zimbabwe.

**Table 2.1: Incremental Capital-Output Ratios for Selected Countries, (1990 -2004)**

| Country | I/Y (1990-2003) | g (1990-2004) | ICOR |
|---|---|---|---|
| Albania | 19.36 | 2.5 | 7.7 |
| Armenia | 21.51 | .41 | 52.5 |
| Argentina | 16.80 | 3.30 | 5.51 |
| China | 36.45 | 10.12 | 3.6 |
| India | 23.74 | 5.75 | 4.1 |
| Zimbabwe | 16.81 | -.9 | -18.7 ?? |

source :calculated from WB, WDI

While simplistic calculations of aid requirements have fallen into disfavor, and aid agencies and others focus more on root problems of development that affect the low productivity of investment: incentives for private investment, governance, the legal system, the quality of public investment, and public sector programs that invest in the poor, such as education and health. However, the technique is resurfaces whenever the question arises ". . . but how much money do they need?", particularly when the issue is rebuilding from some natural or economic crisis.

*Economic Review,* 1966. For even more extensive criticism of it, see William Easterly, *The Elusive Quest for Growth* (MIT Press, 2001).

## The evolution of development thinking: Fads and "Magic Bullets"

Once it became clear that investment was not enough, development thinking evolved into a search for the "magic bullet" that would launch development. At various times, various "gurus" have advocated focusing on (among others):

- Import substitution
- Population control
- Agriculture/ rural development
- Appropriate Technology
- Trade liberalization
- Micro-credit
- Meeting basic needs
- Female empowerment
- Education
- Property rights
- Governance and corruption

All of these have been advocated with messianic zeal by their followers as the key to unlocking rapid growth and poverty reduction. Some have proved very relevant, while others have been abject failures. However, it seems clear that there is no one magic bullet that will automatically launch the growth process. Rather, all of these are important in different degrees to the process, but none offers an easy path to nirvana. Nevertheless, we can expect fads in the thinking on economic development to come and go in the future, as they have in the past.

## Appendix: The Influence of Keynes

The Keynesian revolution in macroeconomics placed great emphasis on maintaining aggregate output to insure full employment. It did not focus on long term growth. For Keynes, labor was not a constraint, rather it was a problem. The question was how to move back to full employment by manipulating aggregate demand. As we see in the classic Keynesian diagram, the economy is not a full employment at output level A, with total demand being the sum of C, consumption, and I, investment. Carefully tuned government spending, G, can bring aggregate demand up to the point where full employment reached.

Fig. 2.4 . The Classic Keynesian Demand Problem

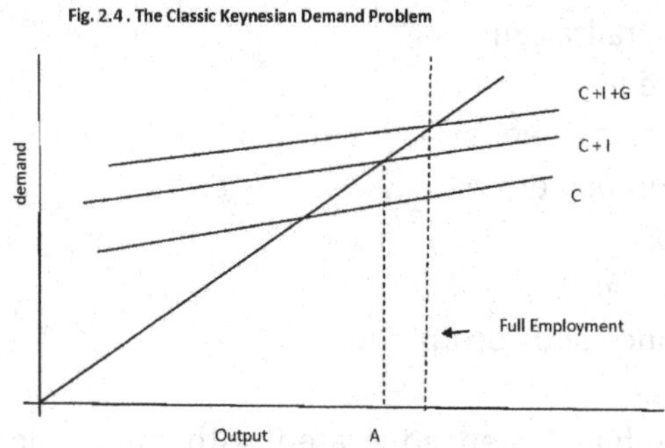


In a closed economy, income can be consumed, saved or used to pay taxes (T), or:

$$Y = C + S + T,$$

While aggregate demand consists of consumption, investment and government spending, or

$$Y = C + I + G$$

If people save more, consumption must fall, aggregate demand falls, and the rate of unemployment increases. In the short run, an increase in savings is bad, since it reduces consumption and aggregate demand and thereby reduces output. In contrast, an increase in savings in H-D increase growth, while in Solow it increases growth temporarily until a new steady state is reached.

# CHAPTER III

# CONVERGENCE AND THE SOURCES OF GROWTH

"If God had meant there to be more than two factors of production, He would have made it easier for us to draw three-dimensional diagrams."—Robert Solow

"I am not a student of development."—Robert Solow[11]

## The Solow Model and the Issue of Convergence

Robert Solow won a Nobel Prize for his work in explaining economic growth, and the development of what has become called the neoclassical growth model. The model was developed to explain growth in developed countries, but it has important implications for developing countries as well. Solow starts with the assumption of a linear production function with capital and labor, which assumes constant returns to scale, but diminishing returns to capital and labor. This is in contrast to the constant returns to capital, and the absence of labor, in the Harrod Domar model. The production function is often cast in Cobb-Douglas version:

$Y = A K^{\alpha} L^{1-\alpha}$

[11] From G. Meier and J. Stiglitz, eds., *Frontiers of Development Economics: The Future in Perspective,* World Bank/Oxford University Press, 2001., p.514

This linear homogenous production function implies that an equal increase in each factor (say 10%) would produce an equivalent increase in output (10% in this case). There are no scale economies or diseconomies. It also implies that there are diminishing returns for each factor. A is a parameter measuring technical change. If this technical change is labor augmenting, then the function can be written as :

$$Y = K^{\alpha} A L^{1-\alpha}$$

Solow assumes that output depends on capital per worker, and adding capital to the existing work force produces diminishing returns. He recasts the Harrod-Domar equation for capital growth by dividing by L, the labor force, and allowing for population growth, n. Hence,

$\Delta K_t = S_t - d K_{t-1.}$ In the HD model, becomes

$$\Delta K/L = s(Y/L) - (n + d) K/L$$

Defining k = K/L, and y = Y/L, we have the fundamental Solow equation:

$$\Delta k = sy - (n + d) k,$$

where the growth of capital per laborer is a function of savings per person, less an allowance for depreciation of the capital stock, and the need to provide an expanding labor force with the same level of capital as the existing labor force, in order to maintain Y/L steady.

The workings of the model can best be explained with a graph (see Fig. 3.1, which shows k (= K/L) and y (= Y/L). The line (n + d)k shows the amount of capital needed to provide for depreciation and the growing labor force. The line sy shows the amount of savings per worker. To the left of point A, savings exceeds what is required to maintain the capital stock, so the capital stock grows, and K/L increases (capital deepening), raising Y/L (or y). However, as K/L increases, diminishing returns arise from adding more capital to a fixed labor force, so the increment to income from additional capital falls. Eventually, a steady state is reached where the economy is just generating sufficient saving to maintain the capital stock, k, given population growth and depreciation (n + d).

Fig. 3.1 Solow Growth Model

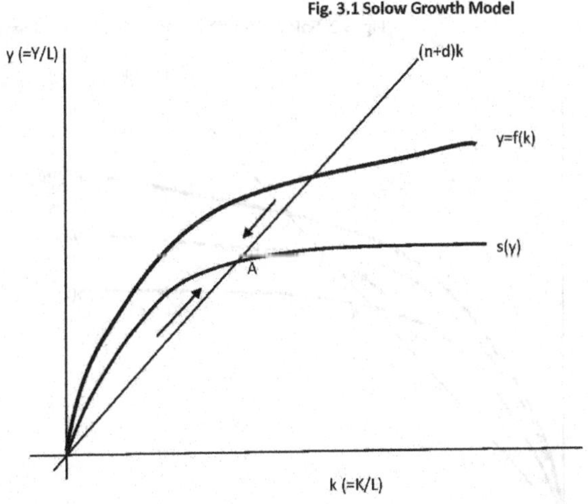


An increase in the savings rate would temporarily increase the rate of growth, until a new equilibrium output level is reached (see point B in Fig. 3.2). If for some reason, output moved beyond point B, there would not be enough saving to sustain the capital stock. Think of an extreme case: an investment is made that generates no income. Since savings is already allocated toward the maintenance of the previous existing capital stock, there are no funds available for maintaining this new (but unproductive) investment, and the capital stock falls back to the equilibrium position. On the other hand, an increase in the population growth rate causes the (n + d) k line to move upward, resulting a new equilibrium at a lower steady state. The only way to raise the growth rate is a continuous shift the Y(k) production function upward, and this can only be done via technical change (see Fig. 3.3, where technical change has raised the equilibrium output level to point C). Thus, the growth factors for total output Y are technical change A, and population growth n. Per capita growth depends, in the steady state, only on A (or Θ in Solow's notation). Technical change allows an existing labor force to produce more with a given capital stock. The growth rate of output per person, y, then is a function of Θ plus the capital stock per person, or:

$$y = f(k, \Theta) \text{ or } Y/L = f(K/L, \Theta)$$

**Fig. 3.2 Solow Growth Model with increased Savings**

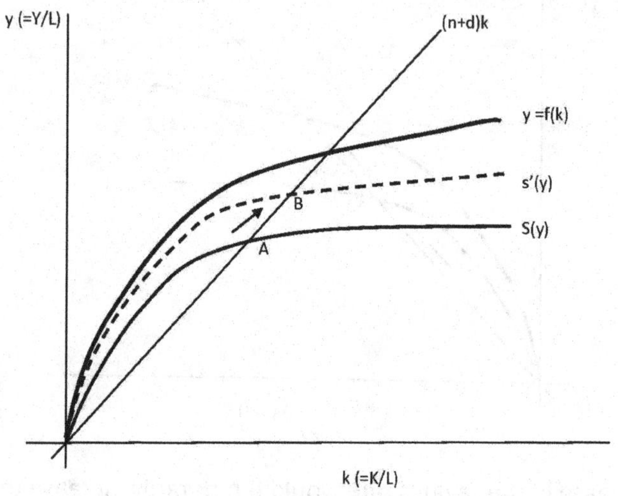


**Fig. 3.3 Solow Growth Model with Technical Change(Θ**

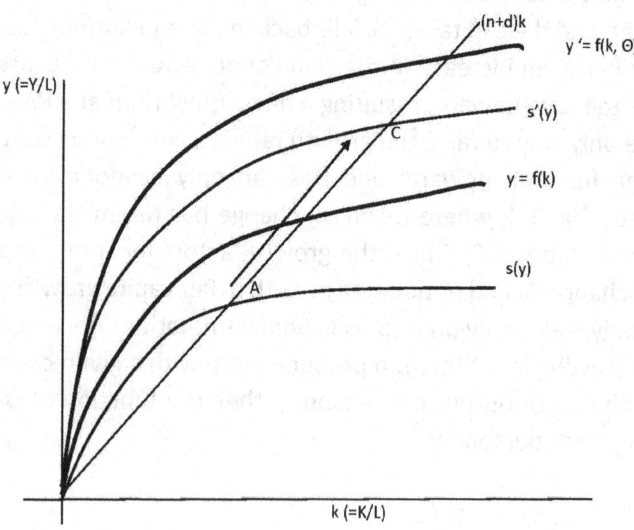

The Solow model is very elegant, and nicely combines basic macro and micro economics. However, it leaves growth theory at a dead end. In the short term, capital accumulation accounts for growth up to the point of the steady state. In the long run, growth depends on technology change, and we have no idea what generates changes in technology[12]. Hence, the neo-classical model is often called an "exogenous" growth model; growth comes from outside of the model.

But the conundrum is even worse than being exogenous. According to the Cobb-Douglas production function:

$$Y = A K^{\alpha} L^{1-\alpha}$$

The coefficients on K and L total to one. This means that output (income) allocated 100% to labor and capital. There is no residual left over to finance research and technology development. But we know that R&D exist, so the production function is missing something.

## Solow and the LDCs

Solow stated he was not a student of development, since his model was not meant for developing countries. It has, however, implications that are important. If it is right, developing countries should be able to advance rapidly by accumulating capital and adopting advanced technology, provided they are not constrained by low savings. In theory, capital should be more productive in LDCs where it is scarce, and therefore have a higher return than in developed countries. Attracted by these higher returns, capital should flow capital surplus rich countries to capital scarce LDCs. The LDCs should eventually be able to reach the steady state levels of growth and output of the developed countries. But do we see this kind of convergence?

Early estimates seem to back up the idea of convergence, but they tended to use only data from more advanced countries. As the body of statistical information became broader (more countries) and longer over time, it became clear that there was actually divergence, not

---

12 For a discussion of this "dead end" and the current state of growth theory, see Lant Prichett, "The Quest Continues" *Finance and Development,* 43 (March 2006).

convergence. Pritchett pointed this out in a classic article in 1997,[13] Pritchett assumes that the bare minimum average income for a country would be $250 (PPP, 1985 prices). By multiple means, he calculates that this is the amount necessary to sustain life at a subsistence level. The richest country, the US, between 1870 and 1960, had an increase in per capita income of four fold. Thus, there would be divergence if poor countries did not also increase their per capita income by four fold over the period. If $250 is the basic minimum, any country with a per capita income of $1000 or less in 1960 must have had less than a fourfold increase (otherwise it would have had a per capita income of less than $250 in 1870, which is insufficient to support life). The Penn World Tables show that there were 42 countries with per capita incomes less than $1000 in 1990. Hence," divergence, big time".

Pritchett lacks data on developing countries going back to 1870. But assuming that the poorest country had a per capita income of $250 back then, he calculates that the ratio of per capita income between the richest (US) and poorest country was 8.7 in 1870. Actual data for 1990 shows that the ratio in 1990 was 45.2. Again, "divergence, big time."

Fig. 3.4 Per Capita Income, 1960 and 2007, selected countries.
(Gross Domestic Income per capita, 1985 PPP prices)

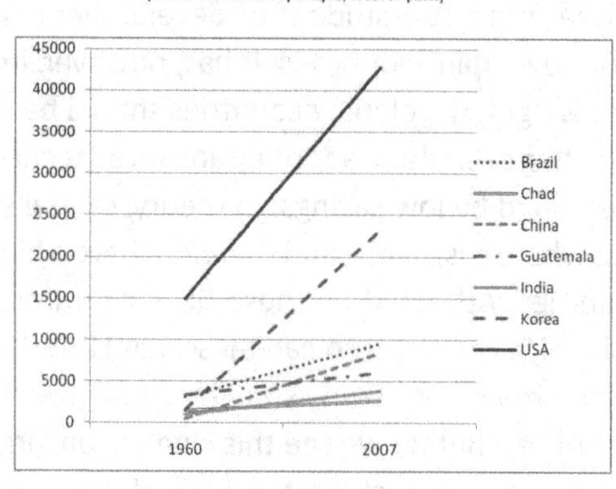


Source: based on data from Penn World Tables, 6.3

But this analysis obscures the fact that there is convergence, by some countries. As noted in Chapter I, there has been substantial growth in recent decades by two of the most populous countries: China

13 "Divergence: Big Time" *Journal of Economic Perspectives,* 11 (Summer, 1997).

and India. A true measure of convergence has to measure the gap in average incomes between rich and poor. As the work of Milanovic has shown, world income distribution has improved, and the gap between rich and poor has narrowed (largely thanks to China). Thus, while there may be divergence between countries, there may be convergence between people, in the sense that the average income gap may be narrowing.

**Table 3.1 Growth Rates, Selected Countries, 1960-2007**
(Gross Domestic Income per capita in PPP $ 1985)

| | 1960 | 2007 | Growth rate, 1960-2007 |
|---|---|---|---|
| Brazil | 3191 | 9504 | 2.34 |
| Chad | 1493 | 2659 | 1.24 |
| China | 477 | 8494 | 6.32 |
| Ghana | 2078 | 1713 | -0.41 |
| Guatemala | 3389 | 6071 | 1.25 |
| Honduras | 2256 | 3576 | 0.99 |
| India | 972 | 3869 | 2.98 |
| Korea | 1615 | 23332 | 5.85 |
| United States | 14953 | 42835 | 2.26 |

Source: data from :Alan Heston, Robert Summers and Bettina Aten, *Penn World Table Version 6.3,* Center for International Comparisons of Production, Income and Prices at the University of Pennsylvania, August 2009.

The debate on convergence is further confused by the difference between absolute and relative convergence. As shown in Fig. 3.4 and Table 3.1, within these 8 representative LDCs, between 1960 and 2007, four had per capita income growth faster than that of the USA(which we take as the standard). These are China, Korea, India, and Brazil (just barely). Thus, these four were converging, while the others in the table were lagging behind and not converging on the US: Chad, Ghana, Guatemala and Honduras. However, even so, the gap between some of the converging countries and the US is widening in an absolute sense because the growth in the US comes from a higher base (illustrated in Fig. 3.4). For instance, the absolute gap between China and the US was about $14,500 in 1960 and about $34,000 in 2007, even though China had an average growth rate three times higher. Even if China could sustain its historical growth rate of 6.3%, and assuming the US also continues to grow at its historical rate of 2.3%, it would take about 129 years for the two countries to converge, i.e. have the same per capita incomes.

## Growth Accounting

The Solow framework led empirical researchers into trying to identify the sources of growth in various countries: did it come from growth of capital, labor or technology? This work starts with assumption that there exists a Cobb-Douglas production function, which has constant returns to scale and diminishing returns to each factor. Since we assume a competitive world, the coefficients on capital and labor add to one, meaning that there is no excess profits.

$$Y = a K^{\alpha} L^{1-\alpha}$$

With some manipulation (trust me) this equation can be transformed into:

$g_y = w_k g_k + w_l g_l + a$; where the "g's" indicate growth rates.

Thus, the overall growth rate of the economy, $g_{y,}$ can be decomposed into a weighted average of the growth rates of capital, labor and a residual, a, which is presumably technology and other factors. Labor growth is adjusted for changes in the quality of labor, which arises from more education. The weights of capital and labor can be assumed in a competitive economy, to be equal to their factor shares, and the residual, a, is a measure of the growth of productivity. This productivity measure reflects changes both in labor and capital productivity, so it is labeled "total factor productivity" or TFP, and is sometimes called the Solow residual. The reason it is a residual is that $g_y$, $w_{k,}$ $g_{k,}$ $w_l$, and $g_l$, are all known or can be calculated; the a is what is left after the capital and labor portions are subtracted. This means, of course, that "a" also includes any errors or omissions in calculating the other variables, a potential source of error.

**Table 3.2 Estimated Growth Shares for K, L and TFP, 1960-1987**
(percent of total growth)

| | Capital (K) | Labor (L) | TFP |
|---|---|---|---|
| Africa | 73 | 28 | 0 |
| East Asia | 57 | 16 | 28 |
| Latin America/Caribb. | 67 | 30 | 0 |
| South Asia | 67 | 20 | 14 |
| 68 LDCs | 65 | 23 | 14 |
| | | | |
| United States | 23 | 27 | 50 |
| Germany | 23 | -10 | 87 |

Source: World Bank, World Development Report, 1991, p. 45

Early estimates of TFP produced some surprising results. Work by Denison on the United States for the period 1948-73 indicated that of the US had an average annual growth rate of 3.9 %, during the period, but capital only grew by .7% per year. Thus, capital accounted for only 18% of growth. Furthermore, the residual or TFP, accounted for 44% of growth, most of which Denison could not identify and simply labeled it "advances in knowledge and not elsewhere classified". Applying the framework to developing countries produced even more surprising results. The World Bank's World Development Report, 1991, calculated TFPs for groups of countries (Table 3.2). Here we see that LDC growth, unlike developed country growth, is largely a factor of capital stock growth, accounting for 65% of total growth, 1960-87. Clearly, there is something happening in high growth economies other than the growth of capital and labor. However, in developing countries TFP growth only accounted for 14% of growth, but this varies from 0% in Africa, to 28% in East Asia. The low levels of TFP growth in developing countries suggests that growth is occurring largely via capital accumulation, not technical change. However, since adopted capital from developed countries embodies new technology, the technical change may be occurring.

## Endogenous Growth

Questions about the Solow model begin to arise when economists began to think about technological change and research and development expenditures (R&D). If in a purely competitive economy with Pareto-optimal conditions the entire product went to pay factors of production, where did the funds come from to invest in R&D? Furthermore, in a competitive world, there would be no monopoly on technology, and ideas would flow freely from one user to another. There would be no incentive to do R&D if the researcher could not realize a return on his investment. Only by using a model involving imperfect competition and a degree of monopoly power, was it possible to have technological progress. Example: in agriculture, firms are small and single farmers do no influence the market. It is as close to pure competition as one can get. Farmers generally do not have profits that allow them to invest in research. Rather, technological change comes from large seed, machinery and chemical firms who operate in oligopolistic conditions, and extract profits to pay for their research.

Furthermore, Paul Romer[14] argued, the assumption of constant returns to scale may not be true. As an economy expands, it offers new possibilities. As Adam Smith pointed out, the degree of the division of labor depends on the size of the market. When computers are wide spread, it pays to develop innovations that make them run better, with improved hardware and software. When computers are uncommon, there is no incentive to invent improvements, because the size of the market is limited. In notation terms, the idea that technical change drives growth, or:

$y = f(k, \Theta)$ (where y is output per labor, and k is capital per labor)

can become:

$\Theta = f(y)$.

In addition, it means the standard Cobb-Douglas formulation itself is wrong ($Y = A K^{\alpha} L^{1-\alpha}$) and that there are increasing returns to scale. This would imply a function like:

$Y = A K^{\alpha} L^{\beta}$; where $\alpha + \beta$ can be greater than one (scale economies). In that case, a 10% increase in each factor would produce an increase in output of more than 10%.

In other words, technological change itself is a function of the level of development. Thus, growth can become endogenous, rather than exogenous, as it was in the Solow model. In that case, then the old Harrod-Domar production function ($Y = AK$) might be right after all; given more and more capital, countries can keep on growing, without being constrained by diminishing returns.[15]

---

14 Romer, Paul. "Increasing Returns and Long-Run Growth" *Journal of Political Economy* 94 (1986).

15 Hussein, K and A. P. Thirlwall, "The AK model of "new" growth theory is the Harrod-Domar growth equation: Investment and Growth revisited" *Journal of Post Keynesian Economics*,22, Spring 2000.

## Conditional Convergence and Growth Regressions

Initially, attempt to prove convergence statistically did not work. Running a regression of the form[16]:

y = a + bY (where y is per capita growth and Y is initial per capita income, a is a constant term)

with non-significant estimated coefficients for b. To prove convergence, the "b" should be negative; at higher levels of income, the growth rate of income should be lower, since countries have reached the "steady state."

This, combined with the intuition that there was a host of other conditions influencing growth, led to a plethora of statistical studies estimating the causal factors of growth, using a more general form:

$$y = a + b_1 Y + b_2 X_2 + b_3 X_3 \dots$$

Where the X's represent other factors that could influence growth. In almost all cases, these regressions found significant and negative coefficient estimates for $b_1$ (growth is slower at higher levels of per capita income). This implies that there is convergence, but it is conditional on other factors affecting growth. Thus, the convergence hypothesis is modified to be *conditional convergence*.

The pioneer in estimating growth equations is Robert Barro[17]. His results, reproduced here as Table 3.3, combine three time periods 1965-75. 1975-85, and 1985-90. They show clearly that level of GDP (first variable in Table 2.3) is significant and negative, showing the presence of conditional convergence. However, the pace of convergence is very slow. Barro's estimates indicate that it would take LDCs 89 years to reach a level of 90% of the income of the richer countries. Health and education variables clearly have a positive effect on growth, and schooling interacts with the level of GDP to accelerate the convergence process. Democracy

16 For a quick review of the technique of multiple regression, see "How to Read a Regression Table", in Gerald M. Meier and James E. Rauch, *Leading Issues in Economic Development* (New York: Oxford Univ. Press, 2000), appendix, p. 587., or any standard textbook on econometrics.

17 Robert J. Barro, *Determinants of Economic Growth: A Cross Country Empirical Study*, National Bureau of Economic Research, Working Paper 5698, (NBER: Cambridge Mass, August, 1996).

is good for growth, but only up to a point, and then has a negative effect (see democracy index squared). Better rule of law conditions are good for growth, but higher government consumption, high fertility, and inflation all have a negative effect on growth. Gains in the terms of trade have a positive influence, suggesting support for Prebisch-Singer. However, the overall system of equations only explain about half of the variance in growth (as shown by the $R^2$), suggesting tha there is still a substantial amount of variance in growth that cannot be explained.

**Table 3.3 Barro's Estimates of the Determinants of Economic Growth**
(estimated regression coefficients, t-values in parenthesis, dependent variable = per capita GDP growth)

| Independent variable | Estimate #1 | Estimate #2 (with dummies) |
|---|---|---|
| log (GDP) | -.0254<br>(8.19) | -.0225<br>(7.03) |
| male secondary and higher schooling | .0118<br>(4.72) | .0098<br>(3.92) |
| log (life expectancy) | .0423<br>(3.09) | .0418<br>(3.01) |
| log(GDP)*male schooling | -.0062<br>(3.65) | -.0052<br>(3.06) |
| log(fertility rate) | -.0161<br>(3.04) | -.0135<br>(2.55) |
| government consumption ratio | -.036<br>(5.23) | -.115<br>(4.26) |
| rule-of-law index | .0293<br>(5.43) | .0262<br>(4.76) |
| terms-of-trade change | .137<br>(4.57) | .127<br>(4.23) |
| democracy index | .090<br>(3.33) | .094<br>(3.49) |
| democracy index squared | -.088<br>(3.67) | -.091<br>(3.79) |
| Inflation rate | -.043<br>(5.38) | -.039<br>(4.88) |
| dummy variables: | | |
| Sub-Sahara Africa | -- | -.0042<br>(.98) |
| Latin America | -- | -.0054<br>(1.69) |
| East Asia | -- | .0050<br>(1.22 |
| | | |
| $R^2$ | .58, .52, .42 | .60,.52, .47 |
| number of observations | 80, 87, 84 | 80, 87, 84 |

Source: Robert J. Barro, "Determinants of Economic Growth: A Cross-Country Empirical Study" NBER Working Paper 5698 (Cambridge, 1996), p. 80. Note that standard errors in original have been converted to t-values. Coefficients estimated in a three stage process using periods: 1965-75, 1975-85, and 1985-90.

Similar results on productivity also reinforce Barro's findings of the strong influence of the role of government and trade were obtained by a classic study of productivity by Hall and Jones.[18] First they note that that average productivity in the top five countries in their sample is 31.7 times that of the and lowest five countries. These differences can be traced to capital intensity (1.8), human capital (2.2) and the residual—productivity (8.3). They relate productivity differences to an index of social infrastructure, which is a composite measure of the role of government, and trade openness. The first is measured by a variety of

[18] Hall, Robert E. and Charles I. Jones. *Why Do Some Countries Produce So Much More Output per Worker than Others?* NBER Working Paper W6564 (NBER: Cambridge, Mass: June 1999).

indicators of law and order, bureaucratic quality, corruption, expropriation risk, and government repudiation of contracts. The second, by an index of openness created by Sachs/Warner. They find significant association of the social infrastructure index with all three parts of the growth equation: the productivity of capital, the level of human capital, and the residual productivity measure.

The development over time of better data, and the computer power to analyze large data sets, has resulted in countless studies of growth determinants, each one with slightly different conclusions. While there are about 80 countries with good data that can be used in a growth regression, there are hundreds of possible variables that can be included. The selection of variables becomes a big issue, particularly when the "right-hand" or "independent" variables are not totally independent of each other. A recent study by Sala-I Martin *et. al.*[19] attempts to examine a wide range of possible variables, and to statistically choose the correct and only important factors. It looks at 67 possible variables explaining growth between 1960 and 1996. It finds that, once again, the initial level of GDP per capita exerts a strong negative effect on the growth rate of per capita income (the conditional convergence effect). Other important policy variables are:

The level of primary schooling;
The price of investment goods (indicating incentive to invest);
The size of government consumption in GDP (a negative);
Two measures of health: life expectancy and malaria prevalence;
Exchange rate distortions; and
Openness of the economy.

Because this study uses variables that measure the state of economies in 1960, it was not able to use some more recent indices of rule of law, government bureaucracy, corruption, etc., that were developed in the 1980s.

The study also found several geographic variables to be important. Countries in East Asia grew faster than average; those in Africa and Latin America, and those that were Spanish Colonies, below average.

19 Xavier Sala-i-Martin, Gernot Doppelhofer and Ronald I. Miller, "Determinants of Long-Term Growth: A Bayesian Averaging of Classical Estimates (BACE) Approach" *American Economic Review* 94 (September 2004).

Religion was important: Confucian, Buddhist and Muslim countries grew faster, but countries with ethnolinguistic fractionalization grew slower. Countries with a high share of mining in GDP also grew faster. However, these are all variables that describe the state of various economies, and do not represent items that can be changed with economic policy. It begs the question as to why East Asia grew more quickly, and Latin America and Africa more slowly, and thus represents an index of our ignorance. Interestingly, this study did not find a significant impact for such economic variables as inflation, government investment, the terms of trade, or population growth rate (compare to Barro's findings).

## Bottom Line—What do we know?

As Pritchett has noted, we still don't know very much about growth (or more charitably, we are still learning). The endogenous growth revolution launched hundreds of regression studies, and thousands of regressions, attempting to find that true set of factors explaining growth[20]. Even the best of the growth equations, however, rarely explain more than 50% of the variance in growth rates between countries. But the idea of conditional convergence remains strong—countries with lower incomes grow faster CONDITIONAL on a lot of other factors being right, and where we have some ideas on what those factors are, but this set of "other factors" is still somewhat uncertain. Part of the problem is measurement—how does one measure well political stability or the quality of the investment climate? We (economists) use proxies that stand for these factors, but these proxies are often very inexact substitutes for what we really want to measure.

Nevertheless, we do see, particularly in the past twenty years, that some countries have "taken off". By making themselves attractive to foreign investment, open to trade, and having reasonably efficient governments, they have managed to accelerate their rate of growth and close the gap between themselves and the richer countries of the world. So in a certain sense Rostow was right. There can be a "take-off", but there is no immutable law that it will happen in all countries at all times.

---

20 Note the title of the article by Xavier Sala-i-Martin, "I Just Ran Two Million Regressions" *American Economic Review,* 87, (May,1997).

The richer countries of the world did not "take-off" because they had to develop new technologies over time. The poorer countries can take advantage of this by adopting present technologies and catch up to their richer cousins. The LDCs do not have to start with factories powered by falling water, introduce steam engines, and then electric motors. They can go right to the final stage—at least In theory.

# CHAPTER IV

## AGRICULTURE AND DEVELOPMENT: MYTHS AND REALITIES

*"If the world is committed to reducing poverty and achieving sustainable growth, the powers of agriculture for development must be unleashed. But there are no magic bullets. Using agriculture for development is a complex process"*

—World Bank[21]

*"Diversity among nations in their physical endowment, cultural heritage, and historical context precludes any universally applicable definition of the role that agriculture should play in the process of economic growth. Nevertheless, certain aspects of agriculture's role appear to have a high degree of generality . . ."*

—Bruce Johnston and John W. Mellor[22]

The most basic need of any person is to eat. Food, along with access to water and shelter, are the fundamental basic needs of all mankind. In primitive societies, the majority of the time of the population is consumed with the production of food. As nations and groups progress, they are able to produce more than enough food, allowing for the development of industry and arts. This natural progression away from agriculturally based societies to those based on industry is a fundamental shift that has been going on for centuries. Even in the US, we see this transformation continuing, where the rural population has declined from 60% of the population in 1900 to

21 From World Bank, *World Development Report 2008: Agriculture for Development*, World Bank: Washington DC: 2008, p. 25.

22 Bruce F. Johnston and John W. Mellor "The Role of Agriculture in Economic Development", *American Economic Review,* 51 (Sept. 1961) pp. 566-593

21% in 2000. In the US today, only about 1 of the labor force is employed in agriculture; in the lower-middle income (developing) countries, the figure is about 40%, and higher in the low income countries.

There is a natural tendency for the share of agriculture to decline over the development process. The share of agriculture declines because new technologies and innovations allow countries to increase agricultural productivity, freeing up labor to move to urban centers and take up non-agricultural pursuits. A study of these trends by Hollis Chenery and Moises Syrquin[23] showed a generalized pattern as shown in the Fig. 4.1. The share in GDP for agriculture gradually declines, while the share for industry, and eventually services rises over time. The same pattern marks stages of development between rich and poor countries, as shown in Table 4.1

**Fig. 4.1: Stylized Facts: The Chenery-Syrquin Patterns of Development**

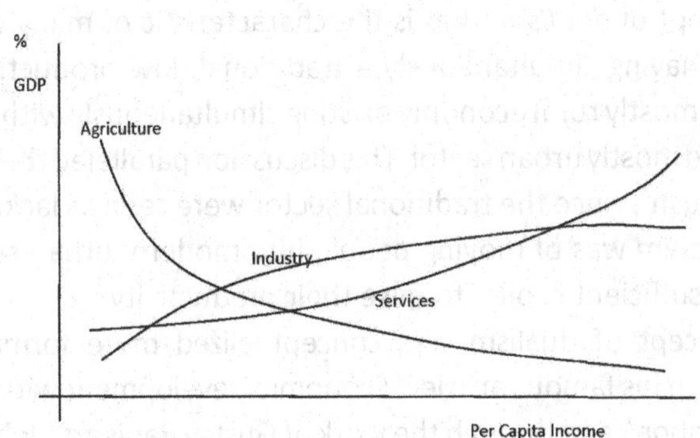


Agriculture represents only 3% of world GDP, but in low income countries the share averages 27%. The share clearly declines with income, with the middle income countries have a 10% share, and the high income countries having a share of only 1.4%. Likewise, rural populations dominate in poor countries even though they produce a less than dominant share of output. Thus, rural populations in Sub-Saharan Africa are about 65% of the total, while producing only 16% of GDP, and the gap is similar in South Asia. Very few countries have large agricultural sectors; the exception is New Zealand, but even here the agriculture sector is only about 7% (compared to 5% in Russia, 1% in the US).

---

23 Chenery, Hollis and Moises Syrquin, *Patterns of Development, 1950-1970,* World Bank: Oxford University Press, London, 1975.

**Table 4.1: Agriculture in GDP and Rural Population, Groups of Countries (%, 2006)**

| | Rural Pop./Total | Agriculture/GDP |
|---|---|---|
| High income | 22.8 | 1.4 |
| Low income | 72.1 | 27.0 |
| Middle income | 52.9 | 9.6 |
| | | |
| South Asia | 71.2 | 18.6 |
| Sub-Saharan Africa | 64.5 | 16.3 |
| | | |
| World | 50.9 | 3.0 |

Source: World Bank, WDI

Much of the early thinking on economic development focused on the problem of moving people from traditional and rural settings to more urban and modern environments. This discussion, therefore, focused on the concept of *dualism*, that is the characteristic of many developing societies of having simultaneously a traditional, low productive, mostly agricultural, mostly rural economy existing simultaneously with a modern, industrial and mostly urban sector. This discussion paralleled the discussion of the "big push", since the traditional sector were seen as lacking capital, and the problem was of moving people into modern, urban settings but armed with sufficient capital to raise their productivity.

The concept of dualism was conceptualized more formally by W. Arthur Lewis in his famous article: "Economic Development with Unlimited Supplies of Labor", and through the work of Gustav Ranis and John Fei, who developed an analytical graphical framework[24]. According to Lewis, there were people in the rural area who were redundant; they could be taken out of rural areas without diminishing the supply of food. In other words, these were workers with zero marginal product. This is sometimes labeled as "disguised unemployment". This phenomenon is seen in a typical small family farm: all family workers are employed, each works at various levels of effort and skill, and each shares equally in the (mostly food) output. Workers are essentially here being paid their average, not marginal product.

---

24 Lewis, W. Arthur, "Economic Development with Unlimited Supplies of Labor", *Manchester School* (May 1954), and Gustav Ranis and John C. H. Fei, *Development of the Labor Surplus Economy: Theory and Policy* (Homewood, Ill.,: Yale/Irwin, 1964).

Such situations provide easy basis for rapid industrialization, reasoned Lewis, since workers could be moved into the more modern urban sector, with no loss of food production, Hence, food prices would remain low and therefore urban wages would also remain low (assuming that urban wages equaled subsistence levels for urban workers, determined largely by the price of necessary foodstuffs). Industrialists would enjoy (reap) large profits, which in turn would be plowed back into new investments, furthering the industrialization process.

Figure 4.2 shows the interactions of the product and labor markets between industry and agriculture in simplified form, following the ideas of Ranis and Fei. Workers in agriculture are paid a subsistence wage, $W_s$, and the wage in industry is equal to $W_s$ plus a small premium needed to attract workers to move from rural to urban communities. Increases in demand for workers in industry ($D_1$ to $D_2$) draw workers from agriculture, but since they have zero marginal product, total agricultural output remains constant, and wages in industry also remain constant. Once demand exceeds $D_2$, and the supply of workers in agriculture drops below $S_2$ (point c on the graph), wages start to rise. Note that agricultural output will actually start falling sooner, at point b, where workers in agriculture start to have a positive marginal product, although still below subsistence.

Fig 4.2 Lewis/Ranis/Fei Model

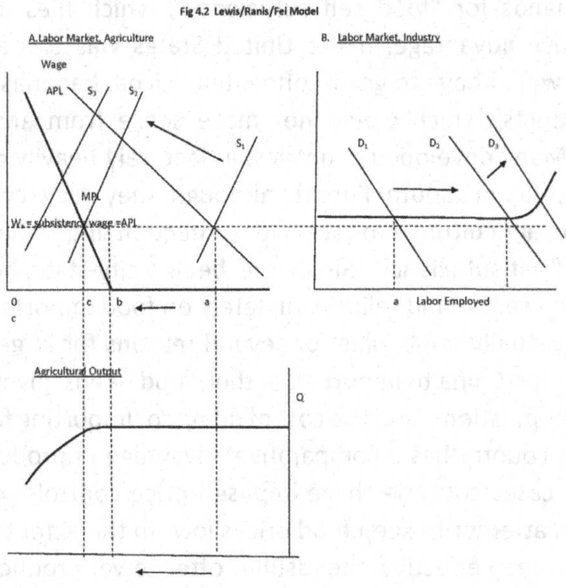

What is missing from this graph is the impact of falling agricultural output on food prices. Once output falls, and food prices rise, the subsistence wage will have to rise, also putting a brake on the industrialization process. However, if higher food prices induce technological change in agriculture, output per worker can expand, and prices remain low. As workers leave rural areas, and food prices rise, farmers have a double incentive to adopt labor-saving and land-saving techniques to increase food production, expand the area under production, as well as to use more fertilizer, irrigation and other inputs. Food could also be imported to keep prices low. The key result here is the need for a parallel development of agriculture and industry, with increased productivity in agriculture allowing the migration of workers to industry, while supplying the same or even greater amounts of food. At the same time agriculture provided important raw materials for industry, illustrating the kinds of forward and backward linkages between the two.

The Lewis-Ranis-Fei model has been criticized on several grounds. Few researchers have been actually able to identify agricultural workers with zero marginal product. Withdrawing workers from agriculture seems to raise wages almost immediately, at least by a small amount. Furthermore, an open economy can import food easily, often more cheaply than a country can produce it. Xenophobic pressures can lead to demands for "food self sufficiency", which flies in the face of comparative advantage. If the United States was to be food self sufficient, it would have to grow coffee, tea, cocoa, bananas and other tropical products, which would not make sense from an economic standpoint. Many developed countries, in fact, rely heavily on imports (Switzerland, Japan, South Korea), although they face considerable pressure from agricultural producers for protection under the banner of the need for "self-sufficiency". Singapore, being a city-state, has virtually no agricultural sector and relies completely on food imports. However, it would be virtually impossible for several reasons for large countries such as India and China to import all of their food needs, given the large size of their populations, and the cost of doing so. Importing food makes no sense if a country has a comparative advantage in producing food. But in many cases countries have imposed price controls on farmers' outputs in an attempt to keep food prices low. To the extent that these controls have been effective, the result is often lower production in the long run, and food shortages.

In general, there is no shortage of food in the world. Between 1970 and 2005, world food production grew at a rate of 2.3% per year, while population growth was 1.6% (see Fig. 4.3).

**Fig. 4.3 World Food and Population Growth, 1970-2005**

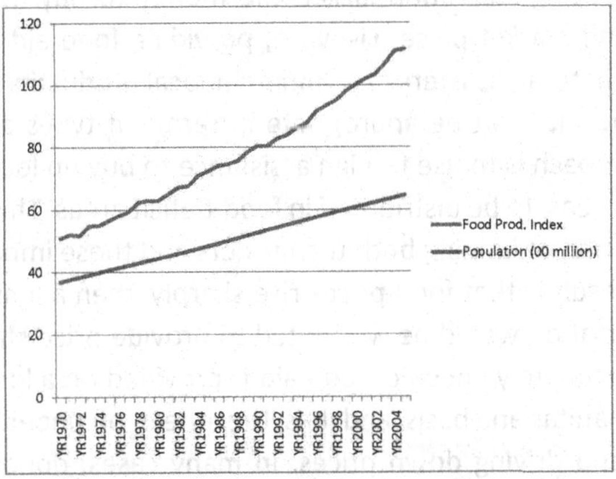

Source: World Bank, WDI data. Food production index, 2000 = 100.

The situation has been less dramatic in the low income developing countries, but even here food production exceeded population growth over the 1990-2005 period (2.7 vs. 2.3% per annum). Only in Africa has food production lagged behind, but here too, since 1990 food production has kept up with population growth (see Table 4.2). Even if food production in a particular country does not keep up with population growth, food would is available for purchase on world markets. The problem is the lack of purchasing power: weak economic development and weak export growth means that countries lack often resources to buy food, and imported food is relatively expensive when foreign exchange earnings are meager.

**Table 4.2 Food Production and Population Growth**

| Growth rate of: | Food Production | | Population | |
|---|---|---|---|---|
| | 1970-2005 | 1990-2005 | 1970-2005 | 1990-2005 |
| World | 2.3 | 2.2 | 1.6 | 1.4 |
| Low Income | 2.3 | 2.7 | 2.5 | 2.3 |
| Africa | 2.2 | 2.7 | 2.8 | 2.7 |

Source: World Bank, WDI

The same logic applies to countries having famines. A.K. Sen found in a classic study that during a famine in India, the areas experiencing famine were actually exporting food to other non-famine areas. The reason for this paradox is that the famine destroyed farm earnings, so that farmers facing starvation lacked the money to buy food that was available in the market place. Likewise, providing food aid to countries experiencing natural disasters may undercut local production efforts, and imported food may not be appropriate in terms of types and tastes. A far better approach is to use foreign assistance to buy up local food from non-disaster areas, to be distributed in food-deficit areas. This produces a win-win situation of helping both the farmers and those impacted by the crisis. If the result is that food prices rise sharply, then a limited amount of food importation would be warranted to provide price stability in the market. Unfortunately, much of food aid is provided on a long-term, not crisis or humanitarian, basis and has the effect of undercutting local production, and driving down prices. In many cases, donors are more interested in dumping surplus commodities or opening up new markets for their agricultural products, than providing development assistance. These lessons have been gradually internalized by aid agencies, and food aid programs today are more limited than they had been.

## Productivity Variations among Countries

The simple-minded approach to the problem is to state that productivity is low in agriculture in developing countries. But what do we mean by "productivity"? Often the solution is seen as raising yields, expressed in terms of tons per hectare (or acre). But yields are not that low in many developing countries compared with richer countries, such as the US. Table 4.3 shows yields on rice, wheat and corn in a selected group of countries[25]. It shows that wheat yields in India, China and Mexico are greater than the US. In the case of rice, yields in China are not that far below those of the U.S. What is low, therefore is labor productivity. Because more people work on farms in India and China, the output per worker is much lower, even if the

---

[25] See David Abler "Agriculture in Developing Countries" at: http://450.aers.psu.edu/agriculture.cfm.

output per hectare is about the same. If we look at wheat yields, one would think that the US is an inefficient producer and not competitive with Mexico, which has yields twice as high. In fact, what the US enjoys is vast open areas for growing wheat with mechanized agriculture and few labor inputs.

**Table 4.3 Comparisons of Yields in Selected Countries**

| Country | Yield (metric tons/hectare), 2003-2005 Averages | | |
|---|---|---|---|
| | Rice | Wheat | Corn |
| China | 6.2 | 4.2 | 5.1 |
| India | 3.1 | 2.6 | 1.9 |
| Indonesia | 4.6 | *nd | 3.3 |
| Brazil | 3.4 | 2.1 | 3.4 |
| Pakistan | 3.0 | 2.4 | 2.6 |
| Bangladesh | 3.6 | 1.9 | 4.7 |
| Nigeria | 1.4 | 1.1 | 1.6 |
| Mexico | 4.7 | 4.6 | 2.8 |
| Philippines | 3.5 | *nd | 2.0 |
| Vietnam | 4.8 | *nd | 3.5 |
| U.S. | 7.6 | 2.9 | 9.4 |
| Japan | 6.3 | 4.1 | 2.5 |
| Germany | *nd | 7.4 | 8.6 |

*nd = no data because crop is unimportant in that country
**Source:** FAO, FAOStat, compiled by David Abler, Penn State University.

However, the differences in labor productivity are not explained by just inputs, such as irrigation or fertilizer. Irrigation rates vary based on climate and available water; many countries have adequate rainfall and do not need irrigation. Developed countries do not necessarily get their higher productivity from using more fertilizer; China and Vietnam use about 3 times as much fertilizer per hectare as the United States (see table 4.4). Tractors, which primarily raise labor productivity rather than crop yields, do show a difference between developed and developing countries. The number of tractors per square kilometer is still larger in the three developed countries than in any of the ten developing countries. However, it is much higher in Japan than the US, because the Japanese operate on very small farms with smaller tractors, using labor-intensive methods. Measuring just "tractors" per hectare is a very crude measure of mechanization.

**Table 4.4 Variations in Inputs and Value Added per Worker, Selected Countries**

| Country | Irrigation (% of cropland), 2001-2003 | Fertilizer (kg per hectare of arable land), 2000-2002 | Tractors (per 100 square km of arable land), 2001-2003 | Agricultural Value Added per Worker (2000 $), 2001-2003 |
|---|---|---|---|---|
| China | 48 | 3.5 | 89 | 368 |
| India | 33 | 1.0 | 141 | 381 |
| Indonesia | 13 | 1.3 | 41 | 556 |
| Brazil | 4 | 1.2 | 137 | 3002 |
| Pakistan | 81 | 1.4 | 149 | 690 |
| Bangladesh | 54 | 1.7 | 7 | 308 |
| Nigeria | 1 | 0.07 | 10 | 843 |
| Mexico | 23 | 0.7 | 131 | 2708 |
| Philippines | 15 | 1.3 | 20 | 1010 |
| Vietnam | 34 | 3.2 | 247 | 290 |
| U.S. | 13 | 1.1 | 270 | 36216 |
| Japan | 55 | 3.1 | 4588 | 33546 |
| Germany | 4 | 2.2 | 801 | 23475 |

**Source:** World Bank, World Development Indicators 2007 . compiled by David Abler.

## Engel's Law and the Price Elasticity of Food

Agricultural development in developing countries is seen as a battle to raise farmer productivity. The key to reducing rural poverty is often seen as a simple matter of raising output per farmer or per hectare. As income rises, food consumption rises but at a slower rate (Engel's Law). In other words, the income elasticity of demand for food is less than one[26]. By the same token, the price elasticity for food is also less than one. Given inelastic demand curves, increases in food production often lead to falling food prices, and less income for the average farmer. As shown in Fig. 4.4 below, a shift in the supply of food from $S_1$ to $S_2$, because of new technology in food production, produces LOWER total revenue ($P_1Q_1 > P_2Q_2$). A productivity enhancement makes everyone worse off, unless there is commensurate increase in demand. However, given the

26 For a fuller discussion of the interplay between demand elasticity and agricultural development see Bruce F. Johnston and John W. Mellor "The Role of Agriculture in Economic Development", *American Economic Review* (Sept. 1961) pp. 566-593. They note, in fact, that the income elasticity itself declines with income. The estimated (in 1961) that the income elasticity for food was .6 or higher in low income countries, versus .2-.3 for Western Europe and North America.

low income elasticity of demand for food, such an offsetting increase in demand is unlikely.

**Fig 4.4 Typical Food Demand and Supply Curves**

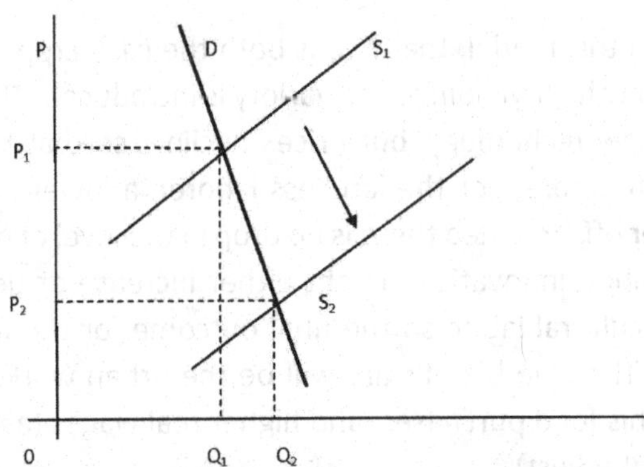


The problems of Engel's Law and the low price elasticity of food can be offset in two ways, neither of them very effective. First, farmers can specialize in crops with high elasticity of demand and high income elasticity. Such crops as lettuce, asparagus, mushrooms, and even flowers, have higher income elasticities. There are also possibilities for some non-food crops, such as cotton, but these also are limited. Finally, farmers can specialize in export crops where the prices of products are determined outside the country, the farmers is a "price taker", and any increase in his output/productivity will not affect the market prices. However, if farmers in one country adopt innovations that increase output, it is also likely that farmers in other countries will adopt similar innovations, and the result in the long run will be the same.

Farmers in developing countries vary in size, abilities, and tolerance for risk. We can distinguish three broad types:

- Small, mostly subsistence farmers, whose output is largely consumed within the farm family, with a small residual that is sold in the market.
- Larger farmers, who typically have a cash or export crop (which may not be food) which occupies the majority of their land, and a smaller plot that covers (a large part of) subsistence needs. The latter may be a garden plot typically managed by women, while

men handle the cash crop. Alternatively, a large farm may only be growing cash crops, and purchasing its food needs.
- Landless laborers, who hire out their services to larger farmers and have little or no land of their own, and cannot survive without wage income.

Let us assume, in this model, that rice is both the cash crop and the food crop. A major new high-yielding seed variety is introduced. The large farmer adopts the new technology, but prices decline, so that his total income is lower than before. For the landless laborer, a lower price for rice makes him better off, provided there is no drop in the level of nominal wages paid for his labor. Innovations might either increase or decrease the demand for agricultural labor, so the final outcome for the landless is not entirely clear. The true beneficiary will be the urban worker, who has lower prices for his food purchases, and higher real wages (assuming nominal wages do not adjust).

For the small farmer, the situation is more complex. The small farmer might adopt the new technology. Since his family need for food is the same, his surplus for the market increases, and he is better off than before, even though rice prices are now lower than before. However, small farmers are notoriously risk adverse, since they have little savings to fall back on and access to only the most expensive forms of credit. It is likely that he will diversify his output over many food crops, in order to limit his risk in case of a major failure of any one crop. He may prefer, for instance, crops that are drought and disease tolerant, even if they have lower potential for profit as a cash crop. He may also lack the financial resources to adopt new technology if it is expensive. For instance, high yielding seed varieties are only high yielding if they receive optimum levels of fertilizer, and often are also more susceptible to pests and disease, thus requiring more careful management and/or the use of pesticides. New varieties may also be risky and may not work out. Small farmers often take a "wait and see" attitude toward the adoption of new technologies. Thus, it is very possible that small farmers will not adopt the new rice seed technology, rice prices will fall, and they will be worse off. At the same time, the large farmer recognizes that he can maintain profitability only by enlarging his operations in terms of scale, putting him in the position of seeking to buy up smaller farmers and consolidate his holdings. The small farmer sells out to the large farmer and moves to the city. Eventually, the large farmer sells out to the giant farmer, and moves to the city. In the end, like the US, you have a country where 1% of the population grow enough food to feed the other 99%, plus a good part of the rest of the world.

During the 1970s, significant progress in raising agricultural production was achieved in Asia and Africa through the introduction of the so-called "high yielding varieties" (HYV), particularly in rice and wheat. New seed varieties were developed through the auspicies of the Rockefeller and Ford Foundations and the establishment of international centers for crop research (such as the International Rice Research Institute in the Philippines). The story of adoption of the HYVs (the so called "green revolution") follows very much along the lines laid out above: larger farmers adopted the new varieties because they had access to credit, and could undertake risks, while smaller farmers did not. The result was more output, which reduced prices, and drove small farmers out of business, or at least made them worse off until they also adopted the HYVs.

The problem of the HYVs or "miracle seeds" is that they produced more output when combined with more fertilizer and irrigation water, and often needed more treatment with pesticides. Traditional varieties of rice and wheat, when given more fertilizer, would become so heavy they would fall over, or lodge. Part of the miracle varieties contribution was to develop varieties with shorter, stronger stems that would remain upright when fertilized. Thus, to get the full benefit of the HYVs, the farmer had to invest in fertilizer, insecticides and irrigation facilities (i.e. private wells), or have access to more publically provided irrigation water. While the "green revolution" produced remarkable increases in output, it is not without its critics (see Appendix A for more details).

**Fig. 4.5 Two Alternative Farm Income Streams -- Illustrative**

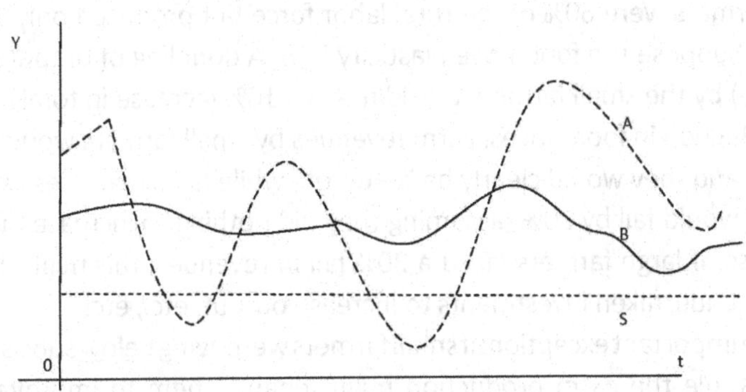

Early "experts" attempting to promote agriculture in developing countries often tried to intro duce Western technologies, and move farmers away from a system of diversified plantings toward one focused on cash or export crops which their farm models showed to be more profitable. Work by T.W. Schultz and others showed that given the risks faced by small farmers, their cropping patterns were in fact often very reasonable and optimal in the long run. Western technologies were often inappropriate for tropical countries. Since small farmers already live close to the margin of existence, a mistake can be very costly, reducing output below subsistence levels, so it is not surprising that they are reluctant to adopt unproven technologies. Consider the situation of two feasible income streams shown in Fig. 4.5, A and B over time. A produces more income over the time period, but greater fluctuations means there are periods when income drops below the subsistence level, S. If credit markets were perfect, the farmer could borrow low interest loans in bad times, and pay them off in good times. However, credit markets in developing countries are far from perfect, and either credit is not available or available only at extremely high interest rates. From the lender's standpoint, there is no guarantee that the farmer's income will rebound, and/or no guarantee that he will use the money to repay the loan. Hence the farmer will choose a cropping pattern reflecting the more stable income stream B, with minimal risk of starvation but a lower total income over time.

Ironically, while helping one poor farmer increase his productivity would have a positive impact, helping all farmers raise their productivity would probably make them all worse off. A program targeted at just small farmers would avoid this problem only if they represented a small share of the total land area, and total output, and technological advances could be limited to them and not taken on by the larger farmers. For instance, suppose small farmers were 60% of the rural labor force but produced only 10% of output. Suppose the food price elasticity is .5. A doubling of output (100% increase) by the small farmers would mean a 10% increase in total output, 20% reduction in food prices. Farm revenues by small farmers would go up by 80%, and they would clearly be better off, while farm revenues by other farmers would fall by 20% (assuming they did nothing to increase output). Of course, if large farmers faced a 20% fall in revenues, this might induce them to undertaken investments to increase output, etc., etc.

One important exception: if small farmers were living <u>below</u> subsistence, it is possible the extra production might enable them to improve their nutrition and that of their families, which would improve their health and welfare. This is particularly important for women and children, since in many developing countries, men eat first, then male children, followed by female children and women last. Adequate nutrition is clearly linked to better health, and improved cognitive ability and performance in school, so the benefits of helping small farmers can be multi-faceted.

## Agricultural Credit

Farmers in developing countries universally complain of the shortage of credit. It is often said that the lack of credit is a case of "market failure". There are profitable opportunities for lenders, but somehow something prevents them from responding. But is this the case? Complaints about the lack of credit are not a proof that market forces are not working.

We can contrast two credit markets in rural areas: first there is often a formal credit market dominated by banks, making loans only to large farmers with substantial collateral, at rates broadly in line with market conditions. Typically formal lenders do not know well local (village) conditions and cannot identify easily which small farmers would be good risks. This is a case of asymmetric information—the farmers know if they a going to repay, but the bankers do not. Information is not equally shared on both sides. Furthermore, their costs of processing small loans are quite high, and fixed regardless of the size of the loan, discouraging them from making small loans.

Second, there are often Informal lenders (money lenders) making smaller loans to farmers who lack collateral. These loans can carry interest rates of 50, 100 or even 200% per annum, but may be for very short periods. Frequently, farmers borrow before the harvest in order to buy food, a loan paid off at the harvest. Money lenders are universally disliked and seen as an evil force. But if small scale lending is so profitable, why doesn't competition enter the market, and drive down the exploitative interest rates? The answer to this is not entirely clear, and there are two main possibilities. First, the net return to money lenders may not actually be that great. Receiving 50% rate of interest on a loan of 3 months is not the same as 100% per year (the money may be idle the rest of the year). The moneylender faces systemic risks—a drought in the village could result in massive defaults, and there would be little he could do. This is in contrast with idiosyncratic risk—the risk that one farmer will default for any of several possible reasons. There is little evidence of money lenders income and return on their investments. However, attempts to increase credit with various agricultural credit schemes in many countries have illustrated how difficult it is to provide low-cost credit in a way that is financially viable. Large scale government sponsored agricultural development banks could be found in almost every developing country in the 1960s and 1970s—most of them have since gone bankrupt and closed. Likewise, attempts to provide credit through cooperatives and local organizations has a mixed record. While micro credit institutions have expanded in recent years, most loans are very small, given to women, and are not for agricultural activities.

Typical money lenders trade on their knowledge—they know their village, and they know who can be trusted, and who cannot. In contrast, formal financial institutions lack this knowledge. Money lenders also have social/religious/ethnic ties so that they are seen as part of the community, so that community members might not trust or accept an outsider. Hence, the second cause of monopoly profits by money lenders might be their ability to keep outsiders from functioning in their village (barriers to entry). But this seems to be a weak reed to hang a case of market failure; the real answer would seem to be that markets function pretty well, and that informal interest rates reflect the real risks and the appropriate return on capital.

## Land Reform

Land reform is often put forward as a necessary first step toward raising output and reducing poverty. Land reform can be broadly defined as dividing up large holdings into smaller farmers, typically giving land ownership to those previous renting or sharecropping "land to the tiller". Such schemes can be accomplished by government seizing land, with or without compensation to the owners, and then enacting a program of land redistribution. Seizure of land without compensation, when land owners are rich and powerful, is rarely an option in most countries, with the exception of those undergoing a socialist revolution (Russia after 1917, Mexico, Cuba, China, Vietnam). Even large scale land reform with compensation is unusual, although in the post WWII years was carried out in Japan, Korea and Taiwan under the pressure from the occupying forces of the United States. Many other countries, such as India, Brazil, Philippines, Bolivia) have instituted land reform programs at various times, but the amount of land transferred has been limited, and the results in terms of output, rather mixed. A new method, called market based land reform, has been introduced in Brazil. Under this approach, a group of farmers are provided subsidized credit from the government and buy a large plot of land from a willing landowner who has already put his land on the market. The government approves the transaction, assists with the subdivision of the parcel, and also provides ancillary inputs, such as technical advice, credit, etc.

The potential impact of land reform is uncertain in terms of output. Empirical evidence is also inconclusive, in most part because of the wide variety of possible land reform scenarios. Consider two illustrative scenarios.

- The original land was owned by an absentee landowner, who did little to invest in the land, provided no inputs, and mostly collected rents. In this case, private ownership in small parcels by former tenants is apt to lead to an increase in output, since the new landowners now have an incentive to invest in their farms, and have collateral on which to obtain credit.
- The original land was part of a large estate producing a crop requiring substantial organization and technical inputs (sugar, bananas, coffee). In this case, land redistribution could result in a fall in production, since the new landowners are not apt to be former tenants but former farm workers who lack the technical expertise to farm efficiently.

For the most part, land reform has the benefit of reducing poverty and income disparities, and providing for a more equitable society. It is not primarily a program to raise output, although in some cases it has.

## Share Cropping

In many parts of South and East Asia, and Latin America, farmers are tenants on land for which they pay a rent in the form of a share of the crop they produce (typically 50%). Arrangements can vary from country to country, both in the share paid as well as the landlord obligations in terms of providing certain key inputs such as seed, fertilizer, etc. Economists have argued (since the time of Alfred Marshall) that share cropping arrangements are sub-optimal, since they give the farmer an incentive to produce less, because they reduce the marginal revenue from additional effort. As shown in the graph (Fig. 4.6) below, a farmer has a marginal cost curve, and this intersects the price line P1, for the output, or the marginal revenue curve, at point A. However, if he now has to pay a fixed share as rent, the marginal revenue from additional output falls to P2, which equals P1 less the rent R owed to the landlord, R.

**Fig. 4.6 Illustrative Farm with and without Share Cropping**

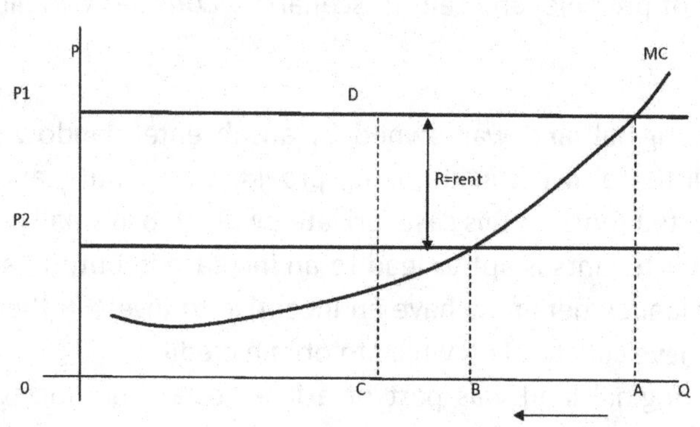


If the landlord changes to a fixed rent, then is the equivalent of a large fixed block of his output (square P1 O C D), but he/she will have the incentive to maximize profits by moving back to point A. However, what happens if output falls below level C? The farmer would have insufficient income to pay the rent, let alone feed himself and his family. With share cropping, since his rent would fall with reduced output, he/she would still have a surplus beyond the rent payment and would be able to survive. In fact, the landlord becomes a partner with the farmer under share cropping, sharing in his good times and bad, and share cropping becomes another means for mitigating risks.

## Discrimination Against Agriculture

Early development thinking was much influenced by the Soviet experience, where forced collectivization of farms, plus controls on output and input prices, were used as mechanisms to extract profits from agriculture and use the resulting surplus to fuel industrialization. Agriculture, furthermore, had a colonial bias. Colonial powers had developed LDC agriculture as a means for providing exports of tropical products, principally by developing large estates and large small holders systems for the production of such crops as coffee, tea, cocoa, bananas, jute, spices, cotton, etc. Marketing Boards set up colonial powers often siphoned off profits by controlling prices paid to the farmer, and many LDC government continued these practices and used these surpluses to finance their industrialization. Newly independent LDC government saw agriculture as backward and colonial, and focused their energies on rapid industrialization and the building up of associated modern infrastructure.

In addition, LDCs tended in the early years to establish fixed exchange rates at a level that produced an overvalued currency. The result was that imports were cheap, and exports suffered. High tariffs were placed on manufactured goods in an attempt to promote import substitution. Farmers engaged in export crop agriculture had to buy expensive imported raw materials but sell crops at the official exchange rate which was overvalued, reducing their income. Imports of food competed with local production, and had low tariffs. Industrialists, on the other hand, enjoyed the protection of high protective tariffs on their products, but lower tariffs on their raw materials. The bias was clearly in favor of industry.

Over time, this bias was corrected, exchange rates brought more in parity with true market values, and tariff systems reformed to be more even. In general, most countries agree that any growth strategy has to combine both agriculture and industrial development, and it is generally cheaper to grow food for domestic consumption in most countries, than to import food from abroad. However, there are some countries which manage to get by with no agriculture at all (Singapore, Hong Kong), and many which import a sizeable part of their food needs (Japan, Korea). Policies should not discriminate against agriculture, or in favor of it. Rather, countries should follow their comparative advantage, and if other countries can produce food more cheaply than it can be produced domestically, they should take advantage of it. This is particularly true if producer countries are willing to subsidize their domestic producers and exporters.

## A Rural Development Strategy

What then should be done in a country with a substantial rural poor population surviving on small farms. Should they be ignored because eventually they will be driven out of business and forced into the cities? Such a strategy would take too long to carry out, and in the meantime millions are living in poverty. What is needed is a strategy of rural development that provides some basic infrastructure and improvements in rural life, while recognizing that many small farmers will eventually become urban migrants. Here are some key points

- Education is key to raising productivity. But it makes no sense to attempt to make small farmers better farmers, if eventually they will migrate. Rather, basic education that raises literacy and numeracy increases skills that can be used in rural or urban settings. Factory workers will have little use for training on farm management.
- Provide better basic infrastructure. One of the best investments in rural areas is in rural roads. Better transport eliminates much economic inefficiency, in terms of reducing the cost of accessing markets, crop losses, and providing greater access to inputs, knowledge, etc. It also provides the rural poor with better access to education and health facilities.
- Health/water/sanitation investments have multiple payoffs. Not only do they raise productivity, but they directly improve the lives of the poor, and lessen the likelihood of migration to urban areas where such services are more abundant.
- Community Driven Development. Providing rural communities with funds which they can invest in a possible range of infrastructure or technical assistance services allows local people the right to identify their own development priorities. Thus, communities can vote on whether a bridge is more important than a school or a health post, or whether they want to contract with a private party to provide advice on crop management, etc.

# Appendix A: The Green Revolution

**Source:** Abridged and edited by author from Wikipedia "Green Revolution", April/September 2010 (http://en.wikipedia.org/wiki/Green_Revolution). See original for sources and citations.

## History

The term "Green Revolution" refers to a series of research, development, and technology transfer initiatives, occurring between 1943 and the late 1970s, that increased agriculture production in many developing nations. The projects within the Green Revolution spread technologies that had already existed, but had not been widely used outside industrialized nations.

The novel technological development of the Green Revolution was the development of new crop varieties suitable for use in developing countries. Agronomists bred cultivars of maize, wheat, and rice that are generally referred to as HYVs or "high-yielding varieties". HYVs have higher nitrogen-absorbing potential than other varieties. Since cereals that absorbed extra nitrogen would typically lodge, or fall over before harvest, semi-dwarfing genes were bred into their genomes. A Japanese dwarf wheat cultivar was instrumental in developing Green Revolution wheat cultivars. IR8, the first widely implemented HYV rice to be developed, was created through a cross between an Indonesian variety and a Chinese variety

The development of hybrid seeds suitable for developing country applications started with the work in Mexico by Norman Borlaug in 1943. Following this success, the Rockefeller Foundation sought to spread it to other nations. The Office of Special Studies in Mexico became an informal international research institution in 1959, and in 1963 it formally became CIMMYT, The International Maize and Wheat Improvement Center.

In 1961 India was on the brink of mass famine. Borlaug was invited to India by the adviser to the Indian minister of agriculture. Despite bureaucratic hurdles imposed by India's grain monopolies, the Ford Foundation and Indian government collaborated to import wheat seed from CIMMYT. Punjab was selected by the Indian government to be the first site to try the new crops because of its reliable water supply and a history of agricultural success. India began its own Green Revolution program of plant breeding, irrigation development, and financing of agrochemicals. As a result, India saw annual wheat production rise from 10 million tons in the 1960s to 73 million in 2006.

India soon adopted IR8—a semi-dwarf rice variety developed by the International Rice Research Institute (IRRI) that could produce more grains of rice per plant when grown with certain fertilizers and irrigation. In 1968, an Indian agronomist published his findings that IR8 rice yielded about 5 tons per hectare with no fertilizer, and almost 10 tons per hectare under optimal conditions. This was 10 times the yield of traditional rice. IR8 was a success throughout Asia, and dubbed the "Miracle Rice". IR8 was also developed into Semi-dwarf IR36.

In the 1960s, rice yields in India were about two tons per hectare; by the mid-1990s, they had risen to six tons per hectare. In the 1970s, rice cost about $550 a ton; in 2001, it cost under $200 a ton. India became one of the world's most successful rice producers, and is now a major rice exporter, shipping nearly 4.5 million tons in 2006.

## ▪ IR8 and the Philippines

In 1960, the Government of the Republic of the Philippines with Ford and Rockefeller Foundations established IRRI (International Rice Research Institute). In 1966, one of the breeding lines became a new cultivar, IR8. IR8 required the use of fertilizers and pesticides, but produced substantially higher yields than the traditional cultivars. Annual rice production in the Philippines increased from 3.7 to 7.7 million tons in two decades. The switch to IR8 rice made the Philippines a rice exporter for the first time in the 20th century.

## ▪ CGIAR

In 1970, foundation officials proposed a worldwide network of agricultural research centers under a permanent secretariat. This was further supported and developed by the World Bank; on May 19, 1971, the Consultative Group on International Agricultural Research was established, co-sponsored by the FAO, IFAD and UNDP. Over time, CGIAR has added many other research centers throughout the world, covering such areas as potatoes, dryland crops, tropical crops, food policy and agroforestry.

CGIAR has responded, at least in part, to criticisms of Green Revolution methodologies. This began in the 1980s, and mainly was a result of pressure from donor organizations. Methods like agroecosystem analysis and farming system research have been adopted to gain a more holistic view of agriculture. Methods like Rapid Rural Appraisal and Participatory Rural Appraisal have been adopted to help scientists understand the problems faced by farmers and even give farmers a role in the development process.

## ▪ Problems in Africa

There have been numerous attempts to introduce the successful concepts from the Mexican and Indian projects into Africa. These programs have generally been less successful, for a number of reasons. Reasons cited include widespread corruption, insecurity, a lack of infrastructure, and a general lack of will on the part of the governments. Yet environmental factors, such as the availability of water for irrigation, the high diversity in slope and soil types in one given area are also reasons why the Green Revolution is not so successful in Africa.

A recent program in western Africa is attempting to introduce a new high-yield variety of rice known as "New Rice for Africa"(NERICA). NERICAs yield about 30% more rice under normal conditions, and can double yields with small amounts of fertilizer and very basic irrigation. However the program has been beset by problems getting the rice into the hands of farmers, and to date the only success has been in Guinea where it currently accounts for 16% of rice cultivation.

## ▪ Effects on food security

The effects of the Green Revolution on global food security are difficult to understand because of the complexities involved in food systems. The world population has grown by about four billion since the beginning of the Green Revolution and many believe that, without the Revolution, there would have been greater famine and malnutrition. The average person in the developing world consumes roughly 25% more calories per day now than before the Green Revolution Between 1950 and 1984, as the Green Revolution transformed agriculture around the globe, world grain production increased by over 250%.

The production increases fostered by the Green Revolution are often credited with having helped to avoid widespread famine, and for feeding billions of people.

## Criticisms of the Green Revolution

There have been many critics of the green revolution. HYVs significantly outperform traditional varieties in the presence of adequate irrigation, pesticides, and fertilizers. In the absence of these inputs, traditional varieties may outperform HYVs. Therefore, several authors have challenged the apparent superiority of HYVs, not only compared to the traditional varieties alone, but by contrasting the monocultural system associated with HYVs with the polycultural system associated with traditional ones.

There are many claims that the Green Revolution has decreased food security for a large number of people. One claim involves the shift of subsistence-oriented cropland to cropland oriented towards production of grain for export or animal feed. For example, the Green Revolution replaced much of the land used for pulses that fed Indian peasants for wheat, which did not make up a large portion of the peasant diet.

The transition from traditional agriculture, in which inputs were generated on-farm, to Green Revolution agriculture, which required the purchase of inputs, led to the widespread establishment of rural credit institutions and greater use of farm credit. The result, critics claim, was that smaller farmers often went into debt, which in some cases resulted in a loss of their farmland. Many small farmers could not obtain credit, and therefore could not adopt the new technologies, and were hurt by the dropping prices resulting from increased production overall. Because wealthier farmers had better access to credit and land, the Green Revolution has been accused of increasing class disparities

The new economic difficulties of small holder farmers and landless farm workers led to increased rural-urban migration. The increase in food production led to a cheaper food for urban dwellers, and the increase in urban population increased the potential for industrialization. However, In some cases, HYVs were nutritionally inferior to standard varieties that they replaced, and in others, consumers preferred traditional varieties because of their taste.

Critics have also focused on the energy and environmental impact of the HYVs. While agricultural output increased as a result of the Green Revolution, the energy input to produce a crop has increased faster, so that the ratio of crops produced to energy input has decreased over time. Green Revolution techniques also heavily rely on chemical fertilizers, pesticides and herbicides, some of which must be developed from fossil fuels, making agriculture increasingly reliant on petroleum products. The heavy use of pesticides and herbicides has had a negative impact on the environment in many cases. For instance, in the Philippines, heavy pesticide use was found to have reduced the number of fish and frog species found in rice paddies.

## ▪ Norman Borlaug's response to criticism

Borlaug dismissed certain claims of critics, but did take other concerns seriously and stated that his work has been ". . . a change in the right direction, but it has not transformed the world into a Utopia".[27] On the environmental criticisms, he noted:

> ". . . some of the environmental lobbyists of the Western nations are the salt of the earth, but many of them are elitists. They've never experienced the physical sensation of hunger. They do their lobbying from comfortable office suites in Washington or Brussels . . . If they lived just one month amid the misery of the developing world, as I have for fifty years, they'd be crying out for tractors and fertilizer and irrigation canals and be outraged that fashionable elitists back home were trying to deny them these things".[28]

27 "http://www.agbioworld.org/biotech-info/topics/borlaug/iowans.html"

28 Tierney, John (2008). "Greens and Hunger". *TierneyLab - Putting Ideas in Science to the Test*. The New York Times. http://tierneylab.blogs.nytimes.com/2008/05/19/greens-and-hunger/?pagemode=print. Retrieved 2009-02-13

# CHAPTER V
# POVERTY AND INCOME DISTRIBUTION

*"God must love the poor. That is why he made so many of them"*—A. Lincoln

## Reducing Poverty

In Chapter I, it was noted that raising incomes through economic development is merely a "means" and not the ultimate "end". What we desire is to reduce or eliminate poverty, or at least a mitigation of its worst aspects. Even the World Bank states, at its front door, that "Our Dream is a World Free of Poverty."

Poverty is common, universal and timeless. Christ noted that "the poor you will always have with you". World religions almost universally demand that people help the poor, and contribute to their upkeep. Concern with the poor and their plight is considered a moral responsibility of most societies, even without religion, and no matter how developed or primitive.

## Focus on Poverty—Historical Perspective

The idea that poverty should be addressed in developing countries is a relatively new idea. The poor and starving millions of places like India and China were accepted as a "fact of life". The countries of Asia and Africa were seen as potential sources of raw materials and markets for manufactured goods under the colonial system of 19th century empire.

Development consisted largely of infrastructure development that aided resource extraction, and assistance for growing export crops such as coffee, cocoa, tea, cotton, copper, etc. plus a certain element of missionary conversion. It was only after World War II that developing countries were seen as deserving independent status as countries rather than colonies, and a potential for being aligned with either the Soviet Union or the US/ Western Europe alliance. Indeed, the World Bank was initially started to help the reconstruction of Europe, and development was a secondary objective tacked on to give it a post-reconstruction purpose.[29]

The dream of the post-war (WWII) world was that countries that were making progress would not be candidates for the adoption of various "isms" that were anti-West (socialism, communism, etc.). It was assumed that growth of GDP would, more or less automatically, raise the incomes of all people within a country, rich and poor alike ("a rising tide floats all boats"). The growing recognition that this was not necessarily happening in the 1950's and 1960s, led several observers to admit that while the gap between rich and poor was widening, the benefits of growth would eventually "trickle down" to the poor. Others suggested that the growth process should not be stopped with early concerns with distribution. Rather, the approach would be to grow now, and redistribute later. Some economists, notably Nicholas Kaldor[30], argued that any kind of redistribution from rich to poor would actually reduce growth. In his model, savings is largely done by the rich. Reducing the income of the rich (e.g. a tax on the rich to help the poor), would mean less overall savings, less investment, and therefore less growth. In the meantime, and at the other end of the spectrum, communist/socialist countries were instituting radical redistribution policies which involved seizing land and productive assets from private owners, and placing them under the control of the state. Only a few developing countries attempted such radical redistribution efforts.

By the late 1960s, there was growing concern among Western observers that what development was taking place in developing countries was not

---

29 Hence the formal name: International Bank for Reconstruction and Development. For a light review of the history of the Bank and its changing focus see Sebastian Mallaby, *The World's Banker*, (Penguin Books, NY, 2004) Chapter 1.

30 Nicholas Kaldor, "Alternative Theories of Distribution", *Review of Economic Studies* 23:2 (1956), pp. 83- 100.

reaching the poor, and development projects were also not concerned about poverty and were benefitting the rich. In 1973, Robert McNamara gave his famous Nairobi speech[31] calling on the World Bank to directly confront poverty, particularly in rural areas, with program of "Integrated Rural Development" which not only addressed increased productivity for small farmers, but also investments in health and education. Increasingly donors turned toward projects that increased the human capital of the poor, and/or helped meet their "basic needs", including nutrition, water supply, sanitation and housing as well as health and education.

Hollis Chenery and his colleagues argued in 1974 in a pioneering book *Redistribution with Growth* (RWG)[32] that countries should aim at redistribution not from the stock of existing assets of the non-poor, or their total income, but from the *Increment* in income. In this way, for instance, high marginal tax rates could redirect basic services to the poor without the trauma of massive income redistribution. Critics argued, however, that a policy of RWG would take a very long time to have a meaningful impact on the poor. Rather, they called for more immediate and large scale interventions designed to meet basic needs. Chenery's RWG had many pioneering aspects, including renewed emphasis on basic service delivery to the poor.

## Poverty is Multi-Dimensional

What do we mean by "poverty"? In general, poverty is often defined as a status of deprivation—a person lacks access to a critical level of goods and services necessary to sustain what is considered to be a "decent" life style. Its standards tend to be relative; the "poor" in any society lack things that are possessed by the "rich". Even in biblical times, people could define the "poor" and the "rich". But while many people can identify

---

31 Address to the Board of Governors by Robert S. McNamara, President, World Bank Group
Nairobi, Kenya, September 24, 1973, available at: http://www.juerguergi.ch/Archiv/EntwicklungspolitikA/EntwicklungspolitikA/assets/McNamara_Nairobi_speech.pdf

32 Hollis Chenery *et.al.*, *Redistribution With Growth,* Oxford Univ.Press, London, 1974.

poverty when they see it, it is not always easy to define exactly what it is. As a judge once said about pornography: "I know it when I see it".

While the first cut on a definition would include income, such a definition risks leaving out other factors that would also cause poverty. The most obvious is assets; a person is rich or poor not only on the basis of the flow of income, but her stock of assets as well. A person with no income but a $3 million house is not considered poor. But the definition could go beyond even assets and income. Would a rich person who was forced to live as a slave be poor or rich? Obviously, on a money scale this person was not poor, but clearly on a scale of human and civil rights, she would be deprived. Thus, we need some broader view of poverty that reflects a low level of "welfare". As noted in Chapter I, we think in terms of a "welfare function" where we can define welfare as a person's total well-being which is made of up many components. A possible welfare function might look like this:

$$W = f(Y, F, V, A, \ldots)$$

where W is welfare is a function (f) of income (Y), political freedom (F), crime and violence (V), assets owned (A) and many other variables. Welfare can be diminished by such non-material factors as a lack of access to health care and education, the absence of human rights, the lack democratic participation in government, and cultural and ethnic discrimination. The problem is that while such a welfare function can be conceptualized, it is difficult to measure welfare. In fact, it is pretty much impossible, since one person's view of welfare will differ from someone else's. For instance, my welfare might depend on the availability of opera tickets, which for someone else such availability has no value. In fact, my friend might say he was better off if he was not forced by his wife to go to the opera. Thus, we say that welfare or poverty is "multi-dimensional".

A.K. Sen argues that looking at access to goods is not sufficient, and this confuses means and ends. Money is a means for raising welfare, but people differ widely in abilities. They do not all have the same "capability" of achieving the same welfare level from the same income. Thus, what we should focus on is a person's capabilities to achieve a certain welfare level. A handicapped person, for instance, will need a larger income to achieve the same welfare level as a normal person. People with the same income will not have the same "capability" if some of them are denied the freedom to educate themselves, or to vote, or other basic freedoms. Thus, the desire is not to have an equality of goods, but an equality of opportunity.[33]

## Social Justice

In general, people living in a most societies do not want to see their neighbors starving to death. Almost all societies have some way of taking care of the old, the infirm, the handicapped and those unable to produce. But how much redistribution to the poor is enough, or how much is warranted?

In the 19th Century, people like Jeremy Bentham developed theories of utility, with the idea being to maximize happiness—the greatest good for the greatest number. But this implied that welfare or happiness could be measured. It was assumed, however, that marginal utility of money decreased with extra income. That is, for every extra dollar of income the marginal happiness or welfare declined. A person received more utility from the first dollar of income than from the 50th or 1,000th. Thus, one could draw a theoretical curve of diminishing marginal utility of money (see fig. 5.1), and it can be shown that a transfer from a rich person to a poor person produces a net gain in utility for the country, since the marginal utility of the rich person's income foregone is less than the added utility of the poor person receiving the transfer. In Fig. 5.1, the marginal loss for the rich person for a one dollar transfer is 4 "utiles" (some arbitrary measure of utility), while the poor person gains 10 "utiles", for a net social gain of 6. On this basis, only a completely equal allocation of income would be that which maximized total utility. However, this assumes that everyone lies on the same utility curve, and that utility can be measured and compared between people, both of which are not true. Who is to say that the marginal utility curve for income is flat, and not diminishing? It may also not be symmetric; people may not value additional income very much, but once used to a certain status and income style, may have a bigger loss of utility when it comes to giving up that income.

---

33 A.K. Sen, *Inequality Reexamined*, Harvard Univ. Press, Cambridge, Mass., 1962.

Fig. 5.1
The Marginal Utility of Income

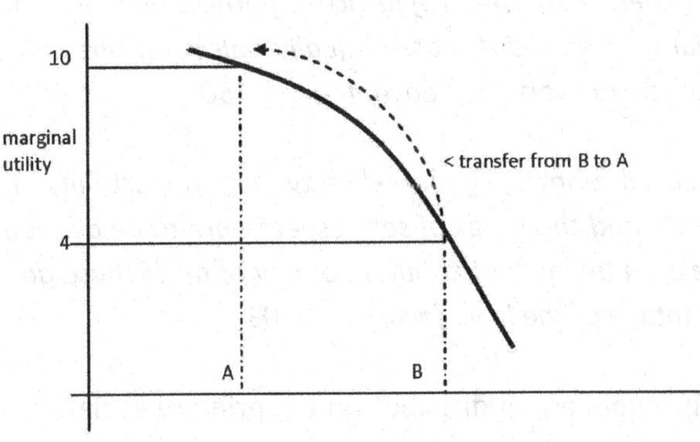


Given the problems of making comparisons, Wilfred Pareto came up with a simple principle that bears his name: any reallocation that makes at least one person better off, provided no one is worse off, is to be preferred. Here Pareto is measuring welfare by monetary values, and escaping from the vagueness of utility. However, his principle is a very constraining guide, as few instances can be found when some action by the state can be undertaken without some one being worse off. A variant of the Pareto principle is called the compensation principle, which states that any action by the state in which the gainers could and would be willing to compensate the losers (because the gainers still come out ahead) is welfare improving, even if the compensation does not actually occur[34]. This then gives the state more room. If we can prove that the incomes of those using a road are greater than the tax money levied to build it, the road is welfare improving and should be undertaken. The social welfare analysis of Pareto led to modern calculations of benefits and costs of public projects.

One of the most famous social philosophers of the twentieth century was John Rawls. His book, called "A Theory of Justice" (1971)[35] laid out a complete theory of social justice. In his view, justice is viewed as "fairness"

34 Also called the Kaldor-Hicks criterion or Kaldor-Hicks efficiency, developed by J.R. Hicks and Nicolas Kaldor. See "Kaldor-Hicks Efficiency" at http://en.wikipedia.org/wiki/Kaldor-Hicks_efficiency.

35 John Rawls, *A Theory of Justice,* Cambridge, Mass.: Belknap Press, 1971.

The foundation of this theory was the so called "difference principle" In Rawls' words:

> *The general conception of justice as fairness requires that all primary social goods be distributed equally unless an unequal distribution would be to everyone's advantage. p. 150*
>
> *All social primary goods—liberty and opportunity, income and wealth, and the bases of self respect—are to be distributed equally unless an unequal distribution of any of all of these goods is to the advantage of the least favored. p. 303.*

So Rawls favors equal distribution of "primary social goods", unless some other non-equal distribution would favor the poor. Rawls defines "primary social goods" very broadly, and includes not only income and wealth, but intangibles such as liberty and opportunity. A more narrow interpretation of Rawls' view is the Basic Needs (BN) approach (see Streeten et. al.[36]). The idea of BN was that minimum or basic needs should be provided by society for its members. What exactly are "basic" of course is questionable. But the BN approach, popular during the late 70s and 80s, suggested that BN should include food, shelter, water, education, health services, and housing. But others would argue that human rights, freedom, voting rights and other intangibles should also be included.

Rawls based his philosophy on something he called the "original position". He suggested the following proposition: suppose you can choose what kind of society you will be born into, but you do not know what your position in that society will be. Rawls argues that most people would choose a more equal society, thus demonstrating that people prefer equality over inequality. However, such a choice might merely reflect a risk adverse approach. If society A has 90% poor and 10% rich, your initial position is more likely to be poor. However, if society B has the same average income, but everyone has that average income (100% middle class), then 9 times out of 10 you would be better off choosing B over A.

---

[36] Paul Streeten et. al., *First Things First*(1981). Oxford University Press

There is also evidence that the difference principle is not viewed as "fair" by people. Konow (p. 1197) offers some interesting examples, two of which are summarized below:

- Example 1: Two workers receive equal pay. Their employer arbitrarily decides to raise each but by unequal amounts. When people were asked to review this example, 86% say it was unfair. Yet this satisfies the difference principle because a more unequal distribution still makes the poorer person better off.
- Example 2: two workers with equal pay. One works harder, while the other is lazy. Employer decides to increase the pay of the productive one, decrease the pay of the other. Opinion: 80% think this is fair, since it is reward for hard work. Yet this violates the difference principle—a distribution is more unequal and the poor person is poorer.

Thus, in these two examples we find that people feel that payments should be linked to effort, or a reward for work. Such payments also maximize incentives for work, which helps maximize total economic output.

## Needs Basis

The ultimate in equalitarianism is the Marxist approach, roughly and frequently summarized as "from each according to his ability, to each according to his needs". Of course, even communist societies had differentiated wage scales and some people were richer than others. Nevertheless, the dominate feature of these societies was their extremely equal income distribution, and low levels of abject poverty. The fundamental problem with this idealistic model, one that is still carried on in communal living arrangements, is that it undermines the incentive to work. If my wage income does not reflect my effort, but my needs, why should I work hard? Thus, we have the classic "free rider" problem. I can coast along doing little and receive income based on the work of others. In an idealistic communal living arrangement, a group of like-minded people might overcome this problem. However, the history of communal living arrangements is usually marked by an eventual breakdown because people feel they are unfairly treated; that some people work harder than others. As the Communist experience showed, eventually the very equal income distribution means so little incentive to work that the growth of income itself is inhibited.

While many people have problems with Rawls' "difference principle" his attention to the needs of the very poorest rings true. The term "primary social goods" is interpreted by Rawls very broadly. However, a more narrow interpretation is consistent with what once called the "basic needs" approach. The philosopher D.D. Raphael (1980, quoted in Konow) states that justice demands that society provide "a basic minimum for all even if some of those affected could achieve it by their own efforts". Paul Streeten notes that "the idea that the basic needs of all should be satisfied before the inessential needs of the few are met is a principle widely accepted."[37] Most people would accept this view, but exactly what is "basic" and what is not is, of course, an open question. A telephone is basic in the United States, but a luxury in Bangladesh. In general, basic needs are considered housing, clothing, food, and some minimal level of education and health care. Beyond this, people are free to earn what they can without restrictions on their income, and thus no limit on their incentives. However, if basic needs are to be paid through taxation, even supplying basic needs can reduce incentives.

While Rawls would say that almost everything should be equally distributed, there are others on the opposite side who strongly reject this approach. For instance, Robert Nozick, a man who studied under Rawls came to exactly the opposite conclusion. For Nozick, the state should only be worried about insuring that transactions are just. People should be free to acquire wealth from their work in an atmosphere that ensures justice in acquistion, and allowed to transfer their holdings equitably. Thus, the state should provide a level playing field, and ensure only that wealth is not accumulated through fraud, theft, enslavement, etc. For Nozick, the state provides for the operation of justice, police, defense and a money supply, but little else. To Nozick, freedom of the individual is more important than "social goods" which are ill-defined. A just society allows maximum freedom for individual to realize his potential.

---

37 Paul Streeten et. al., *First Things First: Meeting Basic Human Needs in Developing Countries*, World Bank/Oxford University Press. Wash. D.C., 1981.

## A Neo-classical View

Modern neo-classical economics does not concern itself with "justice" or fairness. Implictedly what is "fair" is the wage paid by the market. Wages reflect demand and supply of labor; at the margin, the wage paid the last worker hired equals the marginal product (net gain to the firm) of the worker. Put another way, employers will hire workers until the marginal product produced is equal to the wage. However, is supply and demand really "fair"? If we look at wages paid for some jobs in the United States, one has to wonder if the market is fairly valuing everyone's product. Why does the President of the United States receive a smaller income than the football coach of the University of Maryland? Does a CEO need an annual income of $200 million (see table 5.1)? Why does a professional baseball player make $33 million? Naturally, these wages can be rationalized as reflecting the unique skills of the recipients, and their relative scarcity. For sports figures, they also reflect fans willingness to pay to watch them play and the revenues they generate from advertising, etc. However, one has to ask oneself how just and fair is a society that pays $33 million to a baseball player, but whose schools in the inner cities pay only $53,000 to teachers, and whose systems of education prevent poor children from reaching anything approaching their "capabilities"?

**Table 5.1. Some Typical Salaries**
(total compensation, 2009-10)

| | |
|---|---|
| Prime Minister, India (2010) | $ 50,000 (PPP) |
| Beginning school Teacher, Wash. DC | 53,000 |
| US President (2010) | 400,000 (+100,000 for travel) |
| President Univ. of Md (2009) | 498,000 |
| President, GWU (2009) | 900,000 |
| Football Coach, U of Md.(2009) | 1,900,000 |
| Derek Jeter, NY Yankees (2010) | 33,000,000 |
| CEO, Yahoo (2009) | 231,000,000* |

*highest paid US CEO

## Income Distribution and Poverty

The distribution of income between the rich and the poor is a key factor in determining how fast poverty is reduced, and even the very concept of poverty itself. A poor person living in a society of very rich may feel worse off than the same person living in a society where everyone is "poor". Of course, even if one lives in a poor but equal society, in an era of mass communications, it is difficult to avoid comparisons with other, more wealthy, countries.

Consider the following example. Assume there are two countries, A and B (see Table 5.2). The initial income of the rich and the poor are the same in both A and B. Over a ten year period the income of the rich in A grows at 2% per year, while it grows in B at 8% per year. The income of the poor grows at 3% in A and 6% in B (see table 5.3 below). Clearly, the poor are better off in B, since their income is growing faster than the poor people in A. But in A, the poor are catching up to the rich, since total GDP is growing at only 2%. Income distribution is improving. In B, the income of the poor is growing rapidly, but slower than that of total society (and therefore slower than that of the non-poor). Are the poor of B likely to be content when they see material progress, but a widening gap between rich and poor?

**Table 5.2 Example --Income Distribution**

| Initial Income | Growth rate of: | A | B |
|---|---|---|---|
| 1,000 | Income of rich (top 50%) | 2.0 | 8.0 |
| 100 | Income of poor (bottom 50%) | 3.0 | 6.0 |

Of course, it might be the absolute size of the gap, and not the relative gap that is important. For instance, if the rich start with a per capita income of 1,000 (Table 5.3), and the poor 100, after ten years the resulting per capita income is as such:

**Table 5.3 Absolute and Relative Gaps**

| | Initial Income | A | B |
|---|---|---|---|
| Income of rich | 1,000 | 1219 | 2159 |
| Income of poor | 100 | 134 | 179 |
| Ratio rich/poor | 10 | 9.1 | 12.1 |
| Absolute gap | 900 | 1085 | 1980 |

In A the ratio of the incomes has fallen as the poor have caught up in a relative sense (the income of the rich declines from 10:1 to 9.1:1), but the absolute difference between rich and poor widens (from 900 to 1085). Thus, even in A the poor might think of themselves worse off if they measure the gap in absolute terms. In B, the poor are worse off in a relative sense no matter how it is measured, but much better than they were in their initial position (179 vs. 100), and better off than in the slower growing A (179 vs. 134).

Some people argue that the growth of total GDP is unfairly weighted toward the rich, and does not give a valid expression of the growth of total welfare. This is because the income of the rich is so large, any growth in this sector swamps out the impact of growth among the poor. Take the following example. An economy of two people; the poor person has an income of 100 and a rich person with an income of 1000. Total GDP is 1,100[38]. If the income of the poor increases by 10%, with no growth in the income of the rich, the growth of total GDP is about 1%. If the income of the rich grows by 10%, with no growth in the income of the poor, the total GDP growth rate is about 9%. As part of the study *Redistribution with Growth*[39], Hollis Chenery and Montek Ahluwalia proposed that growth rates be weighted by welfare weights. First, they make the point that the normal growth rate calculation can be viewed as the weighted average of the growth rates of the five quintiles of the income distribution, or:

$$G = w_1g_1 + w_2g_2 + w_3g_3 + w_4g_4 + w_5g_5,$$

Where $w_i$ are the weights, and $g_i$ are the growth rates for each quintile. Normally, these weights are the income shares for each quintile. In a typical case, they may look like:

$$G = .05\,g_1 + .10\,g_2 + .15\,g_3 + .25\,g_4 + .45\,g_5$$

In this example, the lowest quintile (poorest) has 5% of total income, and the richest 45%. These weights are typical of what we find in Latin

38 We know that total GDP is not quite the same as personal income, but for this example we use them interchangeably.

39 Hollis Chenery, Montek Ahulwalia, *et. al.*, *Redistribution With Growth*, Oxford Univ.Press, London, 1971.

America, for instance. However, one could recalculate the growth rate using equal weights, or:

$$G = .20\,g_1 + .20\,g_2 + .20\,g_3 + .20g_4 + .20\,g_5$$

A more poverty or welfare focus could be had by only focusing on the growth of incomes of the lower two quintiles or:

$$G = .50\,g_1 + .50\,g_2 + .00\,g_3 + .00\,g_4 + .00\,g_5$$

The result would be a different growth rate overall, one which gives more weight to the bottom of the income distribution.

While an interesting variant of reshaping GDP to better measure welfare, the Chenery-Ahluwalia approach has rarely been used. Perhaps part of the problem is that it deals only with the growth in income, and not the absolute level. In addition, there is no general agreement on which system of welfare weights should be used. Recent interest in "pro-poor" growth, however, has revised interest in this approach (see Appendix to this Chapter for an example of how the adjustments in the weights can affect the overall growth rate).

The intersection of income distribution and poverty comes down to a fundamental question—do we want to focus on increasing the size of the total "pie" (total income), or giving the poor a bigger "slice" (improving income distribution)? Either way, poverty will fall. As shown in the diagram (Fig 5.2) below, one can think of the question of policies that either promote growth, or improve income distribution. Both lead to poverty reduction. But what about the possible interaction between policies(the dashed arrows in Fig 5.2)? Policies that lead to better distribution might reduce incentives to produce, thus lowering growth of GDP. Policies that promote growth could also worsen income distribution. Thus, one set of policies could have offsetting effects, both reducing and raising poverty at the same time. However, it is also true that strong growth policies might have some weak negative effects on distribution, but the net result is still in favor of reducing poverty because of the very strong growth in income.

Fig. 5.2 Policy-Poverty Links

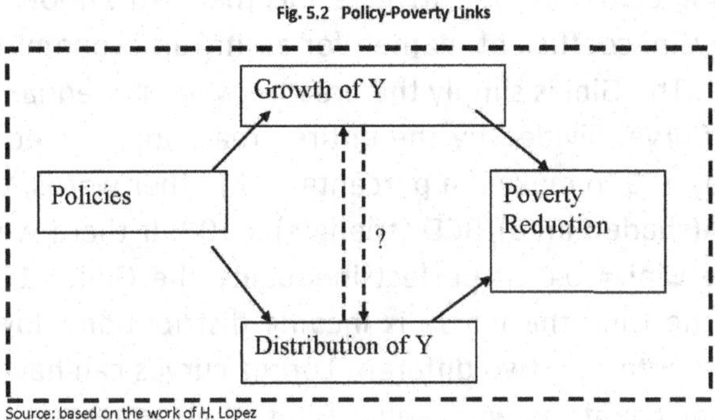


Source: based on the work of H. Lopez

## Measuring Income Distribution

Income distribution is commonly measured with reference to the Lorenz Curve. This diagrammatic approach graphs the cumulative percentage of the population on the horizontal axis, ranked from the poorest to the richest (see Fig. 5.3). The vertical axis measures the cumulative share of total income received by that population share. Thus, the 45° line shows perfect equality—the lowest 20% of the population receives 20% of income, the lowest 50% receives 50%, etc. If there were perfect inequality, the Lorenz Curve follows the horizontal axis up to the point that covers 99.9% of the population, with the last person receiving 100% of income, and then the Lorenz Curve would follow the right-hand vertical axis (line BCD in Fig. 5.3). In reality, Lorenz Curves lie somewhere between these extremes (but the Lorenz Curve can never lie above the equality line).

Fig. 5.3 The Lorenz Curve

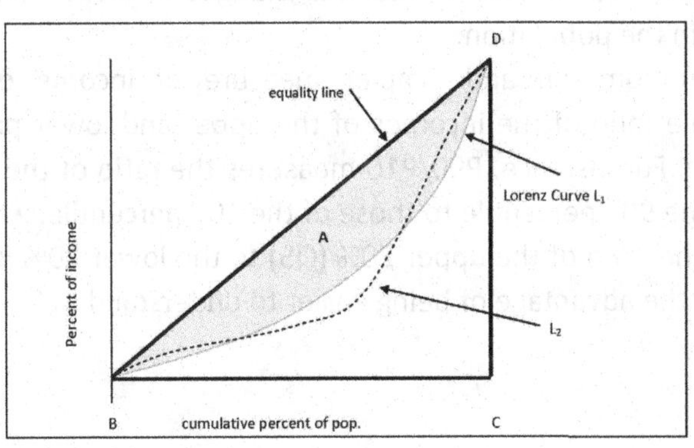

The most common way to give income distribution a numeric value is the Gini coefficient, named for an Italian economist who first calculated it. The Gini is simply the area between the equality line and the Lorenz Curve, divided by the entire area under the equality line, multiplied by 100 to make it a percentage. In other words, the Gini (in Fig. 5.3) = A(shaded area)/BCD (triangle) x 100. If there were perfect equality the Gini = 0.0; if perfect inequality the Gini = 100.0. Thus, the higher the Gini, the worse is income distribution. However, it is important to note that two different Lorenz curves can have the same Ginis, so that countries with equal Ginis need not have exactly the same distribution. In Fig.5.3, Lorenz curves $L_1$ and $L_2$ can have the same Gini coefficient provided the area between the curve and the equality line is equal. (Note: in some cases, Ginis are quoted as decimals such as .45 instead of 45).

While the Gini is the most common measure of income distribution, there are other measures. The Gini tends to give heavy weight to the middle of the income distribution. Other measures (Thiel, Atkinson) give more weight to the top or lower parts of the distribution. Another approach is to measure the variance of each person's income (in the survey) from the mean. This can be done using the coefficient of variation (the standard deviation divided by the mean) or log variance, which is the variance of every observation from the log of income. The advantage of the Thiel and the log variance is that they are exactly decomposable. This means that a changes in these distribution measures can be broken down exactly into the changes in distribution of each sub-group in the population.

> Useful Definitions
> Quartile—25% of a population
> Quintile—20% of a population
> Decile—10% ' " "
> Percentile—1% " " "

Another common and simpler measure of income distribution is the simple ratio of the incomes of the upper and lower parts of the distribution. For instance, P90/P10 measures the ratio of the income of people in the $90^{th}$ percentile to those of the $10^{th}$ percentile, while Q5/Q1 measures the ratio of the upper 20% (Q5) to the lower 20% (Q1). These ratios have the advantage of being easier to understand.

## Income Distribution in the World

While in theory a Gini can range from 0.0 to 100, in fact the actual experience (see Table 5.4) across countries is a range from about 25 (Japan, Sweden) to 60 (Brazil, Guatemala). The United States, at 40.8 is about average. In general, income distribution is very uneven in Latin American countries, and relatively even in Western and Central Europe, particularly the former countries of the Soviet Union.

**Table 5.4 Selected Gini Coefficients**

| | | | | | |
|---|---|---|---|---|---|
| Brazil | 59.3 | Honduras | 55.0 | Sweden | 25.0 |
| Chile | 57.1 | India | 32.5 | Tanzania | 38.2 |
| China | 44.7 | Japan | 24.9 | U.K. | 36.0 |
| France | 32.7 | Kenya | 42.5 | U.S. | 40.8 |
| Ghana | 40.8 | Korea | 31.6 | | |
| Guatemala | 59.9 | Russia | 31.0 | | |

Source: World Bank, World Development Indicators, 2005. Ginis are for income or consumption, latest available year, generally 1999-2003.

What about the world distribution of income? This is complicated, because one has to combine survey data for different countries, and the world distribution has to reflect distribution within countries, as well as distribution between countries, and their relative sizes. Work done by Branko Milanovic[40] taking account of these factors suggests that the overall Gini coefficient for the world was 62 in 1988, and rose slightly to 64 in 1998. The rapid growth of incomes in China and India have helped improve world distribution, but the growing gap between urban and rural incomes in these same countries have tended to worsen the overall Gini. The progress in China and India masks somewhat the growing gap between countries. As Milanovic points out, the gap between the rich countries (Europe, Japan, North America) and the rest of the world is growing; few countries have effectively been able to bridge the gap and join the club of the rich, many several countries have slipped further into poverty. Thus, there is a growing gap between the rich and poor countries, but because of rapid growth in two of the largest countries, world income distribution has remained relatively constant. In fact, the growing gap between the urban rich and rural poor in India and China has tended to worsen world

40 Branko Milanovic, Worlds Apart: Measuring Global and International Inequality (Princeton: Princeton University Press, 2005)

income distribution, but this is offset by the ability of India and China to close the gap between themselves and the rich countries. While there has been little change over time, the level of inequality remains high. Roughly 10% of the world's population receives about 50% of the income.

## Does Growth and Development Lead to Greater Inequality?

Many critics of standard development economics, and development experiences, would argue that they only lead to the greater impoverishment of the poor—"the rich get richer, and the poor get poorer" is frequently heard among the critics of globalization, for instance. There are also arguments that the poor suffer more in a recession than the rich. Most of these statements are not supported by the empirical evidence, however. If they were, there would be a gradual rise in poverty in the world, as the poor would face growing impoverishment both in good times and in recessions.

One of the first economists to think about this problem was Simon Kuznets, working in the 1950s. He reasoned that if a a country started out poor, and rural, and then developed over time, what would happen would be a transformation of poor rural people to a more wealthy urban population. If 95% of the population is poor, and 5% is rich, then the income distribution is fairly even. If the poor become rich, then the income distribution actually is worse, up until the point where 50% are poor and 50% are rich. The distribution will then improve as the country moves to a more developed situation where everyone is rich. Thus, he reasoned, the process of development would tend to result in a period of worsening income distribution, and then improving. It would trace a kind of inverted "U" shaped curve (see figure 5.4 below).

Kuznets did some research with limited data, plotting countries Gini coefficients and income, and found that this inverted "U" shaped relationships seemed to hold. Since that time, economists have sought to prove or disprove this "Kuznets Hypothesis". Most analysis of income distribution data does not support his hypothesis, and finds no relationship between level of income and distribution. Kuznets' work in fact was hampered by a shortage of data. For the middle-income countries, he had mostly data from Latin America, which is notorious for having bad income distribution. At the lower level, he had data from South Asia, which has a fairly even distribution, and at the upper level data from Europe and North America. The result was the "inverted—U" shaped curve (see Fig. 5.4). However, as more countries undertook household surveys, and more data became available, the "inverted—U" pattern disappeared.

**Fig. 5.4 The Kuznets Hypothesis**

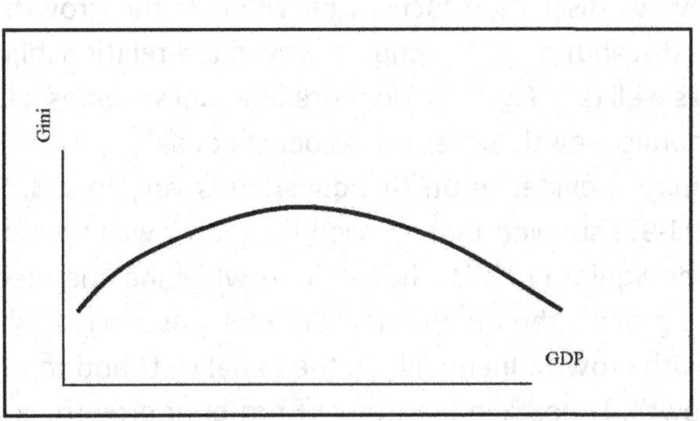


One of the most thorough examinations of this relationship was by Deninger and Squire[41], who carefully constructed a data set of comparable household surveys of similar quality. They found no overall relationship between distribution and income levels, or between income distribution and growth. In fact, they noted that countries tended not to exhibit major changes in income distribution over time. Since income distribution tends to be stable, growth of income tends to be effective in reducing poverty. Similar results were found by Chen and Ravallion[42], who noted that income distribution improved during growth in as many cases as it deteriorated; there was no clear trend. The exception was the developing countries of Europe and Central Asia where declining output was associated with deteriorating income distribution. However, it is also true that the phenomenon pointed out by Milanovic (see above), of the

41 Klaus Deininger, and Lynn Squire (1996). "A New Data Set Measuring Income Inequality" *World Bank Economic Review* 10:3 (1996) pp. 565-9,.and Klaus Deininger and Lynn Squire, "New Ways of Looking at Old Issues: Inequality and Growth" *Journal of Development Economics* 57:2(1998), pp. 259-287.

42 Martin Ravallion and S. Chen "What Can Recent Surveys Tell Us About Trends in Distribution and Poverty" *World Bank Economic Review* 11:2 (1997), pp. 357-82

growing gap between urban rich and rural poor in China and India, is in fact a manifestation of the Kuznets effect.

## Does Inequality Impact on Growth?

The previous discussion focuses on whether the growth of income affected the distribution of income. However, the relationship can go the other way, as well (see Fig. 5.2). Do more unequal societies have faster or slower economic growth, other things being equal?

The empirical evidence on this question is very mixed. Some early studies (1994-97) showed that showed inequality was bad for growth[43]. Deininger and Squire (1998)[44] showed that while income inequality was unrelated to growth the distribution of assets, as measured by land, is correlated with growth. Inequality in the initial distribution of land leads to lower growth. Lopez[45], in his study of pro-poor growth, could find no relationship between inequality and growth. Some recent studies suggest that inequality could be good for growth[46]. However, there seems to be little evidence that savings rates are a constraint on growth, and only a weak relationship between investment and growth. Hence, if inequality

---

43 Alesina, A. and D. Rodrik (1994). "Distributive Policies and Economic Growth" *Quarterly Journal of Economics*, 109: 465-90. Roland Benabou, "Inequality and Growth" *NBER Working Papers*, No. 5658, National Bureau of Economic Research (Cambridge, Mass), 1997. Perotti, Roberto (1996). "Growth, Income Distribution and Democracy: What the Data Say" *Journal of Economic Growth* 1: 149-187.

44 Deininger, Klaus and Lynn Squire, "New Ways of Looking at Old Issues: Inequality and Growth" *Journal of Development Economics* 57:2(1998), pp. 259-287.

45 Humberto Lopez, "Pro-Poor, Pro-Growth: Is There a Trade-ff?" *Policy Research Working* Paper 3378, World Bank, August, 2004.

46 H.Li, L. Squire and H. Zou, "Explaining International and Intertemporal Variations in Income Inequality". *Economic Journal*, 108(1998), pp.26-43, Kristen, Forbes. "A Reassessment of the Relationship between Inequality and Growth." *The American Economic Review,* 90:4 (September 2000), pp. 869-887

is good for growth, it is not because of the reasoning behind the Kaldor hypothesis that increased inequality increases savings and investment.

## Median Voter Theorem

> Definition of an Economist
>
> An Economist is someone who sees something in the real world, and then goes home to see if it works out in theory.

Another model of how inequality can impact on growth is based on the political economy of the growth and distribution process in a democratic system. In theory, if the poor are majority, they will vote for more redistribution, more taxes on rich, lower growth. Hence what is important is the status of the median voter, since he/she determines a majority. If poor are a minority, the median voter is in the non-poor group that will pay taxes, receives no net benefit from redistribution, hence will vote against such programs. If the poor are the majority, the median voter will be poor, and is likely to vote for programs of redistribution.

While this seems to make sense on the surface, in fact, it does not seem to be borne out in practice. It assumes that the poor can influence government enough to ensure that tax systems are progressive, but we know that in most developing countries they are not. It also assumes a working democracy, lacking in many developing countries. Finally, there is some evidence that poor people who are upwardly mobile do not want to impose taxes on a class of people above them, when they hope to enter this class sometime in the future. In societies where there is little or no mobility, but yet a well functioning democracy, it might be possible that the median voter theorem might hold. The Median Voter Theorem is another elegant economic theory, like the Kuznets Hypothesis, which sounds good but fails to be empirically verified, in part because it overly simplifies the real world (see box). The field of economics is full of these failed theories.

But does income inequality lead to greater political instability? On this point the evidence is mixed. Part of the problem arises from defining political instability. Somoza's regime in Nicaragua was very stable for years, without any change, until it was overthrown. The U.S., on the other hand, changes governments every four to eight years. Perotti (1996) found that more equal (income) societies have lower fertility rates and higher rates of investment in education, both of which are growth promoting. He also finds that very unequal societies tend to be politically and socially unstable, which is reflected in lower rates of investment and growth. He does not find any support for the "median voter theorem"—equal societies do not have fewer demands for redistribution. A study by Fajnzylber, Loayaza, and Lederman[47] provides evidence, however, supporting the idea that unequal societies have higher crime rates and more violence. Crime rates do not appear to correlate, however, with the level of poverty.

## Effect of Public Expenditures and Taxes

Changing the distribution of income is not easy, and usually has to be done through actions by the public sector. Government options include:

- confiscation of assets and their redistribution directly to the people, or retention by the state, as was often done under socialist governments in Eastern Europe. These programs may or may not include some form of compensation to the previous owners. Full compensation would, of course, negate the goal of evening of wealth and income.
- Imposition of progressive taxation programs, in which the rich pay a greater share of their income than the poor. Generally, progressive taxation works best via the income tax, and is a common approach in Western Europe and the U.S. Income taxation is generally found in only the more advanced developing countries, and is rarely effective. Most developing countries rely on sales taxes, including the value-added tax, which tend to be regressive.
- Expenditure programs by the government that are directed to benefit the poor more than the rich. In developing countries poverty targeted expenditures are more important than progressive income taxation.

---

[47] Pablo Fajnzylber, Daniel Lederman, and Norman Loayza, "Determinates of Crime Rates In Latin America and the World: An Empirical Assessment" *World Bank Latin American and Caribbean Studies* World Bank, Wash. DC, 1998.

In fact, most estimates of income distribution based on household surveys do not account for free public services received as part of real income. In other words, the value of free services provided by the government is not included in household income and expenditures. This would generally include such things as education, health, child care, job training, subsidized electricity and water. Direct grants, pensions, and other monetary compensation would be included.

We can construct a distribution curve of public expenditures using the Lorenz curve approach to show which programs are progressive or regressive. For instance, in fig. 5.5, we plot the cumulative expenditures and population shares for two programs, A and B. The population is ordered from low to high income, as before. At the mid-point of the population, we see that the lower 50% of the population receives more than 50% of program A, but less than 50% of program B (dashed line, Fig. 5.5). This is one case where the Lorenz curve can be above the equality line, since it is not measuring total income, but share of the government program. In fact, it really should not be called a Lorenz curve. The distribution measure associated with this curve is often called a pseudo-Gini, for the same reason.

**Fig. 5.5**
**Lorenz Curves for the Distribution Expenditures**

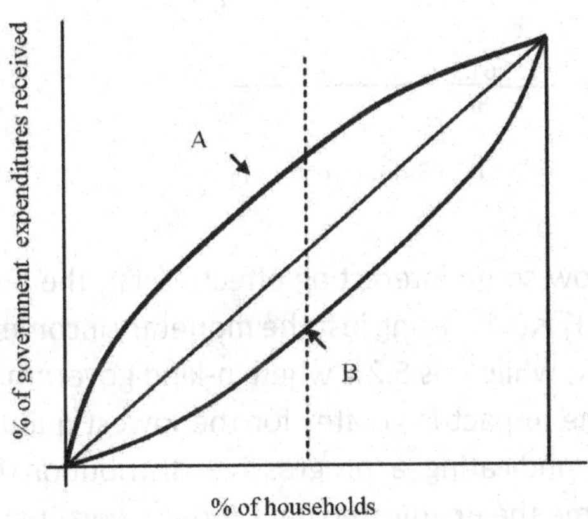


The potential for changing distribution through expenditure programs is considerable. For instance, assume a country in which the government spends 25% of GDP, and poor receive only 5% of GDP. If 10% of government expenditures can be redirected to poor then the result will be a 50% increase in their real income (10% of government expenditures is 2.5% of GDP, which is 50% of their share of 5.0%). This assumes, however, that $1 of government services received has the same value as a $1 of cash income. In fact, the valuation that people place on free government services might be greater or less than this. The value of a program that is ineffective, for instance job training for jobs that do not exist, would not be worth the money the government spends on it. However, if government salaries are less than the market wage, services such as education and health might be more valuable than their cost.

If we were to allow for the welfare impact of government services, the normally calculated Gini coefficient would be changed. In general, such an adjusted Gini would be more equal than the unadjusted one, since universally provided services tend to make income distribution more equal (assuming that they are not provided by a regressive tax). An example of what can happen when this is done is given in the table 5.5 below using Chile as a country example[48].

**Table 5.5**
**Chile: Income Shares Adjusted to Include Government Expenditures**
(Percent of Total Income, 1998)

| Quintile | Before | After |
|---|---|---|
| $Q_1$ | 3.1 | 5.2 |
| $Q_2$ | 6.7 | 8.2 |
| ... | | |
| $Q_5$ | 61.1 | 57.0 |
| Gini | .564 | .503 |

Source: World Bank, Chile's High Growth Economy, p. 54.

These results show some interesting effects. First, the income share of the lowest 20% (Q1) is 3.1% using just the monetary income reported in the household survey, while it is 5.2% when in-kind government services are also included. The impact is greater for the lowest quintile than for the second quintile, indicating a progressive distribution of services. Furthermore, over time the unadjusted data show a worsening of income

48 World Bank, *Chile's High Growth Economy: Poverty and Income Distribution 1987-1998,* World Bank, Washington DC, 2002.

distribution, but since during the 1990-98 social expenditures were being expanded, on an adjusted basis income distribution improved.

The redistribution effects of government spending can occur even if the rich receive the majority of the benefits of a program. What is required is only that the poor receive a share greater than their share in total income. For instance, if the poorest quintile (lowest 20%) receives 10% of government expenditures while it has only 5% of income the effect is still progressive; it does not have to receive 20% of government spending to be neutral.

# Appendix

**Table 5.6 Chenery-Ahluwalia Poverty Weights – An Example**

| | Normal Calculation | | Equal Weights | | Poverty Weights | |
|---|---|---|---|---|---|---|
| Quintile | Share of total income | Growth rate of income | revised share | growth rate | revised shares | growth rate |
| 1 | 0.05 | 9.00 | 0.20 | 9.00 | 0.50 | 9.00 |
| 2 | 0.10 | 8.00 | 0.20 | 8.00 | 0.50 | 8.00 |
| 3 | 0.15 | 6.00 | 0.20 | 6.00 | 0.00 | 6.00 |
| 4 | 0.25 | 6.00 | 0.20 | 6.00 | 0.00 | 6.00 |
| 5 | 0.50 | 5.00 | 0.20 | 5.00 | 0.00 | 5.00 |
| Overall Growth Rate: | | 6.15 | | 6.80 | | 8.50 |

# CHAPTER VI
# POVERTY AND GROWTH

*"What we do learn is that growth generally does benefit the poor as much as anyone else . . ."*—Dollar and Kraay

## Poverty Reduction as the Ultimate Goal

The ultimate goal of development is to improve the welfare of the poorest of the world's population. As we have seen in the previous chapter, incomes are not evenly distributed, so that raising average per capita income in a country may not benefit the poor. Development is not useful if it will only benefit the rich in poor countries, but is is desired in order to improve the welfare of the poor. As we have seen, policies can affect the distribution of income, as well as the growth of income. But how do we define who is "poor"? Is poverty relative to cultural and social settings, or absolute? This chapter focuses on how we measure poverty, and how growth can impact on reducing poverty.

## The classic poverty line approach

How do we define poverty? In general, poverty is usually defined as those without sufficient income. How do we identify those without sufficient income? National accounts do not identify people by income level. To obtain such data, one needs to have a survey of households which asks questions on income and consumption, as well as other household characteristics.

Household surveys can be conducted on a national of regional basis, and are normally done as a sample of the universe of households. In this case, a census of the population defines the base of households from which a small sample is made using randomized selection procedures. In a country having a population of 20 million, there might be 4 million households. A sample of 1% of these households will be sufficient to have an accurate data base; a larger survey does not yield significantly greater accuracy. Even a sample survey of 40,000 household would be excessive, since the sampling error decreases with sample size. Samples above 10,000 have roughly a sampling error of less than 1%. Small samples are adequate, except when countries desire to make breakdowns by regions or cities. In some cases, statistical agencies may "over sample" in certain key regions, or among groups of special interest, in order to obtain accurate data.

Household surveys typically ask a number of questions related to income and consumption. In general, we know that accurate information on income is difficult to obtain. People either want to hide their incomes, or they forget certain types of income. If you ask a single question "what was your income last month" you will get a figure normally reflecting wages received. However, other kinds of income are also important: home produced goods, payments in kind, pensions, gifts, transfers, etc. In agricultural economies income can vary enormously between seasons, and it becomes important to do the survey though the year to get accurate information. In general we know that the more questions that are asked, the more income is identified. Surveys that start in one year asking a single income question, and then later are expanded to ask five or ten income questions, cannot be compared because the later surveys will undoubtedly have higher income.

Under-reporting of income is a common problem. Many people do not want to divulge their incomes for a variety of reasons, particularly to a government survey worker. We know that often a country's household income as measured by a survey does not match the level of income appearing in the national accounts. In the case of India, we know that the gap between the survey data and national accounts data is growing annually. Income in the survey data is not growing as fast as income in the national accounts. Why this is happening is not clear, but it is possible that the new rich or middle class of India are reluctant to admit their success and do not report their full income or consumption.

Income has some other drawbacks as a measure as well. We know that income fluctuates, but that a person's consumption level is more stable. People, even poor people, smooth their consumption by saving in good times, and then consuming out of stocks (dissaving) or borrowing in bad times. In addition, people tend to give more accurate information on consumption purchases. Thus, a measure of consumption is generally considered a better measure than one of income. Many household surveys, therefore, have a consumption module that asks about past consumption patterns, including purchases during the past week, month and year. However, to this information must be added information on home produced goods, gifts received, etc. Gini coefficients based on consumption are generally considered more accurate than those based on income.

Household survey information yield data on household income or consumption. In the discussion that follows, the focus is on income (Y), but it could equally be on consumption(C). While consumption data is the preferred approach, many surveys lack this information, and income data are still used. Total household income $Y_H$ is the total reported as accruing to all members of the household, usually in the past month. Dividing by the number of people in the household (n) we get the average household income per household member for the $i^{th}$ individual:

$$Y_H / n = y_i$$

However, this assumes that income is spread evenly within the household, which we know is not true. Furthermore, even an equitable distribution between family members may not be possible. Women may suffer if income/consumption is controlled by men, for instance. Thus, a woman could be living in poverty even though the average household income of her household is above the poverty line. In addition, this rough division of household income does not allow for differences in family composition. We know that children require less than adults. To account for this, people can be converted into "adult equivalents" (AE). Thus, instead of n, we can use AE, or:

$$Y_H / AE = y_i$$

Converting to adult equivalents is usually based on nutrition needs, where an adult man is taken as 1.0, and others are adjusted accordingly. Some typical conversion factors are: women = .8, children = .5, pregnant women = 1.1.

Scale Economies: We also know that large families can achieve scale economies; that is the cost of living does not go up directly in proportion to the number of people in a household. We all know that it is generally cheaper for two people to share a two-bedroom apartment than for each to live singly in a one bedroom apartment. The reason for this is that the cost of heat, electricity and the use of common facilities such as a kitchen, can be shared. Thus, it is also possible to adjust our per capita household income by a scale economy factor, which would tend to raise slightly the per capita income of larger families compared to the standard method.

There is very little evidence defining scale economies, however, and most practioners either adjust for scale economies or adult equivalents, but not both.

## Poverty Line

The poverty line defines the level of income below which judge people are judged to be "poor". This approach goes back to Seebohm Rowntree[49], who defined poverty in the City of York in 1890 based on establishing a budget sufficient to provide "minimum necessaries". The modern method for defining poverty is based on caloric needs, and is based on the work of Molly Orshansky[50]. Orshansky, a U.S. government official, was asked to set up a definition of a poverty line to be used with the Great Society programs of the 1960s. Her method was to base the poverty line on food needs, measured in terms of calories. For every adult, or adult equivalent, a certain level of caloric consumption is presumed as necessary to carry out life functions. Variations in caloric needs in fact is what defines adult equivalents; children a judged to need .5 of an adult male in terms of

49 Seebohm Rowntree, *Poverty: A Study of Town Life*, London: 1901.

50 For a history of poverty lines in the U.S see Jessie Willis, "How We Measure Poverty: A History and Brief Overview", Oregon Center for Public Policy, February, 2000,

calories, pregnant women 1.1, etc. While we can define required calories, how one obtains those calories offers many possibilities. A basic diet of 2,500 calories per day can be obtained either by eating a balanced and nutritious diet, or drinking lots of wine and eating hot dogs.

There are various ways of estimating the nutritional/caloric needs of the poor. One basis is the definition established by nutrition authorities as a "normal" or necessary diet. However, the more common method to estimate the required food budget is to examine what poor people actually consume. By taking the food expenditures of a group at the lower level of the income distribution, one obtains a rough estimate of a typical diet. This "cost of basic needs" approach usually begins by looking at the actual expenditures of people in the 20th percentile of the distribution. Their food expenditures are then converted into calories.

Suppose that we define as poor those with less than 2200 calories per day. At the 20th percentile we find that households are receiving 200 pesos per month in income and spending 100 pesos per month on food, and this allows them to have a consumption level of 2000 calories per person/day (200 calories below the poverty line). We then assume that with 10% more income they would consume 10% more food. This implies that the poverty line for food consumption is 10% more than the average per capita food consumption at the 20th percentile. Thus, the food poverty line becomes 10% more than the food consumption of 100 pesos, or 110 pesos. This food poverty line is also known as the absolute poverty line or indigence line; it is the level of income necessary just to be able to afford a healthy diet[51].

---

51 An alternative approach, the food-energy intake method, looks directly into the income distribution data to locate the point where people are actually consuming the target caloric intake (2200 in this case). This method produces unstable results, however, since richer people will spend more money to achieve the same level of caloric intake (i.e.there may be more than one place in the income distribution where people are consuming 2200 calories, but with different food costs). Thus, a poverty line for a richer group (say in urban areas) would be higher than a poorer group, which would not be warranted from a welfare point of view (see Matin Ravaillon and Bidu Bidani," How Robust is a Poverty Profile" *World Bank Econ Rev* 8:1(1994), pp. 75-102.

But we know that people need other items to survive. Even people who live below the absolute poverty line spend some of their income on non-food expenditures. To estimate non-food needs, Orshansky's method was to use the inverse of the Engel coefficient. The Engle coefficient is the level of food consumption in the diet, which tends to be stable and to rise more slowly than income as income rises (known as Engel's Law). If people consume 50% of their income in food, then the inverse of the Engle coefficient is 2. Thus the total poverty line will be twice the food poverty line in our example, or 220 pesos, which allows for the consumption of non-food items. The inverse of the Engle coefficient is sometimes called the Orshansky number.

## Alternate Approach—Relative Poverty Lines

But is poverty an absolute or relative concept? We know that national estimates put poverty at about 11% in the US and 10% in China. But clearly those above the poverty line in China would be below the poverty line in the United States with the same level of income, even allowing for purchasing power differences. A person below the poverty line in the U.S., having a car, a television and a telephone, would be clearly considered a rich person in Bangladesh. Many would therefore argue that poverty is not a universal concept, but one that differs between societies based on societal norms. As A.K. Sen points out, while a person can walk down the streets in India without shoes, this would not be socially accepted in London. Thus, many argue that the poverty line should adjust upwards as income rises, and that the poverty line is simply a percentage per capita income. Thus, where Z is the poverty line;

$Z = \alpha \cdot YPC$ e.g if per capita income is 1,000; if $\alpha = .3$, then $Z = 300$.

But α is arbitrary, and is often set at something between .333 and .500. This method quite popular in setting poverty lines in Europe. This approach can produce markedly different poverty levels in countries with bad income distribution. For instance, the World Development Report shows that using a relative poverty line in Latin America of 1/3 of national income would raise poverty from 12% to 51% (for 1998, based on the calculations of Chen and Ravaillon[52]).

However, relative poverty lines have a number of drawbacks. For instance, if GNP were to fall, one would expect that poverty would increase. However, if income distribution stays the same (i.e. all incomes fall by the same amount), the numbers in poverty will also stay the same (it remains the same proportion of a smaller GNP). Alternatively, if income fell, and income distribution improved (e.g. everyone got closer to the mean income), then the numbers in poverty could go down (even though their income had declined).

## Head Count Poverty

Once a poverty line has been established, the poor are those whose income lies below the line (by definition). We define $Q_p$ as the number of people in a population N whose income is less than Z, the poverty line. Then the simplest measure of poverty is then the headcount poverty ratio, H, or:

$$H = Q_p/N$$

One problem with the headcount poverty concept is that it is not affected by improvements or worsening of conditions for those below the poverty line, while it can be affected by small changes in status for those very near the poverty line.

For an example of these problems, look at Fig. 6.1, where the vertical line measures per capita income. In an economy of six people at year 1, three are in poverty (below the poverty line Z), and three are not in poverty. In time period two, the incomes of the three in poverty have risen, but none of them have risen above the poverty line (Z). Thus, headcount poverty remains unchanged (3/6 or 50%), even though "poverty" in a broad sense has been reduced.

---

52 Chen, Shaohua. and Martin Ravallion, "How Did The World's Poorest Fare in the 1990s?" *Policy Research Working Paper* 2409, World Bank, Wash. D.C., 2001.

Fig. 6.1

Case No. 1: Raising Income of Poor Does Note Reduce Headcount Poverty

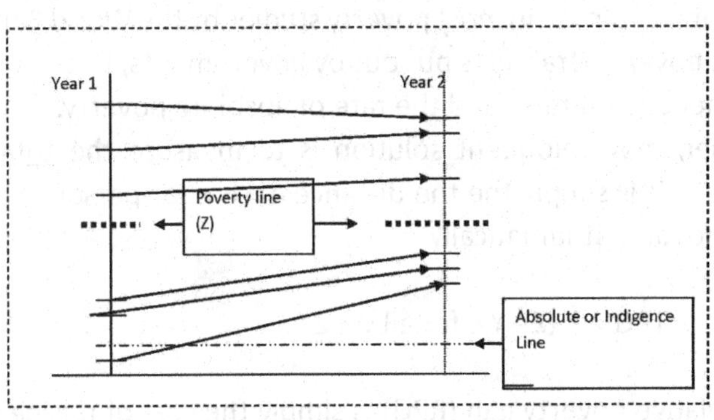


Fig. 6.2 shows another example. Here, again, are three people initially below poverty line. In this case, person A moves up over line, but B and C become worse off. Poverty headcount goes down, but one could argue that the extent of poverty has increased. There is also an incentive if one is designing programs to reduce poverty to focus on those near the poverty line (almost already out of poverty), because one would show the greatest amount of progress (assuming only the headcount index was used to measure success).

Fig. 6.2

Case No. 2: Poverty Head Count Improves, But Poverty Worsens

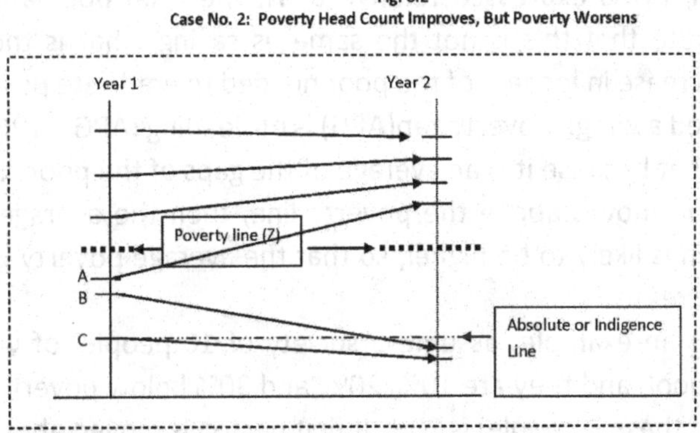


One solution to this problem is to consider both the poverty line and the absolute poverty line. The absolute poverty line, or food poverty line, provides a standard for the poorest segment of the population. Thus, more people moving down into absolute poverty would be a sign of poverty worsening (as in Fig. 6.2), even if the total headcount remained the same. It is common in most poverty studies by the World Bank, as well as in most poverty strategies put out by governments, to see mention of both the headcount ratio and the rate of absolute poverty.

Another, more eloquent solution is to measure the total poverty gap (TPG). This is simply the the distance each poor person is below the poverty line, or mathematically:

$$TPG = \sum (Z - Y_i), \text{ for all } y_i < Z$$

The relative poverty gap (RPG) is simply the cost of raising everyone to the poverty line, as a percent of GDP:

$$RPG = \sum (Z - y_i)/ GDP \text{ (for all } y_i < Z)$$

These measures of the poverty gap also have their own problems as a general poverty measure, the principle one being that if GDP rises, while the income of the poor stays the same, the RPG will decline indicating that poverty has been reduced, when in fact it has not changed. In fact, in a relative sense, it has worsened.

For this reason, most analysis is not based on the RPG, but on the poverty gap index, PG. Since the absolute poverty gap will grow with population, PG is expressed relative to N, the total population in the country. Note that this is not the same as saying what is the average percent increase in income of the poor needed to eradicate poverty. This, the so-called average poverty gap(APG) is misleading ($APG = TPG/Q_p$). The reason is that because it is an average of the gaps of the poor, if a slightly poor person moves above the poverty line, then the average of those that remain is likely to be higher, so that the average poverty gap would actually increase.

Here is an example: assume a society of 10 people, of which only three are poor, and they are 10%, 20%, and 30% below poverty line. The average (of these 3 people) is 20%. If first person is moved above poverty line, the remaining people have an average "poverty gap" of 25% ((20% + 30%)/2). Poverty has been reduced, but the average poverty gap has risen. The solution: average the number over the total number of people in society, not just the poor[53]. Thus, doing the calculation using 10 people, the correctly calculated poverty gap measure declines from 6% to 5%. The problem is the poverty gap is now an index, it has no actual meaning. It is not 5% of anything. However this is the standard measure of the poverty gap that is widely used in poverty analysis.

To this family of the headcount index (H), and poverty gap index (PG), we can add a third measure, the squared poverty gap, or $PG^2$. The idea of the squared poverty gap is to give more weight to those furthest from the poverty line. The choice of the exponent of 2 is itself arbitrary and depends on how much weight one wants to give to the very poor; higher exponents give greater weight to those further from the line. However, it is common practice is to use the squared poverty gap rather than any other formulation.

Most analysis of poverty show four poverty measures: the headcount (H), the poverty gap, the squared poverty gap, and the absolute or indigence poverty level. But in practice, such as in discussions of targeting projects, the focus tends to remain on the headcount poverty measures. Why? The answer is not entirely clear. For one thing, the headcount and

53 **The Foster-Greer-Thorbecke (FGT) formula.** This is an elegant way of combining the three poverty measures, and showing their connection. The formula shows that for the family of poverty measures:

$$P\alpha = \frac{1}{N} \sum \left(\frac{Z - Yi}{Z}\right)^{\alpha} \qquad (\text{for } Y_i < Z)$$

where: $\alpha = 0$, $P_0$ = headcount poverty; $\alpha = 1$ $P_1$ = poverty gap (PG), $\alpha = 2$ $P_2$ = squared poverty gap, N = population, Z= poverty line

When $\alpha = 0$, the expression $(Z - Y_i)/Z$ equals one for every person below the poverty line (since any expression with a zero exponent equals one). Thus it becomes a simple count of the poor, This is labeled as $P_0$ = the headcount measure, and also called $FGT_0$, where FGT stands for the names of the authors. When $\alpha = 1$, the expression sums the percentage deviations of income from the poverty line, divides it by total population, thus becomes the poverty gap ($P^1$ or $FGT_1$). When $\alpha = 2$, the expression produces the squared poverty gap, or $FGT_2$. See James Foster, Joel Greer, and Erik Thorbecke, "A Class of Decomposable Poverty Measures" *Econometrica* 52 (May, 1984), pp. 761-766.

PG measures tend to move together, so that one is a proxy for the other. Secondly, the headcount index is easier to calculate. And finally, there this may reflect a lag between theory and practice. The World Bank after years of reporting total poverty headcount numbers for the world, recently has started also producing estimates of the world poverty gap. Gradually, the poverty gap concept is becoming more common.

## Comparisons: National vs. World Bank global estimates.

Individual country poverty estimates cannot be combined because they use different methods, and use different assumptions about caloric needs. In addition, there is a large element of social and cultural influence over what is "poverty". To estimate world wide poverty, the World Bank uses a single standard applied to the income distribution data of countries. The current standard is a poverty line of $1.25 per day in PPP terms, in 1985 prices (originally the line was $1.00 per day). By this standard, about 1.4 billion people live in poverty, as noted in Chapter 1. This methodology attempts to use a common poverty line across countries, but has several methodological and data problems, and as a result global poverty estimates tend to vary from year to year. One problem is that the global estimates produce very low estimates for some of the richer regions, such as Eastern Europe/Central Asia (4%) and Latin America/Caribbean (8%)[54]. In these cases, the Bank suggests using a higher level of $2 per day, but even so the numbers seem low. Using $2 per day for the entire developing world would raise total poverty from 1.4 billion to 2.6 billion.

National poverty rates differ substantially from the $1.25 per day calculations done by the World Bank, which raises questions about their validity of both. For instance, poverty in China is only 2.8% using the national poverty line, but 16% using the Bank's $1.25 PPP per day. In Argentina, the gap goes in the other direction. National poverty rates of 53% are substantially higher than the Bank's estimate of 10%. Variations seem do not seem to reflect a logical pattern (see Table 6.1) and only in rare cases come close to each other (e.g. Vietnam).

---

[54] S, Chen and M. Ravallion, "The Developing World is Poorer Than We Thought", World Bank Policy Research Paper 4703, August 2009, p. 44.

**Table 6.1. National Poverty Rates vs. PPP rates, selected countries**

| | National Poverty Estimates | | World Bank PPP Estimates | | |
|---|---|---|---|---|---|
| Country | poverty (%) | year | $1.25 /day | $2 /day | year of PPP estimates |
| Argentina | 53.0 | 2002 | 9.9 | 19.7 | 2002 |
| Brazil | 21.5 | 2002-03 | 7.8 | 18.3 | 2005 |
| China | 2.8 | 2004 | 15.9 | 36.3 | 2005 |
| India | 28.6 | 1999-2000 | 41.6 | 75.6 | 2004-05 |
| Kenya | 52.0 | 1997 | 19.6 | 42.7 | 1997 |
| Morocco | 19.0 | 1998-99 | 6.3 | 24.3 | 2000 |
| Nigeria | 34.1 | 1992-93 | 68.5 | 86.4 | 1996-97 |
| Ukraine | 19.5 | 2003 | <2.0 | 3.4 | 2002 |
| Vietnam | 28.9 | 2002 | 24.2 | 52.5 | 2004 |

Source: World Bank, *World Development Report 2010*, Annex Table 2

The comparisons illustrate a fundamental point: poverty is difficult to compare across countries and the concept of poverty varies with the cultural context. While the $1.25/day estimates thus have many problems, they still present the best single estimate of world poverty. They are generally not useful, however, to be used in a country context for identifying the poor. In either case, the poverty headcount measure is best used to track poverty over time, regardless of its initial starting value. Thus, the important thing is whether poverty has risen or fallen over time, not its absolute level. In some cases, such as Chile, countries have radically revised upwards their poverty line, and thereby poverty rates when poverty appears to have fallen too low.

## Alternate Measures of Poverty: Unsatisfied Basic Needs

Another approach, common in Latin America, is the measurement of unsatisfied basic needs (UBN, or NBI from the Spanish acronym). This is particularly useful where countries lack data on a local level with regards to income and poverty, and need a shorthand method of identifying poor areas. In this case, a number of indicators are defined, usually drawn from what is available in the census. These focus on "basic needs", and thus measure school attendance, access to water, quality of housing, overcrowding, etc. The basic needs index might include anywhere from 5-10 indicators. These indicators are not combined, but instead deficiencies are defined. Thus, a community may be deficient in water supply if more than 20% of the population lacks access. It may be deficient in primary education if more than 10% of eligible students are not attending. In this way communities can be classified in terms of how many basic needs are unsatisfied, and priority given to those with the highest number of unsatisfied basic needs in terms of social expenditures. For instance, a program might be limited to serving only communities with three of more unsatisfied basic needs. Households can also be assessed in terms of basic needs deficiencies as a means of determining eligibility. One problem with the NBI approach is that it tends to be heavily weighted toward housing indicators, such as water supply, overcrowding, quality of floor or roof, because this information is often readily available from the census. Other useful measures, such as literacy or health status, are often not available and therefore not included. The UBN approach offers a simple way of determining poverty, particularly at the community or regional level, without the expense and complexity of doing a household survey on income and consumption.

## Does Growth Benefit the Poor?

While the early focus was on growth and industrialization, there was always an undercurrent of dissent concerning the need to focus on distribution as well. However, a greater focus on the problems of income distribution and poverty were made difficult by the lack of adequate household surveys on income and consumption in most countries. As more data became available, there was a growing sense that development efforts benefited the reach but excluded the poor. In their 1973 book, Adelman and Morris[55] concluded, based on data from the 1950s and 1960s, that:

> ". . . development is accompanied by an absolute as well as relative decline in the average income of the very poor . . . . there is no automatic or even likely, trickling down of the benefits of economic growth to the poorest segments of the population." (p. 179)

The Adelman and Morris study was pioneering, and led development practioners to focus much more on the poor, and the distributive impact of their projects and policies. However, the data base used by Adelman and Morris was rudimentary, and more recent studies have come to different conclusions. For instance, Chen and Ravallion(2001) found that

---

55 Irma Adelman and Cynthia Taft Morris,*Economic Growth and Social Equity in Developing Countries*, Stanford Univ. Press, Stanford, Cal., 1973.

the slow rate of global poverty reduction was attributable to low rates of growth in poor countries, and persistent inequality which meant that poor people did not benefit from the little growth that did occur.

The most thorough study of this relationship was done by Dollar and Kraay[56]. Defining poverty as the income of the lowest quintile (Q1), they found that the growth of income of the poorest is highly associated with overall growth. A simple regression of GDP growth on growth of income of the poor has an $R^2$ of .49, suggesting that growth explains about half of the change in the income of the poor. Furthermore, most observations (see Fig. 6.3) are clustered in the upper right panel, which shows positive growth of income overall and the poor, and the lower left panel, which shows negative growth for both. There are some countries, however, in the lower right panel that do show a pattern of positive growth overall and negative growth for the poor. There are even a few observations for episodes of negative overall growth and positive growth for the income of the poor, but these are rare.

Fig. 6.3
Growth of GDP and Growth of Income of the Poor

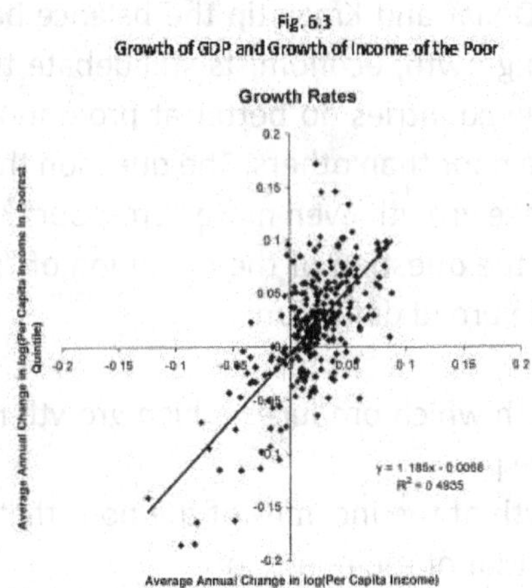


Source: David Dollar and Aart Kraay, "Growth is Good For the Poor", *Journal of Economic Growth* 7 (September, 2002), Fig. 1, p. 1221. Copyright by *Journal of Economic Growth* and Springer Publications. Used with kind permission from Springer Science+Business Media B.V.

In addition, Dollar and Kraay find no difference in negative and positive growth episodes. While open policies benefit the poor as much as the general population, pro-poor measures (improvements in primary

---

56 David Dollar and Aart Kraay, "Growth is Good for the Poor", *Journal of Economic Growth* 7 (September, 2002), pp.195-225.

education, increases in health/educ. spending, democracy, increases in agricultural productivity) do not seem to benefit the poor. Globalization effects (more openness, WTO membership) seem to have no effect on the poor, and there are no differences at different income levels (i.e. no Kuznets effect). They conclude that:

> This does not imply that growth is *all* that is needed to improve the lives of the poor . . . What we do learn is that growth generally does benefit the poor as much as everyone else, so that the growth-enhancing policies of good rule of law, fiscal discipline, and openness to international trade should be at the center of successful poverty reduction strategies[57].

## What is Pro-Poor Growth?

While the work of Dollar and Kraay tip the balance back somewhat toward an emphasis on growth, economists still debate the proper mix of policies. Clearly, some countries do better at promoting a pattern of growth that benefits the poor than others. The question then arises as to what can be done to make growth even more "pro-poor"?

First, we must face the question of the definition of "pro-poor". We can think of two possible broad definitions:

Definition #1: Growth which produces a high growth rate of income of the poor.
Definition #2: Growth of the incomes of the poor that is more rapid than that of the non-poor.

In the first, we are emphasizing the absolute welfare of the poor, regardless of their relative standing compared to the non-poor. Going back to example of Table 5.2 (reproduced below as Table 6.2). Strategy B would be judged pro-poor by definition #1, because it has a high rate of growth for the poor. However, by definition #2, strategy A would be more pro-poor because it favors the poor over the non-poor, even though the

---

[57] Dollar and Kraay, p. 219.

growth of the poor (3%) is lower than in B (6%). Both definitions have some merit, and it is difficult to choose between the two.

**Table 6.2 Example –Income Distribution**

| Initial Income | Growth rate of: | Strategy A | Strategy B |
|---|---|---|---|
| 1,000 | Income of rich (top 50%) | 2.0 | 8.0 |
| 100 | Income of poor (bottom 50%) | 3.0 | 6.0 |

The choice between redistribution and growth depends on where countries stand in terms of distribution and poverty[58]. In very unequal societies, with low levels of poverty, growth is not likely to benefit the poor very much (since it has not benefitted them much in the past). Rather, redistribution is probably the best route, and more feasible, since the poor represent a small segment of the population. However, in very unequal economies with high poverty, redistribution will probably not work as well (since a small rich minority would have to be taxed heavily to benefit the poor, or the poor would have to be taxed to help the extremely poor, thus reducing the poverty gap but not headcount poverty rate). In this case, it would be better to rely on overall growth. In very equal societies there is only a small potential for redistribution, particularly if poverty is high. Here, growth is the main solution, since there is limited scope for redistribution. Thus, redistribution policies seem to work best only where income distribution is bad and poverty is relatively low.

58 What follows comes from the work of Humberto Lopez, "Cross Country Evidence on PPG" (unpublished presentation, 2002).

**Table 6.3. Cross country evidence on pro poor growth**

| Inequality | Growth: Negative | | | | Growth: Low | | | | Growth: High | | | |
|---|---|---|---|---|---|---|---|---|---|---|---|---|
| | Country | N | g | g20 | Country | N | g | g20 | Country | N | g | g20 |
| Worsens | Poland | 20 | -0.2 | -1.4 | Ecuador | 26 | 1.7 | 0.3 | Korea, Rep. | 32 | 6.7 | 6.6 |
| | Iran, Islamic Rep. | 15 | -0.4 | -0.7 | Philippines | 40 | 1.5 | 0.5 | Taiwan, China | 31 | 6.3 | 6.2 |
| | Slovak Republic | 10 | -0.4 | -0.5 | Chile | 24 | 1.4 | 1.1 | Hong Kong, China | 20 | 5.8 | 5.2 |
| | Niger | 32 | -0.6 | -1.3 | Peru | 33 | 0.4 | 0.1 | Singapore | 20 | 5.4 | 5.2 |
| | Sierra Leone | 21 | -0.8 | -7.7 | Costa Rica | 35 | 1.6 | -0.1 | China | 15 | 5.0 | 1.6 |
| | Zambia | 37 | -1.0 | -2.7 | Tanzania | 27 | 1.5 | -2.1 | Malaysia | 25 | 4.7 | 4.1 |
| | Estonia | 10 | -1.7 | -6.2 | Bulgaria | 10 | 1.5 | -3.5 | Thailand | 36 | 4.2 | 3.1 |
| | Latvia | 10 | -4.2 | -7.4 | Panama | 26 | 1.4 | -2.3 | Mauritius | 11 | 3.7 | 1.6 |
| | Russian Fed. | 10 | -5.6 | -14.3 | Nigeria | 38 | 1.2 | -0.5 | Brazil | 33 | 2.5 | 0.3 |
| | | | | | D.R. | 20 | 1.0 | -0.2 | Colombia | 31 | 2.3 | 2.1 |
| | | | | | El Salvador | 30 | 0.7 | -1.2 | Mexico | 38 | 2.1 | 0.9 |
| | | | | | Senegal | 31 | 0.2 | -0.5 | | | | |
| | | | | | Ethiopia | 14 | 0.2 | -1.2 | | | | |
| Improves | Country | N | g | g20 | Country | N | g | g20 | Country | N | g | g20 |
| | Guyana | 37 | -0.4 | -0.1 | Trin. and Tobago | 31 | 1.8 | 2.1 | Gabon | 15 | 7.7 | 9.0 |
| | Jordan | 17 | -0.6 | 1.0 | India | 34 | 1.8 | 2.2 | Indonesia | 35 | 3.7 | 4.4 |
| | Belarus | 10 | -1.8 | -1.1 | Bangladesh | 32 | 1.3 | 1.5 | Tunisia | 25 | 3.4 | 3.6 |
| | Madagascar | 33 | -2.1 | -1.7 | Nepal | 18 | 1.2 | 3.9 | Egypt, Arab Rep. | 32 | 2.8 | 4.5 |
| | | | | | Jamaica | 35 | 1.1 | 1.5 | Ghana | 10 | 2.4 | 4.3 |
| | | | | | Honduras | 28 | 0.5 | 1.3 | Sri Lanka | 32 | 2.3 | 3.4 |
| | | | | | Bolivia | 22 | 0.3 | 1.0 | Hungary | 31 | 2.2 | 2.7 |
| | | | | | Venezuela, RB | 31 | 0.1 | 0.1 | Turkey | 26 | 2.2 | 2.9 |
| | | | | | | | | | Pakistan | 32 | 2.2 | 2.8 |

Notes: N = length of spell (in years); g = average growth rate of per capita income; g20 = average growth rate of per capita income of the lowest quintile.
Source: Louise Cord, Humberto Lopez and John Page, " 'When I Use a Word....': Pro-Poor Growth and Poverty Reduction", World Bank working paper, unpublished (August, 2003), Table 3, available at:
http://siteresources.worldbank.org/INTPGI/Resources/15179_Page_Lopez_Cord_-_When_I_use_a_word.pdf.
Additional details kindly provided by H. Lopez, World Bank.

But how many countries actually have pro-poor growth by any definition? A study by Cord, Lopez and Page examined 54 countries over long periods of time (see Table 6.3). Comparing the growth of overall GDP per capita (g) with the growth rate of per capita income of the lowest quintile (g20), they found that for 41 countries having positive growth, inequality rose in 24 countries and declined in 17. Of the 24 countries with worsening inequality, 15 still showed a positive growth rate for the poor. Thus, these 15 could be considered "pro-poor" by the first definition. However, the 17 which showed improving inequality and positive growth could be considered "pro-poor" by either definition. Of the 13 countries with negative growth rates, inequality rose in 9 but fell in 4. In only one country, Jordan, did the income of the poor rise while overall incomes fell.

Econometric analysis done by Lopez[59] found similar results to Dollar and Kraay, but with some important differences. Lopez found that indeed, there is a Kuznets effect, with income distribution worsening up to a peak of $3000 per capita income, and then improving (PPP, 1985 prices). He

---

[59] J. Humberto Lopez,. "Pro-Growth, Pro-Poor: Is There a Tradeoff?" *World Bank Policy Research Working Paper 3378* (August 2004), World Bank, Washington, D.C.

also found that better education, better infrastructure, and reduced inflation all led to reduced inequality, and increased growth. Thus, these are "win-win" interventions. However, financial development, trade openness, and smaller government led to increased inequality, at least initially, but they promote growth and hence poverty reduction in the long term. Thus, these could be considered "Lose-Win", because they are anti-poor in short term (provided there is no compensation to offset rising poverty). Conversely, financial crises help reduce inequality, because they tend to adversely affect the rich more, but they reduce long-term growth and lead to higher poverty in the long run (hence are "Win-Lose"), Output volatility, however, is "Lose-Lose" because leads to increased inequality and also reduces growth in the long term, both thus leading to higher poverty.

Unlike Dollar and Kraay, Lopez does found that education and infrastructure do help reduce poverty. Both found that inflation is bad for the poor. Other factors which may affect the poor adversely in the short term can help in the long term by accelerating growth. Thus, there does seem to be a positive role for government in promoting pro-poor growth—attention to macro-economic stability, trade openness, education and infrastructure all help.

Thus, while overall growth can explain a large part of the growth of the incomes of the poor, it does not explain it all, and there is considerable variation between countries suggesting room for public interventions. Which interventions work best is the subject of the remaining chapters.

## The "Washington Consensus"—good or bad for the poor?

The prevailing economic philosophy of the 1980s and 1990s was categorized by some as the "Washington Consensus". The term, originally coined by John Williamson in 1989, was simply his attempt to pull together the received wisdom of the time about how to proceed with reforms that would restore growth and economic and financial stability in an era when many LDCs were facing a massive debt crisis[60]. This debt crisis in turn

60 John Williamson, "A Short History of the Washington Consensus", International Institute of Economics, 2004, available at: http://www.iie.com/publications/papers/williamson0904-2.pdf

reflected past action whereby these countries borrowed money abroad to cover deficits that reflected underlying structural problems, rather than deal with their problems. These issues included over-valued exchange rates, budget deficits caused by inefficient government enterprises, inadequate tax systems, and lack of controls on public spending. Thus, the need for "structural adjustment", which implied a trade-off of in-country reforms in return for assistance from the IMF and World Bank, plus debt relief from the commercial bank creditors. Providing this relief without needed reforms would have been counterproductive, as the basic problems would have remained and these countries would have needed a perpetual inflow of foreign capital that was not sustainable. Thus, the "consensus" focused on fiscal and monetary discipline, tax reform, restructuring public expenditures, trade liberalization, removal of price and capital controls, privatization of public assets, property rights, deregulation, financial sector reforms and restructuring, and eliminating over-valued exchange rates. There was little attention paid to the impact on the poor or on social services, which often had to be cut to restore fiscal balance.

In general, the "consensus" policies were effective in terms of reducing inflation, increasing financial stability, eliminating distortions, accelerating exports and providing better incentives for private sector growth. However, in comparison with expectations, the growth performance was often disappointing. After an initial burst of growth in the late 1980s and early 1990s, most of the reforming countries experienced a return to stagnation. This was particularly true of countries in Latin America, Europe/Central Asia and Africa. However, the general prescription worked well in many countries, including China, India, Korea, Chile, Malaysia and Thailand, among others. And while often criticized, few people would suggest going back to a strategy focused on heavy state involvement, controls on prices and exchange rates, and massive deficits and inflation. The lesson learned from this experience, particularly in Eastern Europe, is that "institutions matter". Countries need to do more than just "get the prices right". They also need to focus on having an efficient and less corrupt public sector, strong financial institutions, and a private sector that can rely on a system of justice to enforce contracts and the "rule of law."[61]

---

[61] S. J. Burki and Guillermo E. Perry, *Beyond the Washington Consensus–Institutions Matter*, World Bank Latin American and Caribbean Studies, World Bank, Wash. DC, 1998.

There is also a general agreement that the original "consensus" needs to be broadened to recognize the poverty/equity issue, and that reforms need to protect spending on social services, provide adequate safety nets to the poor, and provide for micro-credit, land reform and other pro-poor programs, particularly education[62]. But a lack of focus on poverty originally was not an oversight by Williamson; he accurately reflected the focus of the leading multilateral organizations, supported by their member governments and the commercial banking interests in achieving financial stability and reform. In the panic to avoid a world-wide financial collapse, the poverty issue was put aside. This pattern repeats itself throughout the period. The initial emphasis by McNamara in the early 1970s gets muted by the oil/energy crisis of the later 1970s and early 1980s. The revival of interest in poverty and basic needs in the late 1970s and 1980s is overwhelmed by the need to resolve the debt crisis. Nevertheless, over time the poverty issue has become more "main stream"; it is generally conceded to be the general objective, and programs of debt relief, such as the HIPC[63], are now fundamentally directed at poverty reduction.

---

62 John Williamson,"The Washington Consensus and Beyond" *Economic and Political Weekly* 38:15 (April 12 - April 18, 2002).

63 HIPC—debt relief for Highly Indebted Poor Countries.

# CHAPTER VII

# HUMAN DEVELOPMENT: EDUCATION & HEALTH

*"People are the real wealth of a nation"*—UN, Human Development Report, 1990

Poor people not only lack income, but they also lack assets. One of their chief assets is their labor services, or their human capital. Improving the quality of this human capital raises the value and quality of their major asset. Thus, programs that provide basic human services to the poor make them more productive, increases their earnings, and helps reduce their poverty. Increasing the supply of improved manpower in an economy will not raise incomes unless there is also growth in employment and demand for these labor services. But growth itself is linked to the quality of the labor force, so the two are intertwined. Almost all studies of growth find some connection between the quality of human capital or human resources, and growth (see Chapter VI). While an emphasis on human capital development is likely to be pro-poor, particularly if it focuses on those underserved by existing public programs, it is also likely to be pro-growth as well.

Improving the quality of the human resources of the poor can also be considered directly poverty reducing if one considers ill-health and poor education as a measure of poverty. On that metric, human resource investments directly reduce poverty even if they did nothing to raise the income capacity of the poor. From the Sen "capabilities" perspective, improvements in human resources allow people to be free to develop to the full extent of their innate capacity, even if all of them are unable to escape poverty. The great tragedy of poverty is the large number of capable poor who could have risen to higher levels if they had had the opportunity for better education (and better health care).

## I. Education

Probably nothing is as important for improving the welfare of the poor as education. Education levels are highly correlated with income, productivity, good health, nutrition, participation, adoption of family planning, and growth itself. Investments in education have both private and social returns, and there is usually a gap between the two. Private returns are simply the discounted present value of the extra income stream generated by an investment in education, counting only the private costs and private benefits[64]. For private returns, the private cost includes the opportunity cost of time spent in school, which is the foregone earnings the person would have earned had she been employed in the labor market, plus any financial outlay required (tuition, books, etc.). In developing countries, financial outlays are considerable even for primary and secondary schools, and include purchases for school uniforms, supplies and even books.The social returns to education include the extra earnings of the recipient of the education (before taxes) in relation to all private costs as well as publicly funded costs (investments in facilities, teacher salaries, etc.) that are not paid for by the recipient of the education.

In theory the social returns should include the benefits to society from education that go beyond the individual benefit (externalities), in practice these are ignored since they are difficult, if not impossible, to measure. However, these social benefits could be very important, and include a better functioning democracy, lower crime, lower rates of population growth, and other benefits from having an educated population.

Calculations of rates of return to education in developing countries generally show high returns, particularly at the primary level, with private returns exceeding social returns in almost all cases (see Table 7.1). Social returns for primary education are highest in Africa, at about 25%, and lowest in the developed (OECD) countries, at about 9%, reflecting the fact

---

64 Private benefits are after income and wage taxes, while social benefits are pre-tax. However, this is more relevant to calculations of returns to education in developed countries that have significant income taxes.

that scarcities of educated people increase their income premium. Returns on primary education generally are higher than those on secondary and higher education in developing countries, but tend to be more even in advanced countries.

**Table 7.1 Rates of Return to Education**
**(%)**

| Region | Social Returns | | | Private Returns | | |
|---|---|---|---|---|---|---|
| Asia | 16.2 | 11.1 | 11.0 | 20.0 | 15.8 | 18.2 |
| Europe/ Middle East/ North Africa | 15.6 | 9.7 | 9.9 | 13.8 | 13.6 | 18.8 |
| Latin America/ Caribbean | 17.4 | 12.9 | 12.3 | 26.6 | 17.0 | 19.5 |
| OECD | 8.5 | 9.4 | 8.5 | 13.4 | 11.3 | 11.6 |
| Sub-Saharan Africa | 25.4 | 18.4 | 11.3 | 37.6 | 24.6 | 27.8 |
| **World** | **18.9** | **13.1** | **10.8** | **26.6** | **17.0** | **19.0** |

Source: George Psacharopoulos and Harry Patrinos "Returns to Investment in Education: A Further Update", *Education Economics*, 12 (August, 2004), pp. 111-134. Country data comes from various years between 1995-99.

The data in Table 7.1 reflect an amalgram of various years, mostly in the second half of 20th century. Psaharopoulos and Patrinos[65] note that where there is time series data, there is evidence of falling returns during the 12 years prior to 2002, on the order of 0.6%. There is also some evidence that returns to secondary and higher education may be rising, while the returns to primary education may be falling, reflecting the shift in demand to higher skilled employment as a function of shifting labor demand brought about through more open trade and globalization, as well as technological advances.

Data in Table 7.2 shows more current data for Argentina for the years 1992 and 1998. This data shows the returns on education in a slightly different form. The numbers represent the percentage increase in wages from years of education shown in the table, and are derived from what is called a Mincerian wage equation (named after Jacob Mincer who first popularized this approach). The Mincerian equations shows the impact of education on earnings using a semi-log formulation of the type:

$$\ln E = k + b_1S + b_2S^2 + b_3EX + b_4EX^2 \ldots b_5FEM \ldots$$

[65] see source cited in Table 7.1

Where E equals earnings, S equals years of schooling, and EX is experience, and FEM is a dummy variable for male and female. EX is generally measured as the age of the worker. Since earnings are expressed as a logarithm, the equation shows the percentage increase in earnings from an additional year of schooling, or experience.

**Table 7.2. Impact of Schooling on Earnings, Argentina**
(% increase in earnings compared to zero education)

| Years of Schooling | 1992 | 1998 |
|---|---|---|
| 2 | 6.8 | 5.0 |
| 8 | 7.9 | 8.3 |
| 12 | 8.6 | 10.4 |
| 18 | 9.8 | 13.7 |

Source: World Bank, *Poor People in a Rich Country: A Poverty Report for Argentina*, Report No. 1992AR (World Bank, Wash. DC, 2000). Vol. 1, Table 6.

The results for Argentina show that between 1992 and 1998, the returns for higher levels of education increased substantially. For 18 years of education, the wage premium went up from 9.8 to 13.7%. Returns to primary education, however, declined. Much of this probably reflects the impact of shifting patterns of demand with increased openness. Argentina's competitive advantage is in more highly skilled areas, not unskilled labor with basic education. It is interesting to note that the coefficient for FEM was estimated at-.477 in 1998. Thus, all the returns shown in Table 7.2 would be about .5 percentage points lower for females.

Private Provision? If education has such high returns, why not rely on the private sector and private individuals to invest in education. Why does the government get involved? One reason is that this is another case where the private markets do not function very well. Rich people can pay for education, poor people would have to borrow against future returns. Generally, people cannot borrow to finance their education because of the lack of collateral. You can repossess a person's car, but you cannot repossess their education. Once they have an education, there is a big incentive not to repay the loan. Knowing this, lenders will generally not lend to finance an education, unless the government guarantees the loan (as in the U.S.). The financial distress encountered by many student loan programs attests to the problem that even governments have in collecting on these loans. In cases where governments collect an income tax, repayments can be added on to a person's tax liability. But in developing countries, income taxes are rare and the government's administrative ability to track and collect is weak. Thus, if left to private provisions, the level of education offered by the private sector would be less than socially optimal. This is another case of "market failure".

In addition, private producers of education do not realize the social externalities produced by education. These involve the benefits from having an educated society; democracy works better, crime goes down, etc. Therefore, there is some case to be made for public subsidies for education, particularly primary or basic education. Finally, there is the "rights", or "social justice" approach. Society may feel that it is important that everyone receive at least a basic education because it is important to enable them to realize their "capabilities" (a la Sen). It helps ensure that not just the rich are educated, but that everyone starts off with a (more) equal footing. Some societies in fact ban the provision of primary education by the private sector in order to avoid having schools that cater to the rich, and give their children a chance to advance more rapidly. Others argue that private individuals should be free to choose private education if they wish, and want to pay for it.

In any case, almost all societies provide public education to some extent, and most provide it at primary, secondary, and tertiary (university) levels. While this would seem to be a pro-poverty kind of policy, in fact it often is just the opposite. The reason for this is that primary education can be provided relatively cheaply, while secondary education is more expensive, and tertiary education is very expensive. However, the students who make it to the public universities typically come from the upper classes (or at least upper middle—many of the rich in developing countries send their children abroad). As Table 7.3 shows, there is a wide variety in country experience. In Vietnam, the government spends $34 on a primary student, but $191 on a tertiary student, or a ratio of 5.6:1. In Madagascar, the ratio is 16.5:1, while in Mozambique it is extremely high at 82:1. Why these high costs? Some of the reasons can be traced to a tradition of small classes, light teaching loads, and high salaries for staff in tertiary education in developing countries. Public universities are not always very efficient, in many ways, including the use of classroom space. Very few LDC universities collect tuition and fees, or what they do collect is only a small percentage of the costs. In some countries, the constitution guarantees free education at all levels.

**Table 7.3 Unit costs for selected countries (US$)**

| | Vietnam | Mozambique | Madagascar |
|---|---|---|---|
| Spending Per Student | | | |
| Primary | 34 | 20 | 24 |
| Secondary | 38 | 74 | 106 |
| Tertiary | 191 | 1640 | 397 |
| Vocational | 239 | 159 | n/a |
| Spending by Type (% of total) | | | |
| Primary | 36 | 47 | 51 |
| Secondary | 26 | 22 | 28 |
| Tertiary | 13 | 17 | 16 |
| Vocational & Other | 25 | 14 | 5 |

Source: World Bank, *A Sourcebook for Poverty Reduction Strategies* (World Bank, Washington DC, 2002), Vol. II, Table 19.1. Data are 1998 for Vietnam and Mozambique, 1999 for Madagascar.

Nevertheless, Table 7.3 also shows that despite the higher costs of tertiary education the bulk of education spending goes to primary education, since there are so many more students enrolled at that level. Thus, even in Mozambique, 47% of total education spending is for primary education, while it is only 36% in Vietnam. Since the poor are more apt to be represented in this group, they benefit to a greater extent (more so, if the non-poor send their children to private schools). This effect is helped by the fact that the poor often have larger families, hence more students in school. Thus, if we look at the distribution of benefits by income group, we see more even pattern.

**Table 7.4 Distribution of Education Expenditures and Income**

| Country | Year | Quintile 1 | Quintile 2 | Quintile 3 | Quintile 4 | Quintile 5 |
|---|---|---|---|---|---|---|
| **Madagascar** | | | | | | |
| Education | 1993/94 | 8 | 15 | 14 | 21 | 32 |
| Income | 2001 | 5 | 9 | 13 | 20 | 53 |
| **Vietnam** | | | | | | |
| Education | 1992/93 | 12 | 16 | 17 | 19 | 35 |
| Income | 2002 | 8 | 11 | 15 | 21 | 45 |

Source: World Bank, *Source Book* (2002), Table 19.1 and World Development Indicators, 2005, Table 2.5

Thus, the lowest 20% in Madagascar receive 8% of total education expenditures while the upper 20% receive 32%. On the face of it, this seems wildly regressive with the rich receiving much more than their share. However, if we compare these expenditures to their share in income, we see that in Madagascar the richest quintile receives 53% of income, and the poorest only 5%. Thus, the overall impact of education expenditures has the effect of slightly evening welfare, provided that education expenditures come from taxes that fall equally on the rich and the poor. However, it is also true that education expenditures, if they could be distributed more evenly between income classes, offer a great potential for evening income distribution and reducing poverty.

## Supply Factors in Education

Enrollment alone is not enough to ensure adequate education. The quality of the education received once enrolled is critical. In many LDCs, quality issues are paramount. Schools are poorly maintained, teachers often do not have an adequate education (some primary level teachers often only have a primary education themselves), textbooks and materials are in scarce supply, etc. In many cases, curricula are outdated, overly academic, and the material is not relevant to life of the poor. In rural areas especially, there are language barriers. Teachers often do not come from the locality in which they teach, do not speak the local language, and lack of sensitivity to local culture and traditions. In many rural areas, children are only exposed to local dialects up until school, and then are expected to perform in the main language, usually English, French or Spanish. Teachers from urban areas assigned to rural posts are not prepared to live in primitive conditions without electricity, running water, etc. Pay is often low, with little compensation for hardship posts. Hence, many spend long "weekends" in the city, deserting their schools during school days. Teaching methods in many countries still emphasize rote learning and other inflexible methods. Modern teaching methods, and equipment, are often in scarce supply.

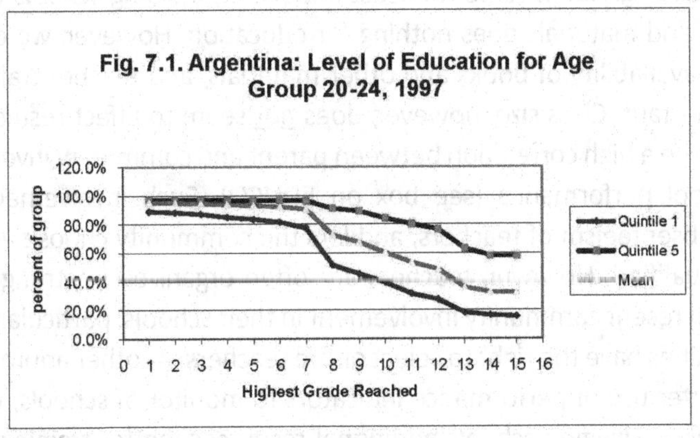


**Fig. 7.1. Argentina: Level of Education for Age Group 20-24, 1997**

The results of these factors are high dropout rates, and high repetition rates among the poor. Many of the poor leave school before 12th grade. Data for Argentina (fig. 7.1) shows almost 100% enrollment for the highest quintiles in the early years, while the poor average about 85%. After grade 7, however, the drop in enrollments in quintile 1 becomes more rapid. By the time of university enrollment, while 60% of children from quintile 5 are enrolled, enrollment for quintile 1 is less than 20%. Thus, while higher education is theoretically available to all, most of the students in university level come from the non-poor. The overall effect is what might be called the "intergenerational transmission of poverty". The poor receive less education, earn less income, have larger families which are also poor—and poverty grows. Breaking this chain of causality is difficult.

Education reform is, and has been, a major issue in most countries. The need, in general, is to shift to a focus on <u>results</u> measured by such factors as achievement tests, and lower repetition and drop-out rates, rather than level of enrollment. Most of the past has focused on inputs (school enrollment, teachers/student, number of schools, number of trained teachers, books available), or outputs (% graduated).

While the goal is to monitor results, how are those results affected by various inputs? What is the education production function? What is most critical? books? teacher training? classrooms? class size? Here the answer not clear, and varies among countries[66]. Generally speaking, we know that

---

[66] For a quick review of the problems of relating education inputs to learning outcomes, see: Robert Picciotto, "What is Education Worth?—From

school buildings seem to be the least important; building schools that lack teachers and materials does nothing for education. However, we do know that the availability of books and other materials, and teacher training are very important. Class size, however, does <u>not</u> seem to affect results. There seems to be a high correlation between parent and community involvement and school performance (see box on EDUCO). Such involvement helps reduce absenteeism of teachers, and lets the community choose a teacher that is qualified. However, teachers are often organized in strong unions, and often resent community involvement in their schools, particularly when communities have the right to select or fire teachers. Another approach is to make better use of performance indicators to monitor of schools, with the goal of giving lagging schools additional resources, better training, etc. to close gap. Another approach is to publish test score results so that parents can see which schools are performing below par. Publication of such results, however, is often opposed by Ministry of Education and school teacher unions since it can be used by parent to force changes in teachers, principals, etc.

## Demand Factors

The issue involves not only the supply (schools) but also the demand for education. While schools may be available for the poor, often the poor do not send their children to school. This may be a product of various factors. One of the main factors is that the poor see low value in educating their children—perhaps because of they see the poor quality of education in the schools (a supply-demand interaction). Children in poor families have a high <u>opportunity cost.</u> Children can earn income for a poor family, particularly in rural areas, that may be essential for the family. Often farm work takes students away from school for long periods—result is sporadic attendance and eventual dropout. Older students are often required to be at home for child care of younger siblings, or to haul water. Many parents do not see the value of educating girls whose future is focused only (in their view) on

---

Production Function to Institutional Capital", World Bank, unpublished, no date, available at: siteresources.worldbank.org/**EDUCATION**/Resources/278200 . . . ./picci.doc

marriage and reproduction. Interestingly enough, attendance at school often rises as families migrate to urban areas—as the opportunity costs go down, school attendance goes up. Other issues related to gender are also important: in some cultures, parents do not want older girls going to schools with boys, taught by men, or walking long distances, particularly at night. Schools are often not equipped with adequate and separate toilets, making it embarrassing for girls who need to use these facilities.

Another factor might be called economic myopia (nearsightedness). People place a high value on the present, and a low value on what might be future benefits. In economic terms, they have a high discount rate on future consumption. Thus, poor people prefer certain and low return on children working now, to possible (uncertain) higher returns from more education. Of course, if without the child's contribution the family starves to death, the present value of the long term benefit is zero. Myopia doesn't only affect poor people—people smoke cigarettes knowing there is a risk of cancer, but do it anyway because they believe that somehow they will escape untouched, and/or cannot picture the pain and misery of an early death. If people could clearly see the future, their present behavior might change.

Financial costs of schooling in most LDCs are formidable obstacles for the poor. Even though schools are free, often schools require that students purchase school books, materials, and uniforms (common in most LDC school systems). Helping poor families meet these out-of-pocket costs is often an effective way of increasing school attendance and helping to reduce poverty.

In fact, a variety of public programs have been tried in an attempt to influence the demand side. These are normally some form of cash grants to families with school age children, conditional on school attendance (Progresa in Mexico, Bolsa Escolar in Brazil). They are often, but not always, aimed at families with secondary school students (higher opportunity cost, more likely to drop out), and may include a requirement for medical visits as well. Another variant of this is "Food for School" programs—free food distribution to a family linked to attendance at school. Some people question whether these demand side programs are enough if they occur without an increase in supply quality. Having more students sitting in bad schools so their families can collect their grant does little for education. In fact, both demand and supply have to be managed together.

<u>EDUCO: Education Reform in El Salvador</u>

The EDUCO program in El Salvador is a classic example of an education reform designed to increase community management and "empowerment". In the aftermath of the peace accords, there was a large increase in demand for schools. The Government decided (1991) to adopt a new model in new areas that delegates management decisions to a local school association, including allocation of money. The local ACE—Parents Associations—receive financial transfers directly to hire teachers, buy books, etc. There was some resistance to this model from teachers and administrators—some saw this as a form of school privatization. Teachers preferred to report to the Ministry of Education, not the ACE, and the Ministry officials saw it as a reduction in authority. Hence, it has only been applied to schools in new areas.

Results of EDUCO are unclear. It has allowed a rapid expansion of education in areas not previously served. Teacher and student absenteeism has fallen, and there is less evidence of delayed entrance to school. There has been a build-up of social capital—the communities who came together through the ACEs have branched out to cooperative community ventures in other areas, such as repairing infrastructure. But there is no evidence that <u>performance of students is materially better.</u> This is a surprising finding—perhaps reflecting the difficulty of finding a valid comparison group. It would suggest, also, that increased student and teacher attendance have no impact on learning.

Source: Darlyn Meza, with José L. Guzmán and Lorena De Varela, "EDUCO: A Community-Managed Education Program in Rural Areas of El Salvador", paper prepared for Scaling Up Poverty Reduction: A Global Learning Process and Conference, Shanghai, May 25–27, 2004. World Bank, 2004. See also E. Jimenez and Y. Sawada, "Do Community-Managed Schools Work? An Evaluation of El Salvador's EDUCO Program", Impact Evaluation of Education Reforms, Working Paper No. 8, World Bank, February 1998.

Vocational or job training is often put forward as a way of raising the productivity of poor people. Sadly, most vocational training programs seem to have little impact (true both in LDCs and Europe and the US). Training institutes are badly run, have out of date equipment, and teach skills often not needed in the market place. Often a better route is to subsidize training in the workplace, or to emphasize general education and let employers provide the technical training they think appropriate.

## II. Health

Health is directly related to a person's welfare, and his/her productivity. It is hard to work productively if one is sick with malaria, diarrhea, worms, or countless other diseases common to developing countries. The links between health and poverty work both ways—ill health is a cause of poverty, and poverty is a cause of poor health. The poor in any country always have health indicators that are inferior to the non-poor in any country, rich or poor. The poor have less access to clean water, sanitation and preventive health measures such as immunizations, they have limited access to effective curative health services, and they cannot afford substantial out of pocket expenditures for medicines or medical services.

Fig 7.2 Child Mortality and Income, by Country

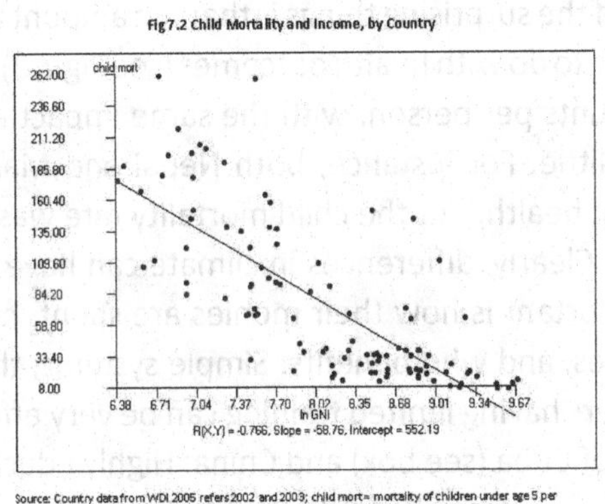


Source: Country data from WDI 2005 refers 2002 and 2003; child mort= mortality of children under age 5 per 1,000; ln GNI is the log of per capita Gross National Income in PPP dollars; developing countries only.

While health status is often related to the level of per capita income, the relationship shows a wide variation in country experience. As shown in Fig. 7.2, if we measure health status by the level of child mortality, some countries with relatively low per capita income have relatively low levels of child mortality, especially when compared to countries with similar income levels. Some of the best performers are countries such as China, Jamaica, Costa Rica and Sri Lanka. For instance, Jamaica with a per capita income (PPP) of $3510 has a child mortality rate of only 20, while Kazakhstan, with a per capita income of 6290, has a much high rate of 73. The champion of all countries is Sri Lanka, with a per capita income of only 3740, and a child mortality rate of 15. The worse performers are the poorer African countries, such as Angola, Rwanda, Senegal and Swaziland, all with child mortality rates over 100, and some over 200. Some of the greatest progress in reducing child mortality has taken place in the middle income and high income countries, not the in poorest countries. As shown in Table 7.5, under five mortality has fallen between 1990 and 2009 by 30% in the richer countries, and only 28% in the poorest, including Sub-Saharan Africa.

**Table 7.5 Under Age 5 Mortality**
**(per 1000)**

| Group | 1990 | 2009 | %Δ |
|---|---|---|---|
| High Income | 12 | 7 | -42% |
| Middle Income | 85 | 51 | -40% |
| Low Income | 171 | 118 | -28% |
| Sub-Sahara Africa | 181 | 130 | -28% |

Source: World Bank, WDI data bank. SS Africa includes developing countries only.

Why is there such large variation? Clearly this depends on a range of factors, but one of the surprising things is that the amount a country spends on health has little to do with health outcomes (see Fig 7.3). Some countries spend large amounts per person, with the same impact as countries that spend relatively little. For instance, both Nepal and Mali spent $12 per person in 2002 on health, but the child mortality rate was 220 in Mali and only 82 in Nepal. Clearly, differences in climate can have an impact here, but also very important is how their monies are spent, how effective are these expenditures, and who benefits. Simple systems, that provide local health care workers having limited training can be very effective, as shown by the examples of Cuba (see box) and China. Highly educated doctors, on the other hand, often are reluctant to work in primitive and rural areas where facilities both for living and working are less than optimal.

**Fig. 7.3 Health Expenditures Per Capita and Child Mortality, Developing Countries, 2002**

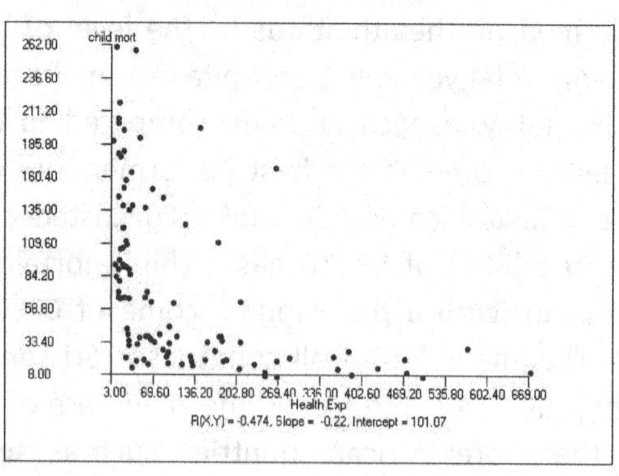


Source: WDI 2005. Health expenditures in US $ per capita.

Health care systems in many developing countries often focus too much on curative health, rather than preventive care. Rich people, and people in richer countries, tend to die from diseases such as cancer, heart disease, diabetes and other non-communicable diseases. Poor people, particularly in developing countries, are affected by infectious or communicable diseases, including respiratory infections, malaria, AIDs, and diarrhea (see Table 7.6). In Africa, 53% of deaths are caused by infectious diseases, compared to only 21% in Europe. The leading causes of death in Africa are HIV/AIDs, malaria, gastro-intestinal and respiratory diseases. In Europe, the leading causes are cardiovascular diseases and cancer.

Thus, health expenditures can be biased, if they focus on curative care for cancer or heart disease, for instance, and ignore programs of hygiene education, vaccination, and other measures designed to prevent infections and the spread of communicable diseases. Simple preventive measures are often much more cost effective than expensive curative measures. In addition, the treatment for many of these infectious diseases is relatively simple and well known, such as oral rehydration therapy (ORT) for treatment of diarrhea. Many diseases, such as diarrhea, malaria and respiratory diseases are a reflection of the poor living conditions of the poor, including inadequate shelter and sanitation. It is estimated that 45% of diarrheal diseases could be eliminated by improved hygiene in the home, including washing of hands, and 35% simply by household level treatment (chlorination) of drinking water[67].

---

[67] Barbara Evans, "Securing Sanitation—The Compelling Case to Address the Crisis", WHO/SIWI (Stockholm International Water Institute, 2005).

**Table 7.6 Causes of Death – Africa vs. Europe**

| | | |
|---|---|---|
| Africa | | |
| Infectious and parasitic diseases | | 52.7% |
| HIV/AIDs | 19.6 | |
| Malaria | 10.7 | |
| Diarrehal diseases | 6.6 | |
| Respiratory Diseases | | 10.5 |
| Cardiovascular | | 9.7 |
| Injuries | | 6.7 |
| Europe | | |
| Cardiovascular diseases | | 51.5 |
| Malignant neoplasms (cancers) | 19.2 | |
| Injuries | 8.3 | |
| Infectious and parasitic diseases | | 2.0 |

Source: tabulations by author from WHO, World Health Report, 2004. http://www.who.int/whr/2004/annex/topic/en/annex_2_en.pdf

What is required is a health care system that provides services in remote rural areas and in urban slums where poor people live, and not highly specialized services in urban centers. The effectiveness of any health system is measured by the results that it produces, not the kinds of inputs that it provides. Cuba offers an excellent example of a health system that provides extensive services at the local level, and excellent monitoring of health conditions (see box). However, the Cuba health system has proven expensive to maintain.

This raises the question of who should provide health services, and who should pay. Is this a public sector responsibility or private? We can envision three possible systems (see table 7.7), in which the provision of health services is done either by the private or public sectors, and the funding of health care is done either by private or public sectors.

**Table 7.7 Health Provision -- Public vs. private?**

| Model | Funding | Provision |
|---|---|---|
| A | private | private |
| B | public | private |
| C | public | public |

Model "A" leaves everything to the private sector. Private households pay private providers (doctors, hospitals) for the cost of medical care. The random nature of medical events presents the risk of facing very large, and unanticipated, expenditures at various times in one's life. Private or public health insurance can even out expenses over time by pooling these risks across the population. However, in developing countries, private health insurance is rarely an option for the poor, and few governments can afford to provide public health insurance. The poor do use, however, a wide range of private providers. These include everything from formal doctors (sometimes "moonlighting" from the public sector), informal practioners, faith healers, herbalists, mid-wives and druggists. Poor people generally have a good idea of what works and what does not and often rely on their own home remedies or traditional herbal cures. For more serious conditions, they turn to the more formal providers if they can be afforded, or to free and low quality services available from public sector clinics and hospitals.

Mixed systems exist, such as model "B", of public financing and private provision. In these cases, characterized by countries like Brazil, all members of society are enrolled in publicly provided health insurance, which is paid for by a payroll tax or out of general tax revenue, or both. The state reimburses private providers for services rendered, usually on either a cost-sharing basis, and with a limit on total charges per procedure. The problem arises when state reimbursements are out of line with costs of provision, which leads providers to discourage or discontinue these procedures, or disguise them as something for which the reimbursement is more profitable. The US Medicare and Medicaid systems are further examples of public funding and private provision.

**Cuba: Health Care Achievements and Problems**

In 1958, Cuba already ranked among the top four Latin American countries in indicators of social well-being. However, it suffered severe inequalities and limitations in the access to health services, particularly among the rural and marginal urban populations where the poor were concentrated. The revolution of 1959 brought radical socioeconomic reform that significantly improved the availability and quality of social services. By 1989, the country was among the top socialist and Latin American and Caribbean countries in achieving access to social services, despite its relatively low gross domestic product per capita.

After the revolution, the government set as a primary goal the expansion of free health care to rural areas and low-income urban groups, which had been virtually excluded. It also put a priority on a massive effort to vaccinate children. Real per capita expenditures for health care jumped 162 percent between 1976 and 1989. As access became universal and free (with few exceptions), the results were remarkable. The infant mortality rate, the number of children born underweight, maternal mortality, and the mortality rate of the population over age 65 all fell. Most contagious diseases were either eradicated or sharply reduced. Finally, the gap between access to facilities and health personnel and in health standards between urban and rural areas was greatly reduced. On the other hand, there were several problems and inefficiencies. The health care system was highly dependent on imports of medical equipment, drugs and other essential inputs from the Soviet bloc.

The crisis of 1989 produced a sharp cutback in exports to, and aid from, the Soviet Union. Health indicators deteriorated in the first half of the 1990s, and improved in the second half. But as of 2000, several had not recovered to their 1989 levels, particularly in the poorest eastern provinces. The deterioration is explained by several causes. Soviet food imports virtually stopped after 1989, Cuba's hard-currency allocation for imports was halved in 1989–97, and domestic food production sharply decreased. All these problems had an adverse effect on nutrition: the proportion of Cuba's population that was undernourished increased from 5 percent in 1990–92 to 17 percent in 2000. Real health care expenditures per capita in 1999 were 21 percent below the 1989 level. The cut in real expenditures and in imports led to a severe scarcity of medicine, spare parts for equipment, inputs for tests, anesthesia, hygiene goods, and other essentials. The crisis did not affect the separate and costly health care scheme that provides better services for privileged elite (military, internal security, Communist Party). The government also instituted a new separate scheme that provides services for foreigners who pay in dollars. However, these systems create inequalities resented by the non-privileged.

Excerpted from Carmelo Mesa Largo, "Cuba: Achievement and Deterioration of Access to Universal Access to Social Services', case study written for the World Bank conference "Reducing Poverty, Sustaining Growth", Beijing, 2005, available at: http://info.worldbank.org/etools/docs/reducingpoverty/case/60/fullcase/Cuba%20Health%20Full%20Case.pdf

Model "C" provides for both public funding and public provision. This system is common in most developing countries, the UK, Canada and Europe. Health care is provided free or at nominal charges through a system run by the public sector. Its costs come largely from taxation, with some limited amount of user charges, usually low and nominal. Since doctors and staff are paid a fixed salary, there is little incentive to provide quality services, but all patients receive the same treatment regardless of income. Model "C" type systems often exist with a parallel model "A" private-private system in place, which generally provides superior services to those (non-poor) who can afford to pay. In Latin America, an additional variant is often found, where workers pay into a social security fund, and the fund runs social security hospitals which provide medical care for members only. The services in the social security hospitals are generally better than those in the pure public sector, because of better financing, but not as good as those in the private sector.

But why should the public sector be involved at all? There are several reasons;

- health is a <u>basic need</u>—access to some sort of minimal level of health service should be available to all, particularly the poor. In addition, the non-poor may feel better knowing that people are not dying because they lack medical care.
- <u>externalities</u>: we are all better off if society is healthy, especially with regards to communicable diseases (e.g. HIV/AIDs). Hence, it is in everyone's interest to promote public health and preventative health measures.
- <u>Insurance/credit</u> problems (market failures): poor people cannot obtain insurance that is affordable, not can they borrow in the market to cover most health costs (although they often do borrow in informal markets).

Fig 7.4 . A Typical Public Health Structure

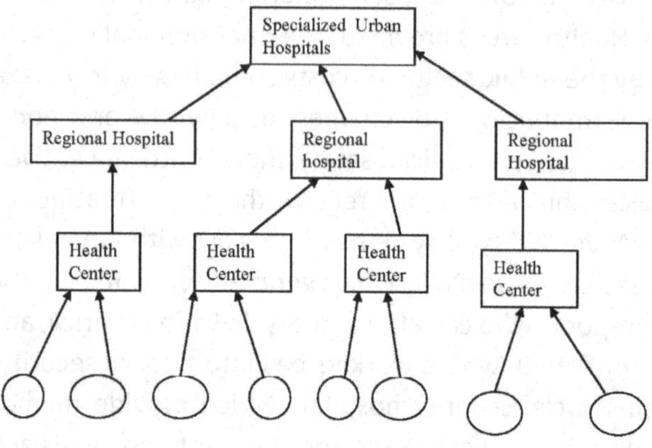


Most LDCs have a public sector health system structured along the lines of Fig. 7.4. Small health posts or primary health care clinics in rural villages and urban neighborhoods provide "front line" support, and can handle routine and simple problems. They may be staffed with one or two community health workers or nurses, but no doctors. For more complicated problems, patients are referred up the chain, to the health center. The health center is typically a larger operation, with a staff of at least one doctor and support staff, and perhaps 5-10 beds for overnight stays. The health center can handle child births and some simple surgeries, especially those that can be done on an out-patient basis. For more complicated problems, patients are referred to the regional hospital, which provides a full range of surgical and other services, and is staffed by a number of doctors with appropriate specialties. Even more complicated cases can be referred to the urban center, which typically has the best hospital in the country and may have additional specialized hospitals focusing on cardiac, cancer or other illnesses.

While the system looks great on paper, it often is beyond the capacity of developing countries to manage and fund. Inadequate funding for the operational expenses means that health posts lack medicines, hospitals lack bandages and X-ray film, and equipment is out of date and not operating because of inadequate maintenance or lack of spare parts. Patients are often told that they must go to private suppliers to find drugs, or come to the hospital with their own bandages or other supplies in order to receive patients. The problems are often more acute at the health center and health post levels, so people by-pass the system and crowd into regional and large urban hospitals because they know the quality of treatment will be better, and drugs and supplies will be available. Often shortages in the public sector arise because materials are being diverted for sale in the private sector.

Because salaries are relatively low, public sector doctors and nurses often work less than a full 40 hour week, and run private practices on the side to supplement their incomes. They often refer patients to their private practices when conditions prevent them from being easily treated in the public sector. Medical staff do not want to work in remote rural areas, and are often absent. Publicly trained medical staff often migrate abroad in search of higher incomes, leading to chronic shortages despite extensive training programs. Cuba's success stems in part from its ability to keep a large supply of medical personnel at home by limiting migration. In many countries,staff from international NGOs provide critical services in rural areas where there would otherwise be no health services. In extremely poor countries, such as Haiti, the NGO community provides practically all of the functioning health services at all levels.

As a result of these factors, there is conflicting evidence on the impact of PHC centers and indicators of health, but in general the typical public sector health system seems to have very little impact[68]. Many PHC clinics are underutilized, seeing as few as 2-3 patients a day (compared to private clinics who see 2-3 patients per hour). The key is demand elasticity—when people have time, as in non-emergency cases, they can shop around and use the cheapest source. In an emergency, they tend to go to the nearest facility. Often traditional healers and practioners are as useful, and often cheaper, compared to local community health workers. The study by Filmer and colleagues found that 63% of health expenditures in low income countries are in the private sector, and this is as high as 75% in South Asia.

The poor quality of the public health system leads to a *defacto* two tier system ; poor people use it or traditional healers, while the rich can afford private doctors and hospitals. What is the solution? The answers are not easy, as we know that few countries have been able to provide

---

68 D. Filmer, J. Hammer, and L. Pritchett "Health Policy in Poor Countries: Weak Links in the Chain" *Journal of Economic Literature* 27 (December, 1999).

an affordable and fully effective health system without setting up some negative incentives and side-effects. Some possible solutions, currently being tried in various places include:

- Decentralization: Allow community based management of PHCs, so that local people can select staff, monitor their performance. While this is being tried in some countries, there is considerable resistance often from the entrenched bureaucracies of the traditional health ministries.
- Privatize: use of private system providers with reimbursement from public sector on a fee for service basis.
- Cost Recovery: Highly controversial, because charging fees more likely will exclude the poor, and many countries cannot or do not want to differentiate between rich and poor, or those who should pay and those who should receive free services. Even where it has been tried, it often does not solve the budget problem if budget revenues merely go into a general account without increasing the amount available for health expenditures. Even if such revenues are segregated, the central government may be tempted to reduce its own allocation to health in the general budget.
- Preventive Care: Shift focus of public sector from curative to preventive care, including sanitation, health education, vaccination, vector controls (e.g. mosquitoes) and public health information campaigns (AIDs, smoking, hygiene).
- Traditional Healers: Upgrade traditional healers with modern techniques, separating out what works and what is ineffective in what they offer.

# CHAPTER VIII
# GUIDING DEVELOPMENT: THE ROLE OF THE PUBLIC SECTOR

A wise and frugal government, which shall leave men free to regulate their own pursuits of industry and improvement, and shall not take from the mouth of labor the bread it has earned—this is the sum of good government.—Thomas Jefferson

## Why the Public Sector?

Fostering development is seen as a proper role for the public sector. Since the early days of the "big push" and national planning, it was generally accepted that development needed to be guided, directed and even undertaken by the public sector. Years of bitter experience with state planning, state industries, subsidies and incentives, have called for a major rethink of the role of the public sector. While the perceived role of the public sector has changed in the eyes of many, few people would question that a public sector is needed. The debate centers around how big a public sector, and what should it do to foster development[69].

[69] Note that "public sector" as used here is larger than just "government". "Government" includes federal, national and local government bodies, including executive, legislative and judicial branches. "Public sector" includes these plus publically owned corporations, authorities and other entities. A country's central bank, for instance, is part of the public sector but not of the government, as are public universities and publically owned utilities.

## Tools of the Public Sector

The public sector has tremendous power that can be used to shape development. These can be grouped into four broad groups:

- Taxation power, including the power to reduce or increase taxes and tariffs as an incentive to produce or invest;
- Expenditures—the allocation of public expenditures between physical infrastructure, health, education, agriculture, finance, etc. can have a major impact on the pace of development, as can a system of subsidies to the private sector;
- Regulation—even without spending money, the public sector can control economic activity by how it imposes (and enforces) regulations concerning prices, interest rates, land development, foreign exchange use, labor conditions, etc. Public sector regulation is key to providing a secure money supply and a financial system that facilitates economic growth and development.
- Legal Framework—the public sector provides a framework for the enforcement of justice, including crime prevention, as well as a system of courts to provide for a (hopefully) orderly and just resolution of civil disputes, including those involving economic activities (e.g. enforcement of contracts)

All of these tools have been used in various degrees in the past by both developed and developing countries to foster economic development. Typically, developing countries often:

- Impose differential import tariffs to encourage industrialization and limit imports of goods that the government wants to have produced at home (import substitution);
- Invest in industries to produce domestically goods and services where private investment is inadequate;
- Build infrastructure (roads, power grids, water supply, irrigation works, etc.) that facilitate private development;
- Provide some degree of free or subsidized health care and education, including higher education

- Provide subsidies for the production of essential goods, such as food, or subsidies for essential services, such as water, electricity, urban transport.
- Provide low cost credit (a form of subsidy) for what are considered to be key or essential activities, including small and medium scale industry, exporters, agricultural producers, etc.
- Set price controls on key commodities and services, such as food and energy products, and/or provide public services at below cost (electricity, irrigation water, drinking water).

## Why Do We Need a Public Sector?

In theory, the market should provide a perfect solution to the problem of the allocation of resources. The so-called "Pareto Optimum" occurs when, in an economy with perfect competition and perfect knowledge, the prices of goods and services are equated to their marginal cost (P = MC). Price is determined by consumer demand, and supply by the cost of producing the last unit put on the market. Any other allocation would be less than optimal, since its cost would be above the price consumers would be willing to pay, and such consumption could be achieved only with some sort of public intervention (subsidy, tax, etc.). Oscar Lange, a famous economist from Eastern Europe, demonstrated that even with state planning, planners should allocate resources so that P = MC, and that any other allocation was inefficient.

However, the conditions of the" Pareto Optimum" do not exist in practice, although the theory states the basis for allowing the markets to allocate resources. In a complex society, markets can work relatively efficiently and well. However, the basic assumptions that there exists perfect competition and perfect knowledge differs from real world experience. The existence of monopolies or near-monopolies means that prices are set to maximize profits, rather than consumer welfare. People do not have perfect knowledge of all products in the market, or the quality of what they are buying. Thus, competitive market equilibria are not necessarily optimal, and "market failures" are common.

In addition, even with perfect competition, game theory suggests that competition can result in sub-optimal solutions. Consider the famous parable of the "Prisoners' Dilemma". Two thieves (A and B) rob a bank, steal $100,000 which they hide, and are caught. The police have no witnesses or evidence, and the thieves are interrogated in separate rooms. As shown in the table below, if neither thief admits to the crime, they go free (zero jail time). However, if A testifies against B, he will get only 5 years of jail time, and B will get 25 years. A can then unearth the money which has been hidden. Likewise, if B testifies against A, he gets only 5 years and access to the money. Now if A and B really trust each other, they will keep quiet and reach an optimal solution of zero jail time. Cooperation produces the best solution. However, if A and B feel they are competitors and do not trust each other, they will end up in a sub-optimal solution where both do jail time[70].

**Table 8.1. Example of the Prisoners Dilemma**

| Strategy | | Jail Time (years) | | Loot ($ 000's) | |
|---|---|---|---|---|---|
| 1 | Neither talk | 0 | 0 | 50 | 50 |
| 2 | A testifies against B | 5 | 25 | 100 | 0 |
| 3 | B testifies against A | 25 | 5 | 0 | 100 |
| 4 | Both talk | 20 | 20 | 50 | 50 |

This game theory approach is sometimes known as the "Theory of the Second Best", and economists frequently refer to "second best solutions". For instance, the best solution is for everyone to pay taxes. However, if tax laws are not enforced and practically no one pays taxes, your tax bill is higher to cover the non-payment of others. The second best solution is not to pay taxes either.

The economist John Nash pointed out that there can be multiple stable solutions in a competitive game, particularly when there are multiple players. Thus, there is no necessary reason that competition produces an optimal solution, and in fact, it is likely that one of these multiple sub-optimal solutions will be the result. Examples of sub-optimal solutions in the real world abound: the QWERTY keyboard for typewriters was designed in the early 20th Century to make typing difficult, so that

70 The game can be analyzed with or without reference to the money. The money introduces a new dynamic in the trade-off, since if A testifies against B, he would get the whole $100,000, rather than $50,000, and may feel that five years in jail is worth the extra $50,000. Also, the cooperative solution is optimal for the crooks, but not for society. The competitive solution puts both crooks in jail, which is a better social solution.

people would slow down and not jam the machine. Modern computers still use it, although it makes typing more difficult.

What does this have to do with development? One can think of the low level equilibrium trap (Chapter 1) as a sub-optimal solution in a competitive environment. Inadequate savings and investment keep countries from raising their output; efficient public sector interventions can push the country to a higher equilibrium and a more optimal solution. The problem is to find interventions that promote growth and reduce poverty, and do not inhibit growth and worsen income distribution.

## Public Goods and Externalities

Another problem driving an economy away from a Pareto Optimum is that not all goods will be produced in adequate amounts purely as a response to market signals. The classic case is the "public good". Public goods are characterized by:

- Non-rival consumption—The consumption by one person does not diminish the supply available for consumption by someone else, and
- Non-excludability—It is impossible to restrict the consumption of those not willing to pay for the good (or service).

There are very few pure public goods, but many goods and services that are "quasi-public goods", or have public goods characteristics. The classic public good is national defense; the government cannot provide a national defense for some people in a country while excluding others. Likewise, including one more person in the national defense umbrella does not diminish the level of defense for everyone else. Since public goods can not be rationed and sold on an open market, they will be *under produced.* That is, the level of production will be less than that desired by the general public—market signals do not provide enough incentive for the optimal production level. Suppose I form a private army to provide defense for my community, and ask people to voluntarily contribute for this service. Some people will enjoy the benefit without paying the fees, since I cannot exclude their being covered. These are the so—called "free riders". A few good natured and public spirited citizens will pay, but the level of defense will be much less than needed.

**Externalities** work in a similar way. Some goods and services have positive and negative externalities. That is, they produce costs that are not paid or realized by the producer, or create benefits that the producer is unable to capture in the form of profit. Likewise, one can think of consumption externalities, where the private benefit from consumption exceeds or is less than the public benefit. Thus, there are positive and negative externalities, and production and consumption externalities (see Table 8.2)

**Table 8.2 Four Kinds of Externalities**

| | Positive | Negative |
|---|---|---|
| Production | Local Roads<br>Good architecture<br>Public music performances<br>Educational TV | Air and water pollution<br>Noise<br>Bad architecture<br>Crime<br>Poverty? |
| Consumption | Education<br>Exercise<br>Inoculations<br>Seat Belts/Bike Helments | Cigarette smoke<br>Addictive drugs<br>Loud music<br>Reckless Driving |

Cigarettes have clear negative consumption externalities; smoking in public subjects others to dangerous carcinogens. The pain cause to others is not realized by the consumer of cigarettes. Inoculations can have positive consumption externalities since they reduce the risk of disease being spread to others (besides the personal benefit to the direct consumer).

The role of the government, then, is to correct this misallocation and make producers and consumers *internalize* the negative externalities, and provide incentives and subsidies to expand production and consumption of goods with positive externalities. Take the following example (Fig 8.1)

**Fig 8. 1 Production Externality Example**

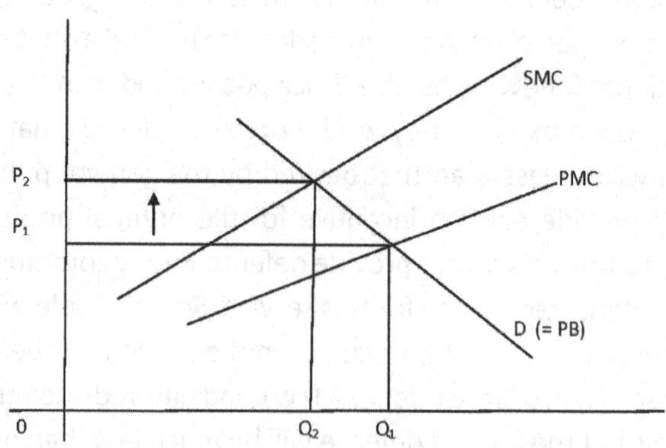

Here we have classic supply and demand curves in which the supply of good X (think electricity) is based on private marginal costs (PMC), which is equated with the demand (D) or private benefit (PB). However, the social costs (SMC) are much higher than the private costs (PMC) because this electricity is produced using coal, which creates air pollution and causes lung cancer. In this case, the good is produced in quantity $Q_1$. Some form of government action is necessary to limit production back to $Q_2$, which is the social optimum. This can be done with a tax that raises the price to the consumer from $P_1$ to $P_2$.

In the case of cigarette consumption, the social benefits are much less than the private benefits of consumption. Thus, the social demand curve is lower than the private demand curve. A tax here would restrict the consumption of cigarettes. In both cases, the government could use the tax revenue to pay for the social costs incurred. But not everything done by governments is because of externalities. Some goods, called "merit goods", are provided publically because people want the government to do these things—subsidized health care, mail service, agricultural subsidies, high speed passenger trains, low cost symphony orchestras, etc. While there may be some elements of public goods and/or externalities involved, these are not often the main reasons for public provision.

In addition, not everyone agrees on what are positive and negative externalities. If I play my violin in the subway station, I can collect donations. But some people will enjoy the music and not donate (free riders). Music in subways will be therefore "underprovided" and a case could be made for public subsidy. However, some people could equally be annoyed by my music, especially if I play badly. They might consider such acts as having serious negative externalities, and insist that playing music in subways stations should be banned. In a developing country, the president may feel there are significant positive externalities in terms of enhanced national prestige in having a fancy airport, an expensive presidential palace, a large football stadium, or a modern steel mill. Others (particularly those in the political opposition) would label these as wasteful white elephants.

The final rationale for public intervention is the decreasing cost industry. In such an industry, (see Fig. 8.2) average per unit cost (AC) decreases with size of the firm. Thus, firm B being bigger, has lower cost than A, which is smaller. The end result is that B can out compete A, and eventually drive it out of business, with the result that it is a monopoly (controls all of industry production at point C). Using profit maximizing principles, the monopolist at point C will set marginal revenue (MR) equal to marginal cost (MC), and the level of production will be less than socially optimal. The socially optimal point is at F, where demand sets price equal to marginal cost (MC). However, at this point the industry would lose money, since average revenues per unit exceed average cost. In a regulated environment, it would be more likely that the regulators would set prices to equal average cost. These kinds of natural monopolies exist particularly in infrastructure, such as in electricity distribution,

**The Washington Consensus Defined**

The term "Washington Consensus" emerged from the writings of John Williamson, an economist then with the Institute for International Economics. He was merely trying to summarize the emerging philosophy of the major multilateral and bilateral development institutions, on their prescriptions for restoring fiscal balance, reduce inflation, and restore growth. The areas emphasized by Williamson included:

- Fiscal discipline (keeping expenditures more in line with revenues);
- Reordering public expenditures to be morepro- growth and pro-poor;
- Tax reform
- Liberalization of interest rate controls;
- Maintaining competitive exchange rates;
- Trade Liberalization;
- Liberalization of foreign direct investment;
- Privatization of state-owned enterprises;
- Deregulation of the private sector; and
- Maintaining property rights

As can be seen, the emphasis was on reducing the role of the public sector, "getting the prices right" by removing actions that led to price distortions.

Williamson was criticized on several grounds, mostly for ignoring issues of poverty and the social sectors. However, as he was not preparing an agenda, but merely codifying the agenda then being used. He did coin the term "Washington Consensus", which was a bit inaccurate since the agenda was pushed also by donor countries in Europe and elsewhere. However, this was shorthand term invented for a one-time conference. No one was more surprised than Williamson when it because internationally famous and widely debated, and became the focus of much of the anti-globalization movement.

Source: John Williamson "A Short History of the Washington Consensus", conference paper, Barcelona, 2004, available at: http://www.iie.com/publications/papers/williamson0904-2.pdf

water supply, sanitation, fire protection, and telephone (land lines). Hence, public sector ownership or quasi-ownership, and/or public sector regulation is frequently found in these industries.

**Fig. 8.2 Decreasing Cost Industries**

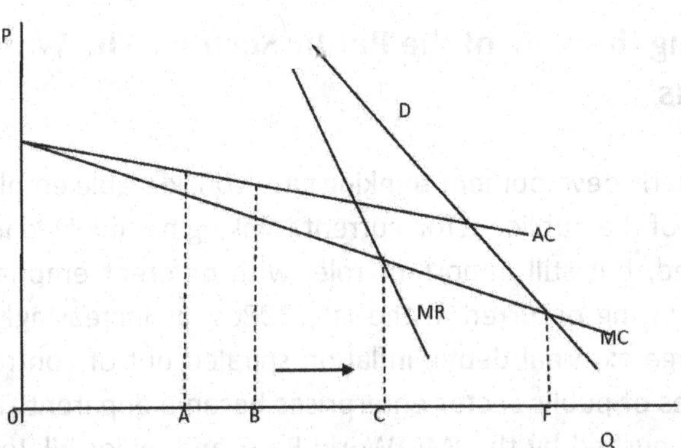


So much for the basic theory, but what does this have to do with development issues in poor countries? Externalities are easy to identify, but the issue is this; does the government need to correct every externality that it finds? Government intervention is costly, in terms of bureaucratic waste and inefficiency. Taxes and regulations create the opportunity for "rent seeking"; that is, government officials taking advantage of their unique position to grant subsidies or levy taxes. It is not hard to see that if an underpaid government official has the power to set tariffs that would protect an industry, and thereby generate millions of dollars of profits for the owner, he might be tempted to ask for part of the "rent", the unearned increment in profit generated by the tariff protection afforded. In countries with weak bureaucracies and limited ability to impose sanctions on corrupt officials, one needs to think twice about setting up new regulations, taxes, etc. that give officials yet more power to extract "rents".

However, development itself generates externalities in terms of new opportunities for investment. The idea of the big push (Rosenstein-Rodan) and balanced growth was based on the idea that a simultaneous development of all industries would create demand between industries (a shoe industry creates demand for leather tanning, shoe machinery, etc.).

While this theory underestimated how easy it would be to industrialize through government intervention, the idea of externalities as a source of growth is one of the basic principles of endogenous growth theory. It is these externalities that permit growth to continue beyond the "steady state".

## Rethinking the Role of the Public Sector—The Washington Consensus

While early development thinking gave considerable emphasis to the critical role of the public sector, current thinking has evolved into a much more limited, but still important role, with different emphases. Much of this rethinking occurred in the late 1980s, as increasingly countries piled up large external debts, inflation spiraled out of control, and the inefficiencies of public sector enterprises became apparent. This reform movement, pushed by the IMF, World Bank and major bilateral donors, became known as the "Washington Consensus"(see box).

The "stylized facts" of how a typical developing country got into problems would go something like this:

- Eager to implement a "big push" toward industrialization, the public sector invests in many basic industries (steel, paint, pharmaceuticals, chemicals, transport, textiles, garments);
- In addition, the government investments in supporting infrastructure includes some dubious projects built in the name of national prestige;
- Because industries and key services (water, electricity) are in public hands, the government keeps prices low to enhance political popularity;
- Because unemployment is high, enterprises are mandated to add employees that they do not need;
- Large enterprise deficits are financed by printing money,or by borrowing domestically or internationally, since raising taxes is politically unpopular and tax laws are weakly enforced;
- Large domestic borrowing raises interest rates, and squeezes out money from the private sector;

- Easy credit from foreign banks encourages foreign borrowing to close public sector deficits, rather than needed adjustments;
- The government sets interest rate controls and imposes lending targets on private banks, who either stop lending or go bankrupt;
- The government establishes public sector banks, who lend for dubious projects in the private sector often influenced by political connections,
- Public sector enterprises are squeezed by insufficient revenues to cover costs, so maintenance and further investments are curtailed, leading to reduced quality of services or goods;
- Inflation spirals out of control, further undermining fixed prices for goods and services, leading to spiraling demands for increases in wages;
- Eventually, foreign donors and bankers refuse to lend, and promise debt relief only if the government adopts an IMF/World Bank program of structural reform (based on the Washington Consensus—see box).
- The IMF/World Bank push the reform which reduces spending, eliminates price controls, liberalizes markets, privatizes failed industries and banks, eliminates redundant employment in the public sector, etc.
- The government blames the IMF/World Bank for the negative impact of the austerity measures.

The Washington Consensus (WC) generated much criticism and debate, particularly as it was seen as imposing Draconian budget cuts on social sectors in order to achieve budget balance, and paid little attention to poverty or income distribution. Over time, the IMF/WB became more sensitive to the need to provide safety nets and protect social expenditures. In general, however, most countries adopted some version of the WC reforms, which generally speaking meant taking steps to "get the prices right", reducing the size of the public sector where possible, opening up the economy to the outside world, and maintaining an overall public sector fiscal balance. Even such countries as Russian and China moved in this direction, although not without much debate and many mistakes. If the WC failed, it was in that it was too simplistic. It assumed that once inflation was controlled and price distortions were eliminated, the economy would "take-off" a la Rostow. In many cases, such as in Latin America, the initial reforms produced positive results in terms of growth that were short lived. In the case of countries formerly in the Soviet Union, these reforms produced a drastic decline in output that required ten or more years just to recover to initial levels. Nevertheless, few countries have made serious attempts to go back to the prior system of distortions and inflation, and/or to renationalize industry and trade[71]. The recent growth record in countries like China and India, among others, is a testimony to the overall correctness of the philosophy.

What was missing from the WC reform package was attention to the deeper problems that limited growth: weak governance, corruption, lack of infrastructure, and weak institutions to support growth, particularly the legal system and the judiciary. The overall result is the recognition that the public sector has a critical role to play in development that it must do well: providing social services and safety nets, providing key infrastructure, and providing an environment that permits and encourages private sector investment and growth.

## The Privatization Debate

One of the most hotly debated aspects of the Washington Consensus reforms was the push to privatize state-owned enterprises, particularly those which were losing money and adding to public sector deficits. Attempts were made in some countries to introduce more private sector management through the negotiation of management contracts, rather than outright ownership. In general, these management contracts were not successful in resolving problems because of the residual influence of public sector officials and politicians. Management contracts and concessions are still popular in the water and electricity sectors, where governments are reluctant to turn full ownership over to the private sector (see box on types of privatizations). Nevertheless, the overall outcomes from privatizations, despite some failures, seem positive on several fronts. In a review of privatization in Latin America, Chong and Lopez-de-Silanes concluded that:

71 Although there have been some partial regressions, such as in Venezuela and Bolivia, involving renationalization.

> Overall, the empirical record shows that privatization leads not only to higher profitability, but also to large output and productivity growth, fiscal benefits, and even quality improvements and better access for the poor. Instances of failure exist, but in light of the overwhelming evidence, this should not be turned into an argument to stop privatization.[72]

Part of the problems of privatization began with the process. In many cases, privatization was not done in a transparent way, and special interests were able to realize large windfall gains by acquiring assets substantially below market prices. However, one has to separate the process of privatization from the results in terms of efficiency of the privatized firms after privatization. Birdsall and Nellis[73], in a study of privatizations in Eastern Europe and Latin America, also find clear evidence that private firms are more efficient than public ones. The distributional aspect of the privatization, however, tended to be anti-poor in that the rich tended to benefit from corrupt privatization practices. They found that this tended to be more true in Eastern Europe than Latin America, and more true for banks, oil and other natural resource producer privatizations. They conclude that while distribution, particularly wealth distribution, is likely to become more adverse in the short term, the long term impact of increased growth in output is likely to benefit all strata of the population. In addition, by reducing the need for government subsidies, government funds a freed up for more worthy government expenditures, such as health and education.

In general, there are fewer issues with privatizations of enterprises involved in production of goods and services that face domestic and international competition (oil, chemicals, steel, textiles, banks, etc.).

---

72 Chong, Alberto and Florencio Lopez-de-Silanes. "*The Truth About Privatization In Latin America*" IDB/NBER Working Paper No R-456, October 2003. Also in **Privatization in Latin America: Myths and Realities,** Inter-American Development Bank, 2005.

73 Birdsall, Nancy and John Nellis, "Winners and Losers: Assessing the Distributional Impact of Privatization" Center for Global development, Working Paper No. 6, May 2002. See also Alberto Chong and Florencio Lopez-de-Silanes, eds., **Privatization in Latin America: Myths and Realities,** Inter-American Development Bank, 2005.

These kinds of firms will not be able to achieve monopoly profits because they face market competition, and the rationale for privatization remains fairly strong. In fact, very few countries have reversed privatizations of these types of industries (exceptions: Venezuela[oil] and Bolivia [oil and gas]).

> **Types of Privatization**
>
> There are different types of private sector participation (loosely all labelled "privatization") common in water supply/ sanitation and electricity. These are:
>
> - management contract, under which the private operator is responsible only for running the system, in exchange for a fee (usually performance-related). Investment is typically financed and carried out by the public sector, but implementation may be delegated. Assets remain publicly owned.
> - lease contract, under which assets are leased to the private operator, who recoups the cost from end users. Investment is typically financed and carried out by the public sector, but implementation may be delegated. Assets remain publicly owned.
> - concession, under which the private operator is responsible for running the entire system, including planning and financing investment. Concession contracts usually run for 20-30 years. Assets remain publicly owned.
> - Asset sale (full privatization), under which the operator owns the assets for an undetermined period.
>
> Source: Wikipedia, "Water Privatization" July, 2010.

More problematic for several reasons are the privatizations of the "natural monopolies" providing essential services: water, electricity and to a lesser extent telecom. Failures in this area stem largely from poorly designed privatization efforts, with private providers not being given clear rules and/ or there being inadequate regulatory agencies in place to supervise their actions. For instance, in Argentina, a concession contract for water supply in Buenos Aires tried to recover from new customers the cost of expanding the network over only two years, a cost of $1100 to $1500 per connection. The result was a charge that equaled almost 25% of the monthly income of poor residents[74]. Eventually regulators changed the agreement to allow amortization of connection charges over a longer period. Overall, Estache et. al. report

74 Estache, Antonio et. al. "Utilities Privatization and the Poor: Lessons and Evidence from Latin America" **World Development 29**(2001), no. 7, p.1195.

gains in services in many cases. These include a 40% drop in electricity prices in five years in Argentina. In Chile, electricity coverage of the poorest 20% families increased from 2% to 94%, and telephone coverage increased from 3% to 40%[75]. In countries where privatization results in expanded services, it is only natural that the poor benefit, since they are the group normally lacking significant access. However, stories of privatization failures, particularly in water and electricity abound. Management contracts have been terminated in country such as Guyana, Bolivia, and Tanzania[76] when contracted firms failed to expand services and make agree improvements, and/or raised prices. Likewise, electricity privatization failed in Guyana for similar reasons.

In theory, the poor should benefit from more efficient services, since they are typically the ones excluded from service provision when service provision is less than 100%. In urban slums, it has been found that water delivered by truck or vendor is 10-20 times more expensive than piped water delivered to a local standpipe. In Guatemala, it was found that a poor family paid $.10 per kilowatt hour for electricity to light up their homes, while those without electricity relied on candles that cost the US$ 5 per kilowatt-hour[77]. Often the poor are adversely impacted because weak utility administration has permitted illegal connections for water and electricity, or has failed to collect bills, and failed to disconnect non-payers. Thus, privatization often results in better and more efficient management, which means poor people have to pay their bills, thus making them in some sense worse off. However, they still stand to gain in terms of more regular and better quality service (fewer outages, cleaner water).

Negative impacts can be offset by creative ways of setting up privatizations and management concessions or contracts. If the regulator specifies its goals in terms of profit maximization, then the purchaser is free to adopt whatever policy it wants with respect to coverage and tariffs. However, privatizations/ concessions can also be tendered with

---

75 Estache, et. al., p. 1181,1183.

76 Paul, John. "Flagship Water Privatization Fails in Tanzania", **The Guardian,** 25 May 2005

77 Based on the unpublished work of V. Foster and J.P. Tre, as quoted in Antonio Estache, Vivian Foster and Quetin Wodon "Making Infrastructure Reform in Latin America Work for the Poor", CEPAL Review 12 (December 2002), p. 112.

certain clear social targets, including the expansion of coverage, quality of services, and tariffs, including the possibility of cross-subsidy to the poor. Thus, a tender can specify that the winning bid will be awarded to the bidder with the highest revenue generated to the government, given agreed targets for extending coverage to underserved areas and limiting tariffs to some given maximum. Problems often arise when regulators realize only ex post that these social goals are important and try to impose new conditions on an already agreed contract. But other problems also arise when bidders, especially foreigners, fail to understand the political and social environment and what is and what is not possible.

Even so, there are countless cases of bidders simply overestimating the gains to be made from the purchase of assets or operating a concession in developing countries. The so called "winners curse" idea indicates that winning bidders tend always to overvalue assets. Consider the case shown in Fig. 8.3. The true value of an asset exists, but is not known precisely by the bidders (or anyone else for that matter). Bids are made on the basis of given information and are made by six firms, A thru F. These are ranked along a line, from low to high. Who wins? Bidder F, the one who makes the most outlandish overbid of the six, wins. Since by definition he/she has overpaid for the asset, we can predict that trouble lies ahead for this bidder.

**Fig 8.3 The Winner's Curse Illustrated**

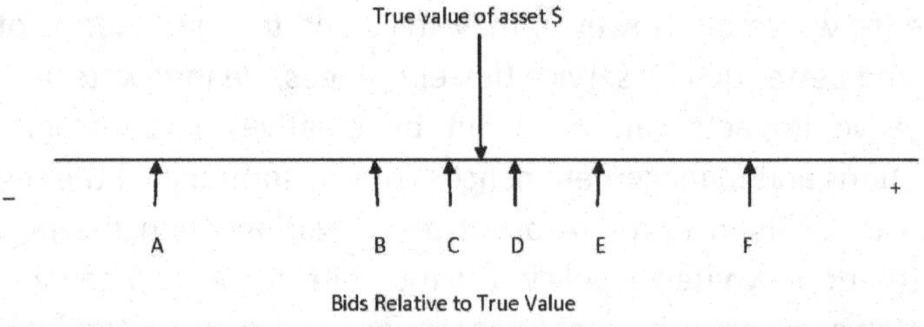

True value of asset $

– A B C D E F +

Bids Relative to True Value

Of course, bidders can adopt a "buy in" strategy, where they purposively overbid in order to establish a presence in the country, and then renegotiate its terms once they "discover" that the contract is not profitable. Alternatively, the country can do the bidding in a "two-step" process. Once bids are received, all bidders are informed of the other bids submitted, and invited to rebid. In this case, F might realize it is overbidding for this asset compared to the other valuations made by its industry colleagues, and lower its bid. However, C, D and E might raise their bids. Other forms of auctions can be used, including the Dutch auction, in which the seller announces a price, which is then lowered until someone agrees to purchase at that price. Whatever system is used, the process has to be open and transparent, with adequately detailed specifications, and clear procedures on ranking bids and making the award.

## Unintended Consequences and Privatization

At one time, advocates were calling for the privatization of practically everything. In developed countries, privatization has been experimented with in such areas as jails, hospitals, schools, police and other government services. The initial idea that the private sector could do things more efficiently, however, ran into the reality that the private sector is guided largely by the profit motive, and not social benefits. These efforts ran into what has been called "The Law of Unintended Consequences". Every policy or public sector initiative designed to correct some externality or social inequity raises the possibility of a change in incentives that produces perverse results[78]. Unemployment insurance, for instance, can encourage people not to seek work, exactly the opposite of what is wanted. Buying surplus farm products to ease the impact of low farm prices can serve as an incentive to produce yet even more. Each of these and other problems can be mitigated with appropriate policies, constraints and regulations, both those in turn increase the cost of administering the program.[79]

In the case of privatization, many early efforts did not fully detail what was required. In the case of privately run jails, for instance, it would appear that the private operator could indeed do it more cheaply. But these cost savings often came because private operators employed cost cutting measures in terms of reduced food quality, untrained staff, overcrowding, etc. To correct these problems, governments had to rewrite contract specifications with more detail. To meet these new criteria, the

[78] Popularized by the sociologist Robert K. Merton. Unintended consequences can actually be positive or negative. See http://en.wikipedia.org/wiki/Robert_K._Merton

[79] Elliot Sclar, *You Don't Always Get What You Pay For*, Cornell University Press, 2000.

private operators had to raise their prices, and eventually the cost savings disappeared. These "transactions costs" involved in privatization resulted in many governments bringing these services back into the public sector, since this turned out to be less costly than the effort required to manage the private operators. This is an example of what is called "the principal-agent problem." Every principal contracts with agents to do things for him/her. For the principal, the challenge is to provide appropriate guidance so as to have the proper response with minimal supervision.

## Regulating the Environment—Externalities in Action

The case of regulation of environmental activities is an excellent example of the complexities involved in correcting an externality. As shown in Fig 8.4, we have an industry whose private marginal costs are much lower than the social costs (this is a repeat of Fig 8.1).

**Fig. 8.4 Correcting an Environmental Externality**

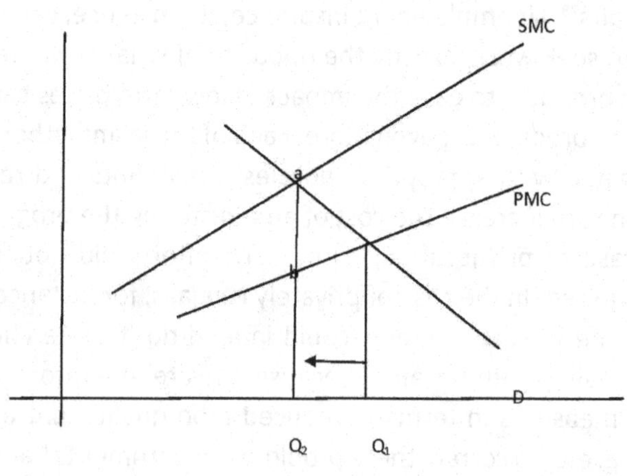


The socially optimal level of production is $Q_2$, and the policy problem is to reduce it from the point of private profit maximization, $Q_1$. There are three alternatives:

- The first is a tax equal to ab, the difference between social costs SMC and PMC, which reduces demand and hence output to the social optimum. From an efficiency perspective, this is the best approach, and also generates tax revenue for the government;

- Second, issue permits or licenses to firms, so that the total output allowed is $Q_2$. Selling permits would be better than outright gift, and if done in a bidding framework, would be equivalent to the tax solution; or
- Third, regulate by law that no firm can produce if it creates the given externality (e.g. smoke), thus driving up costs and reducing output.

Market based solutions are always preferable. Allowing firms to trade permits means that firms with low costs for abatement can sell off their permits to firms with high abatement costs. This assumes, however, that there is a socially optimal level of pollution that is acceptable, e.g. we don't want to eliminate all smoke, only that amount that causes harm. In some cases, such as mercury or arsenic pollution of water, an outright ban may be the social optimum. In cases like smoke, sulfur dioxide or carbon dioxide some limited emission may be acceptable. Regulations that limit pollution can be imposed on all firms in an industry. Generally speaking, such regulations are inefficient, because they are imposed on all firms, regardless of their relative cost of abatement. Economists prefer a system of tradable permits, which would mean that firms with low abatement costs would abate their pollution, and sell their permits to firms with high abatement costs. The total amount of permits issued would be set to the socially optimum level of pollution.

Tradable permits have the advantage of being kind of semi-automatic, letting market forces work things out. However, it ignores the fact that government still needs to regulate and monitor the situation. Otherwise, firms not having pollution permits will continue to pollute, since they know that enforcement is weak or where officials can be paid to look the other way. This is particularly a problem in developing countries with weak administrations, and where rent-seeking by officials is common.

Environmental issues in developing countries also start from a different perspective. Given high levels of poverty, developing countries may place a higher value on the use of natural resources to raise their incomes in the present, rather than postpone consumption now in order to have more consumption in the future. This may be particularly true if the gains are in the form of the world-wide impact on global warming, in which case its actions may have little if any impact on the (small) developing country in the present or even in the near future.

Environmental regulations illustrate the idea of unintended consequences. If a country wishes to conserve a fishery by limiting fishing, it will often limit the number of boats. The result is that fishermen will invest in larger boats. If it limits the number of days of fishing, the industry invests in more boats that are faster, and have greater capacity. Licensing or permits can be used, especially if permits can be traded, but this requires monitoring to insure that all catches are within allowable limits, and that all boats have the required permits.

There is much talk about promoting sustainable development. In general, this means extracting from natural resources only that much that can be replenished naturally. This would not apply to oil, gas or minerals, but to those resources that can naturally replenish themselves, such as forests, fisheries, and soil. Sustainable development makes sense, however, only if the present value of the sustainable yield exceeds the value of an immediate exploitation of the resource.

**Fig. 8.5 Sustainable Yield vs. Immediate Use**

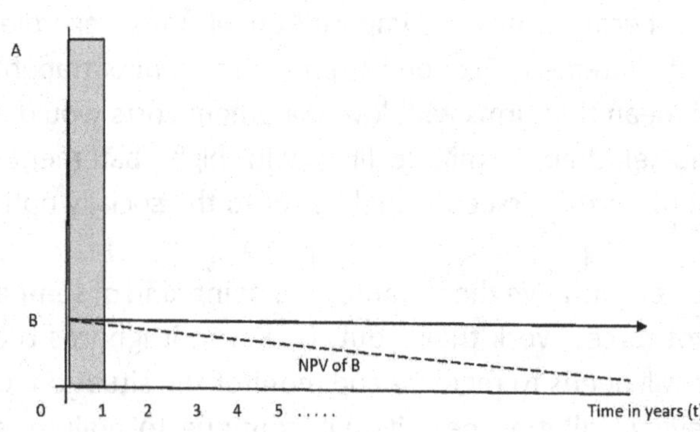


In the example in Fig 8.5, a country faces the choice with regards to a renewable resource, such that it can exploit the whole resource in one year at use level A, and receive the whole income in the shaded box. Alternatively, it could opt for a sustainable yield of B, which can continue yielding indefinitely. Off hand, one would think the sustainable yield is preferred, because the total return over time is greater.

However, future values are not the equivalent to present values. A dollar in hand today is better than a dollar promised five years from now.

But which is beter, a dollar today or two dollars in five years? The answer depends on the *social rate of time preference,* or the discount rate. In simple terms, if you postpone spending the dollar today, you could earn interest on the dollar and have more in the future. How much interest I would have to pay you to choose a future payment is your private discount rate. For instance, we know that with 6% interest compounding, $1 today will be worth $2 in 12 years. If you are indifferent between the two, then your rate of time preference is 6%.

The social rate of time preference reflects the opportunity cost of money, that is, what money could earn if invested in useful projects in the economy. It reflects the time preference of society as a whole. Thus, in the example above, the future benefit stream needs to be discounted and expressed in *present value*. The present value of the benefit stream B is the sum of each year's benefit (Bt) divided by that year's discount rate (1+ d)t, or

$$PVB = \sum (B_t / (1 + d)^t)$$

Then, the comparison is not between A and B, but between A and the PVB, such that the country chooses strategy A if A> PVB, or B if PVB > A. Thus, the answer depends on the discount rate. Table 8.3 shows the present value of $1.00 at three discount rates: 6%, 8% and 10%, for various time spans. Thus, the present value of $1 in 30 years, if the discount rate is 8%, is only 10 cents.

**Table 8.3 Discount Rates for $1 in the future.**

| | 10 years | 20 years | 30 years | 50 years |
|---|---|---|---|---|
| 6% | .55 | .31 | .17 | .05 |
| 8% | .46 | .21 | .10 | .02 |
| 10% | .39 | .15 | .06 | .01 |

Which discount rate is appropriate? In a poor country, where consumption is already low, people may not be willing or able to postpone consumption to the future (i.e. they have a high rate of time preference or a high discount rate). For instance, if the sustainable yield case B involves so little present income that the person starves to death, the knowledge that sustainable practices will eventually produce more income is meaningless. He needs income today. It is for this reason that we see denuded forests and over exploited land all over the third world. This is particularly true when land is abundant, and farmers can move to new plots once land has been exhausted. Practices that feature sustainable yields have to be not only sustainable, but capable of producing sufficient income in the present as well.

A classic case is the drive to introduce contour plowing on hillsides. Farmers often traditionally will farm on hillsides running furrows vertically up and down the hill (A in diagram 8.6). This makes plowing easy, but introduces natural watercourses that lead to soil erosion. Contour plowing and terracing involves working across the hill side, and planting crops that serve as buffers that hold back the soil (see hill B in diagram). The problem is the better, longer term and more sustainable practices also reduce immediate yields and farmers are often unwilling to adopt them.

**Fig. 8.6 Bad and Good Hillside Farming Techniques**

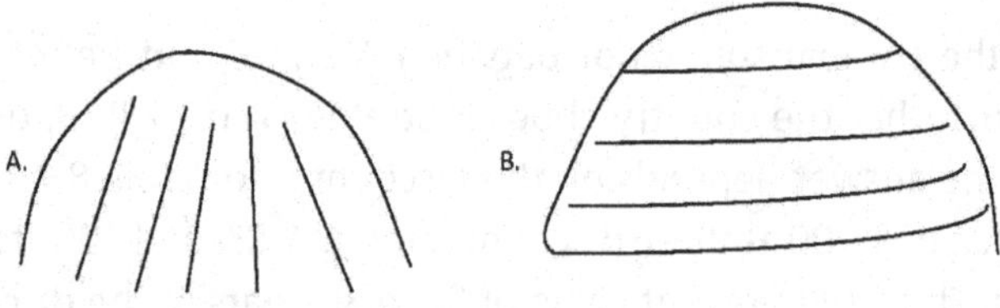


Conflicts over environmental policy can arise over the global impact of pollution and deforestation, which contribute to global warming, a major case of negative global externalities. Developing countries may be less interested (have a higher discount rate) in policies designed to reduce global warming if (as is likely) these policies raise the cost of output, are costly to adopt, and limit production levels. This may be particularly true if the major polluters are the developed countries who have not yet adopted policies to reduce $CO_2$, limit fishing or deforestation themselves. Developing countries see this as a kind of environmental imperialism. However, the impact of global warming is an externality that affects LDCs as well as developed countries. Many small island nations, such as The Maldives, are already imperiled by rising sea levels and have become strong advocates for controls to limit global warming.

# CHAPTER IX
# PUBLIC EXPENDITURES AND REVENUES

*Politics is very much like taxes—everybody is against them, or everybody is for them as long as they don't apply to him."*—Fiorello La Guardia

*"The art of taxation consists in so plucking the goose as to obtain the largest possible amount of feathers with the smallest possible amount of hissing"*—Jean Baptiste Colbert

Early experts on development advocated the creation of detailed economic development plans, using fancy models to predict output and inputs, styled after the Soviet planning experience. Unlike the Soviet Union, most developing countries were mixed private-public economies, so that any plan for the private sector tended to be very speculative. Plans were rarely followed, and the increased emphasis on promoting private sector led growth has diminished their usefulness even further. The net result was that national planning died out in all but a few countries. However, the need to prioritize and plan expenditures in the public sector, particularly at the national government level, continues to be an issue. How effectively the Government spends its resources, and how it raises resources, can have a major impact on promoting, or discouraging, development efforts.

**Table 9.1. Prototypical National Budget Structure.**

A. Total Revenue (= a + b)
 a. Tax Revenue
  i. Taxes on Income and profits
  ii. Consumption taxes (VAT, sales, excise)
  iii. International Trade (import duties)
 b. Non-Tax Revenues
  i. Profits from state enterprises
  ii. Interest income
  iii. Grants from abroad
B. Total Expenditures (= c + d)
 c. Current Expenditures
  i. Wages and Salaries
  ii. Goods and Services
  iii. Subsidies and Transfers
  iv. Interest (domestic and foreign)
 d. Capital Expenditures
C. Overall Fiscal Balance (A – B)
D. Financing
 a. Foreign Loans (less repayments)
 b. Domestic Borrowing (bonds, Central Bank)

## The Budget Process

The budget is essentially a one-year plan for how the government plans to spend anticipated revenues, and what it expects those revenues to be. Table 9.1 gives a rough schematic of the structure of a typical government budget (presentations vary, this is meant to be illustrative).

A budget is roughly divided into three parts: first, revenues, then expenditures, and finally financing items that insure that there is a balance between financial inflows and outflows. Expenditures are in turn divided into a current budget for recurring operating expenses, and a capital budget for investment items that add to the capital stock. Some countries redivide the budget into a development budget and a non-development budget. While capital expenditures might normally be considered pro-development, not all such expenditures promote growth. For instance, capital expenditures by the military, or to build a palace for the president, are not development. Conversely, some current expenditures could be considered pro-growth, such a expenditures for education, health care, and labor training (investments in human capital). Where to draw the line between development and non-development is problematic, however. For instance, are health expenditures investments in human capital or merely recurrent costs needed to stay alive? Should expenditures to maintain the capital stock, such as road maintenance, be considered as development? This has been a typical problem of foreign donors, who want to show they are financing increments to the capital stock, and not recurrent costs which are considered a drain on resources. Developing countries all over the world, but particularly in very poor countries, are littered with the remains of well meaning foreign funded development projects that are either sitting idle for lack of operating funds (for books, seeds, doctor salaries, medical supplies), or are deteriorating for lack of maintenance. It often easier to arrange for financing to build a road that lasts five years without maintenance, and then obtain financing to rebuild the entire road, then it is to build the road once and have the donor fund the maintenance so that it lasts 20 years (a much cheaper alternative).

Note also that foreign loans and grants come into the budget in two places: grants are part of the current budget since they are short-term disbursements, whereas loans are considered a financing item "below the line", or something that helps finance the overall fiscal balance. A switch of a donor from giving loans to grants would actually reduce the fiscal balance, although the material effect would be nil. Likewise, it is useful to note that debt service on debt, either domestic or foreign, appears as interest in the current account, while amortization is netted out against new disbursements in the financing section.

Somewhat ironically, considering our discussion of national planning in the opening paragraph, the new thinking on budgets for developing countries is to place the annual budget within a framework of 3-4 years. The rationale for this is that decisions taken today will often have a big impact on future budgets. For instance, a decision to start a large capital project has not only additional capital expenditures in future years, but also operating and maintenance expenditures. A change in tax policy will have a bearing on revenues for years to come, and so on. These frameworks have been advocated by the IMF and are known as the MTEF—Medium Term Expenditure Framework (or a MTBF—Medium Term Budget Framework when it includes projected revenues as well as expenditures). MTEFs are often included in annual budget documents, with the first year of the MTEF being the current year's budget. There is considerable debate about the utility of the MTEF exercise, since any kind of projection exercise involves dozens of somewhat arbitrary decisions, and often government officials do not follow the outline of the MTEF when preparing the annual budget.

## Performance Based Budgeting

The problem with most standard budgets is that while they detail expenditures, they do not identify programs and objectives. A typical old-style standard budget for a unit, such as a Ministry of Agriculture, would detail line-item expenditures for categories such as wages and salaries, consultants, travel, maintenance of facilities, etc., plus a list of new capital investments. The problem faced by a budget office in the Ministry of Finance is that they have no idea if these expenditures are realistic, and what they might accomplish.

New style budgeting emphasizes a programmatic approach, in that it identifies the programs within the overall Ministry budget, and their cost. Thus, an agriculture budget could be divided into research, extension, and training programs, and each major program could be subdivided into areas such as rice research, cotton research, etc. Extension expenditures could be further subdivided by province. This program budget becomes a performance budget if we can identify output or results targets to be achieved. The research program could be judged on the number of new varieties developed, the extension program on the number of farmers visited, etc. In this way, we have an idea of what the Ministry is trying to do, and can judge the impact of prior year expenditures and their success. Program budgets or performance budgeting is currently being introduced in more and more countries, and is a much better way of understanding the rationale for government expenditures. It is particularly liked by legislators who have to review and approve national budgets[80].

Performance budgeting, to be really effective, should focus on ultimate results, not intermediate products. For instance, what is

80 Robinson, Marc and Duncan Last, "A Basic Model of Performance Based Budgeting", IMF, Technical Notes and Manuals, (Wash., D.C.) September 2009.

important is that farmers increase productivity, not how many times they are visited by an extension worker. Likewise, producing more and more new varieties is not very useful if farmers do not adopt and use these new varieties. Measuring results is much more difficult, however, because of the causality chain may be difficult to trace. Did farm productivity rise because of good extension work, or because the weather was better last year and fertilizer prices were lower? To really appraise the results of government programs requires careful evaluation with a treatment group (farmers receiving extension advice) compared to a similar group not receiving the "treatment". We could then compare the increment in output from one group to the other, the so called "double difference" approach (i.e. the difference between the increments of output between the two groups). The problem is to identify a comparable non-treatment group that is similar in all ways. If one uses differences between two regions or districts, there may be underlying differences between the two regions or districts, such as weather, availability of irrigation water, etc., that invalidate the results. If we select farmers at random within the same district we would have a better comparator group, however, there is always the danger of contamination: farmers can learn from each other and the "non-treatment" group might adopt the trial methods of the treatment group. Given these problems with results indicators, often governments rely on output indicators instead. However, any good budget system needs to also have continuous and careful evaluations of programs.

Performance budgeting, even if centered on outputs rather than results, has an additional problem. This the effect that the output targets impact on bureaucratic incentives and behavior (another "unintended consequence"). If the target is school enrollment, for instance, then there is an incentive to crowd children into classrooms regardless of the supply of teachers or books. If the output variable is school completion, then there is an incentive to graduate students regardless of their academic performance. Thus, even output targets need to be carefully constructed to give the right incentives. School completion rates, for instance, should be based on student performance on standardized tests. Having a working program budget or performance budget can be a real challenge in a low income country, however, where staff resources are limited and data on results or outputs hard to come by. Even so, the alternative is worse.

## Moving Away from Generalized Subsidies

Fiscal problems in developing countries are a result of many factors on both the expenditure and revenue sides of the budget. One of the most frequent is the presence of large, untargeted subsidies. These subsidies consist of the provision of cheap or free services, ostensibly to help the poor, such as basic food products, housing, gasoline, cooking gas, drinking water, irrigation water, electricity, urban transport, fertilizer and seeds, and even candy (formerly in Egypt). While the goal might be to help the poor, untargeted subsidies benefit the rich and poor alike, and often do not reach the poor. For instance, gasoline subsidies benefit those with cars, who are not often the poor. Large untargeted and underpriced basic goods provides incentive for non-optimal behavior, such as when rich people use subsidized cooking gas to heat their swimming pools (Ecuador) or feed subsidized food to the chickens. In some cases, these subsidized goods and services should be eliminated altogether. Where that is not possible, one wants to at least restrict their provision to the truly deserving. There are a number of ways programs can be better targeted:

- <u>Means Testing</u>. This involves finding out the level of income of each applicant for assistance. While practical in advanced countries with good income tax registries, this is rarely possible in LDCs.
- <u>Proxy Means Testing</u>. This means developing a system that correlates life style with income. Normally a survey is done of the applicant's household and points awarded for having a concrete floor, metal roof, running water, TV, appliances, etc. Too many points and the applicant is considered not eligible; the ownership of assets is considered a proxy for his/her income status.
- <u>Geographic Targeting.</u> Basic goods can be made available through outlets only located in areas having a high percentage of poor people. While there is apt to be some leakage, the cost of targeting here is extremely low.
- <u>Categorical Targeting.</u> Programs can be made available to only certain types of people, such as single mothers, widows, veterans. It is assumed that these characteristics are related to need, but obviously it then cannot restrict access by rich widows, etc.

- Self-Targeting. This involves focusing the subsidy on those "inferior goods" which rich people will not want to consume. A subsidy for turnips, for instance, could help the poor, but as poor people move up the income ladder, they are apt to drop turnips in favor of potatoes, regardless of the low price of turnips.

Where a good or service is costly, it is worth spending money on more expensive forms of targeting, such as proxy means testing. For cheaper goods, a less expensive targeting approach is appropriate. The general rule is that the marginal cost of targeting the program (MCT) should always be less than the marginal benefit to the recipient (MBR), or MCT < MBR. Studies summarized by Grosh[81] show a range of targeting costs in developing countries of .4% to 29%, with an average of 9%.

Targeted programs can exhibit two types of errors:

- Type I Error: including people who are not eligible; or
- Type II Error: excluding people who are eligible.

If type I errors are a large percent of total errors, then the targeting is too lose and needs to be tightened up (but cognizant of the need to keep MCT < MBR). The tradeoff is between the cost of increased targeting efficiency and the amount saved in the process. Likewise, a large share of Type II errors means that the targeting has been too rigorous, and needs to be relaxed.

Political Economy Factors. Even while given the foregoing, there is a political economy argument for continuing untargeted subsidies. If the middle class is cut out from a subsidy, they may then drop their political support. In a democratic government, politicians can then cut the program without an adverse voter backlash. Maintaining some access by the middle class may be the price one has to pay to have the program operate at all. This is particularly true of programs that largely benefit the rich, such as free higher education.

---

81 Margaret Grosh, *Administering Targeted Social Programs in Latin America: From Platitudes to Practice* (Washington DC, World Bank, 1994), Chapter 2.

## Cutting Government Expenditures

In crisis times, governments often have to reduce expenditures in order to maintain a proper, non-inflationary fiscal balance. It has been generally assumed that governments protect defense spending, and focus cuts on capital expenditures, which can often be postponed. Cuts in current expenditures tend to avoided, because they might imply reducing the government labor force, which could have negative political repercussions (riots, etc.). Cutting non-wage recurrent spending is common, resulting in hospitals without medicines, roads without maintenance, etc. It is often alleged that social spending also takes a heavy burden of the cuts. There have been very few studies of how governments actually respond to cuts. In my 1991 study[82], I looked 28 episodes covering 24 countries during the 1970-84 period where there was a decline in *real* government spending of 5% or more (nominal spending is rarely reduced). The average reduction for all countries in the sample was -17%, with a -28% for capital spending and a -7% for current spending (see Table 9.2)

**Table 9.2 Average Expenditure Reductions, 1970-84 (%)**

| By Types | | By Sectors: | |
|---|---|---|---|
| Total expenditures | -17 | General Public Serv | -9 |
| Capital Expenditures | -28 | Defense | -6 |
| Wages | -14 | Social | -11 |
| Others | -14 | Productive | -19 |
| Interest | +34 | Infrastructure | -25 |
| Subsidies | -11 | Others | -1 |
| | | | |

Source: Hicks, 1991

Some interesting conclusions from this study are:

- The heaviest cuts were in productive and infrastructure sectors, not social sectors (health, education);
- Defense spending was the most heavily protected showing the smallest percentage decline;
- Capital spending was indeed reduced severely, accounting for the declines in infrastructure spending;

82 Hicks, Norman L. "Expenditure Reductions in Developing Countries Revisited" *Journal of International Development* 3 (January 1991).

- The sharp rise in interest expenditures in this period is a major factor explaining cuts in other areas.

## Investment Analysis

Good budget management implies, among other things, being able to choose useful development projects. Government officials need a way of determining which are the most productive projects, that should have priority over less productive projects. To do this, we return to the concept of present value, or net present value, and the calculation of internal rates of return.

We recall from chapter VIII, that the present value (PV) of anything is its expected future value (FV), deflated by the discount rate that reflects the opportunity cost of capital, or the social time preference rate. Thus,

$$PV = \sum (FV_t /(1 + d)^t)$$

Investment projects, however, consist of both future costs and benefits, so both must be discounted, producing an estimate of the net present value (NPV). The formula for the NPV of a project is simply the benefits minus costs in every year, deflated by the discount rate for that year, or

$$NPV = \sum (B_t - C_t) /(1 + d)^t$$

This can also be calculated by discounting the benefits and costs separately, and then subtracting, or:

$$NPV = (\sum (B_t) /(1 + d)^t) - (\sum (C_t) /(1 + d)^t)$$

A commonly used device for ranking projects is the benefit-cost ratio, which is simply the above formula as a ratio, or:

$$BCR = \sum (B_t) /(1 + d)^t) / (\sum (C_t) /(1 + d)^t$$

Obviously, projects with higher BCRs are preferred.

Here is a simple example (Table 9.3). A project has the following expected cost and benefit streams into the future, where year 0 is the present year, and where a 6% discount rate is to be used:

**Table 9.3 Benefit Cost Analysis Example**

| Year(t) | 0 | 1 | 2 | 3 | 4 |
|---|---|---|---|---|---|
| Benefits | 0 | 0 | 100 | 200 | 200 |
| Costs | 100 | 100 | 20 | | |
| Net | -100 | -100 | 80 | 200 | 200 |
| $(1.06)^t$ | 1.00 | 1.06 | 1.124 | 1.191 | 1.262 |
| NPV | -100 | -94.3 | 71.2 | 167.9 | 158.5 |
| ∑NPV = 203.3 | | | | | |
| BCR = 415.1/212.1=1.96 | | | | | |

In theory, if one had a long list of projects with appropriate analysis, one would undertake those projects with the highest BCRs, working down the list until the investment budget was exhausted. A better way to look at it is an objective of maximizing NPV, since in some cases BCR can give misleading results. For instance, if a project is discovered to produce a by-product (e.g. sawdust) that can be sold, does this reduce its costs, or add to its benefits? Either is possible, but will result in different BCRs. Another example is a small project might have a very high BCR. If the project were done more extensively over a larger geographic area, the BCR would be lower, but still generate positive increments in NPV. If money is available, the larger project should be chosen. Nevertheless, it is common practice to focus on BCRs rather than NPV.

## Internal Rate of Return

While in theory one would want to allocate investment funds over a portfolio ranked by NPV or BCRs, in practice, few development practioners are faced with such a choice. Rather, each project is evaluated individually, and undertaken based on having a sufficient high internal rate of return (IRR). The IRR is defined as that discount rate which equates the NPV of benefits with the NPV of costs, and reflects the return on the investment, much the same way the interest rate on a bond determines its yield. Alternatively, it can be viewed as the discount rate at which the NPV of the project equals zero.

IRR rule: choose a level of d such that:

$$\sum (B_t) / (1 + d)^t) = (\sum (C_t) / (1 + d)^t \text{ or:}$$

$$NPV = (\sum (B_t) / (1 + d)^t) - (\sum (C_t) / (1 + d)^t) = 0.$$

An acceptable IRR is one which exceeds the opportunity cost of money, or exceeds the social discount rate. Multilateral development banks, such as the World Bank, have pioneered the use of IRRs to project returns on projects. However, calculating IRRs assumes that benefits can be correctly identified and measured. For many projects, it is difficult, if not impossible, to calculate IRRs. These would include projects in health, education, governance, general policy reform, technical assistance and the like. At present, IRRs are calculated on less than half of all World Bank loans. IRRs have an additional problem. If used to select among projects, they will be biased toward projects that have short pay backs. The reason? Since one is effectively raising the discount rate to the point where NPV of benefits equals costs, this implies (for projects with substantial positive benefits) a very high discount rate applied to benefits in the distant future.

## Shadow Pricing

In general, benefits and costs are priced at market prices. However, if benefits and costs do not reflect the relevant opportunity costs, then an adjustment is needed. For instance, if exchange rates are distorted and do not reflect the true international value of goods, then project costs that contain imported components should use a true, market based, exchange rate. Likewise, if there are large amount of underutilized labor, the true social cost of labor is zero, and a lower or zero wage should be used to calculate project costs. This technique is called shadow pricing. In the days when economies had substantial distortions the need for shadow pricing was more acute and more common in project analysis. A variant of shadow pricing is called *social pricing*. In this case, benefits going to the poor would be given a higher weight than those going to the rich. The bias in favor of the poor, however, is somewhat arbitrary and could be used as a convenient way to distort project returns.

## Other Concerns in Project Analysis

While shadow pricing is less relevant to project analysis today than it was 20 years ago, there are a host of other factors that influence project choice, and are often outside of the calculation of the IRR. Some of these include

- Environmental issues. Projects today have to have careful assessments of their environmental impact, and develop environmental mitigation plans to reduce or eliminate this impact. This includes both the "green" impact (forest destruction, wildlife habitat) as well as the "brown" concerns (water and air pollution).
- Transmigration. Projects that require that people be moved from one location to another have to have clear plans on how these people will be resettled, and with what services and facilities they will be provided. It is often difficult, for instance, to resettle people on land with equal productivity, or suitable for the growing of crops with which they are familiar.
- Fiduciary Management. Projects need to have adequate controls to insure that money is appropriately used, including the undertaking of competitive bidding and appropriate procurement procedures, auditing of financial statements, etc.
- Participation. There is increasing evidence that projects in which the beneficiaries participate in project planning, design, execution and operation have a higher probability of success. Listening to the ideas of affected peoples can often improve initial project design, and head off potential problems down the road.

## Taxes and Other Revenue

Taxation is a necessary evil, in that it provides the bulk of the funds needed for public expenditures. Other sources include user fees, foreign loans and grants, and domestic borrowings, but taxation remains the source of the majority of revenues in developed and developing countries. There are four main sources of tax revenues;

- Taxes on Good and Services: includes sales, excise and value added taxes, which are levied at the point of production or sale of goods and services
- Taxes on Income and Profits: these are taxes levied on incomes of households or corporations;
- Taxes and International Trade: taxes on imports or exports, are really a special kind of taxes on goods and services.
- Social Contributions: taxes levied, usually on wages (think social security,) to pay for social benefits such as old age and disability pensions, unemployment insurance, or medical care.

For poor developing countries with limited administrative capacity, the easiest taxes to collect are those on international trade, since most countries have only a few viable ports through which most international trade passes (and limited overland trade with neighboring countries, so called "South-South" trade). Where tariffs are high, of course, smuggling can be a problem, including undervaluation of goods and "technical smuggling", where goods are claimed to be a product with a lower tariff (e.g. declaring shoes as raw leather).

Most developing countries also levy excise and sales taxes. Excise taxes apply to specific goods, normally luxury goods (whiskey, perfume, cigarettes). Sales taxes are more general, and collected either at the point of production or point of sale. Since developing countries often have many informal sellers in the market place, LDCs prefer to levy taxes at the production or even wholesale level. One problem with these kinds of taxes is the cascading effect which occurs when goods are taxed on importation, taxed again when the materials are turned into a final product, and then again at the wholesale or retail level. To avoid this effect, many LDCs have moved (as have most developed countries) to a value-added tax (VAT), which is levied on the difference between input costs and sales revenue (or the value added). In terms of tax administration, the VAT is levied at the same rate at every level, with the taxpaying unit (store, factory) allowed to deduct from its VAT payments any VAT payments made on inputs. This means that every tax paying unit has a big incentive to obtain proof that the VAT has been paid on its inputs, and this provides a type of self-enforcing mechanism. The only way to escape the VAT (legally) is to not buy anything. Thus, the VAT is a tax on consumption, and should encourage savings, while an income tax is a tax on both consumption and savings.

**Table 9.4. Taxes Collected**
(Selected Countries 2006)

| country | Tax/GDP (%) | Taxes on Goods & Services | Taxes on Income & Profits | Taxes on International Trade | Social Contributions |
|---|---|---|---|---|---|
| | | % of total revenue | | | |
| **LDC** | | | | | |
| Uganda | 12.3 | 29.9 | 18.8 | 20.5 | - |
| Bangladesh | 8.2 | 28.6 | 14.6 | 30.9 | - |
| China | 9.4 | 57.2 | 25.1 | 5.1 | - |
| Turkey | 19.7 | 48.5 | 21.9 | 1.1 | - |
| Georgia | 15.5 | 50.9 | 9.9 | 4.0 | 15.3 |
| **Developed Countries** | | | | | |
| France | 22.4 | 23.8 | 25.0 | – | 42.3 |
| UK | 28.5 | 28.0 | 38.3 | – | 21.3 |
| US (Federal only) | 12.0 | 2.8 | 56.9 | 1.0 | 35.3 |

Finally, some more developed LDCs have imposed taxes on income and profits, although this is a relatively small source of income for most LDCs (see Table 9.4). Reliance on income taxes requires a great deal of self-compliance, and a population able to read and fill out income tax forms, and a government with a credible enforcement capacity. Even in Latin America, where income taxes apply mostly only to the rich, compliance with personal income taxes is very low, perhaps as little as 10%. The Surprising thing in these countries is not that 90% do not pay, but that these 10% do. As countries develop, however, there is a gradual shift first, from taxes on international trade to those on sales or consumption (VAT), and then gradually to taxes on income. These trends are illustrated in Fig. 9.1. As shown in Table 9.4, a low income country such as Uganda derives 21% of its revenues from trade taxes, and 30% from domestic sales taxes, whereas a more developed country such as Turkey relies more heavily on domestic sales taxes, while trade taxes constitute only 1% of it revenues. In general, the overall tax rate (as a % of GDP) is also lower in low income countries. Compare Bangladesh at 8% with France at 22%. However, there are exceptions to this rule.

Fig 9.1 Approximate Tax Levels Relative to GDP Per Capita

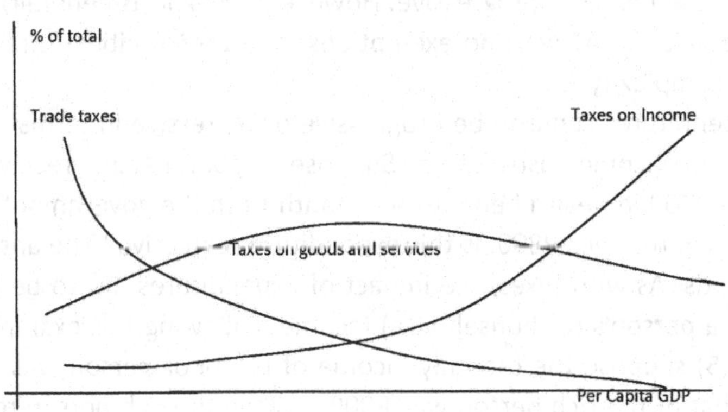


## Progressive and Regressive Taxes (and Expenditures)

Like rain, taxes fall on rich and poor alike. We say that a tax is *progressive* if the tax as a *percentage* of the tax relative to income is higher for those with higher incomes, and *regressive* if the percentage paid by the poor is higher than those who are rich. A tax in which everyone pays the same percentage of his/her income is proportional. In fact, taxes can be both regressive and progressive at the same time. Suppose the government levies a flat tax of P500 (where P stands for Peso) on every person, but exempts those with incomes under P5000. The tax rate for someone with P2000 is zero, for P5000 it is 10%, and for P50000 it is 1%. The tax is progressive in the lower end, and regressive in the upper end. The US social security tax, which applies to all wages up to $100,000 is a regressive tax. The US income tax, which exempts those under about $9000 (single individual) and has increasing marginal tax rates up to 35%, is clearly progressive (rates are for 2009 tax year).

The VAT tax, because it is effectively a tax on consumption, is mildly regressive since savings rates are higher at higher income levels. Since the poor are spending a larger share of their income on consumption, they will pay a larger amount of VAT relative to their income[83]. Some developing countries exempt such items as food or other basic goods from the VAT, or

83 However, to the extent that the poor purchase goods, especially food, in informal markets that escape the VAT may offset this regressivity.

have a dual rate system with a a lower rate for these goods, in an attempt to make the tax more progressive. However, tax experts generally prefer a single valued VAT with no exemptions in order to mitigate fraud and reduce complexity.

Expenditures can also be progressive or regressive in terms of their impact on income distribution. Suppose a poor person receives, on average P200 in health benefits per month from the government, and a rich person receives P800. Is this expenditure regressive? The answer is: it depends. As with taxes, the impact of expenditures has to be judged against a person's (or household's) income. Following this example (see table 9.5) suppose the monthly income of the poor person was P1000, while that of the rich person was P8000. While the rich person receives four times the benefits (800 vs. 200), as a propotion of his/her income it is much lower (10% vs. 20%). The net impact of the program is to raise the relative income of the poor person (7.3 vs.8.0), and thus Is progressive, just the same way that a progressive tax also reduces relative incomes.

**Table 9.5. An Example of a Progressive Expenditure**

| | Poor Person | Rich Person | Proportion |
|---|---|---|---|
| Income (per month) | 1000 | 8000 | 8:1 |
| Health benefit | 200 | 800 | |
| Benefit % of Income | 20% | 10% | |
| Income + Benefit | 1200 | 8800 | 7.3:1 |

The importance of this is the relative impact of basic social services in improving income distribution. Programs that give a certain basic benefit to everyone equally, such as primary and secondary education, basic health care, or food distributions all tend to work to improve income distribution. Even programs in which the rich seem to be receiving a greater benefit (such a secondary education) can have the effect of evening income distribution. As discussed in Chapter V, the case study of Chile showed that expenditures had a major effect in reducing income inequality, whereas the tax system was roughly proportional and not a major factor in promoting equality.

One problem with measuring the impact of taxes is that stated rates and actual collection rates vary widely, particularly in poorer countries. Not only is there tax evasion, but liberal tax credits and tax forgiveness and rebates used as investment incentives often reduce effective rate far below rates on the books. Improving tax administration in developing countries is a major challenge, particularly when tax officials are generally underpaid, and the temptation to skim off tax revenues for personal profit is great. In some countries, tax officials have been placed into special civil service categories that give them much higher than normal civil service salaries, in an attempt to reduce corruption.

# CHAPTER X

# GOVERNANCE AND CORRUPTION

"We have the best government money can buy"—Mark Twain

## Governance Defined

Governance issues are central to development in third world countries. Poor governance and high levels of corruption appear key to explaining why some low income countries are able to make significant progress (convergence) and why others are not. Research by many scholars shows that improved governance strengthens development, and not the other way around.[84] However, it also true that many developing countries have governance indicators equal to those of such developed countries such

> What is Governance?
>
> Governance consists of the traditions and institutions by which authority in a country is exercised. This includes the process by which governments are selected, monitored and replaced; the capacity of the government to effectively formulate and implement sound policies; and the respect of citizens and the state for the institutions that govern economic and social interactions among them.
>
> Source: "Governance Matters 2009", World Bank / World Development Institute, June 29, 2009. See http://info.worldbank.org/governance/wgi/pdf/WBI_GovInd.pdf

---

84 Kaufmann, Daniel, Art Kraay, and Massimo Mastruzzi, "Governance Matters VIII—Aggregate and Individual Governance Indicators, 1996-2008", *World Bank Policy Research Working Paper 4978* (June 2009) and summary in World Bank Institute, "Governance Matters 2009", June 29, 2009 (at http://info.worldbank.org/governance/wgi/pdf/WBI_GovInd.pdf)

as Italy or Greece. These include such countries as Slovenia, Chile, Botswana, and Costa Rica.[85] Thus, good governance is not a "magic bullet" that guarantees rapid development, but it is a key factor explaining success.

Good governance is more than the absence of corruption. It includes having an adequate rule of law, political stability, absence of violence, and the ability of people to participate in government (see box for a more precise definition). The World Governance Indicators (WGI) tracked by the Brookings/World Bank researchers include six indicators, which themselves are the composite of 9-13 sub-indicators used as inputs. These six indicators are[86]:

- **Voice and Accountability:** the extent to which a country's citizens are able to participate in selecting their government, as well as freedom of expression, association, and the press.
- **Political Stability and Absence of Violence:** the likelihood that the government will be destabilized by unconstitutional or violent means, including terrorism.
- **Government Effectiveness:** the quality of public services, the capacity of the civil service and its independence from political pressures; the quality of policy formulation
- **Regulatory Quality:** the ability of the government to provide sound policies and regulations that enable and promote private sector development
- **Rule of Law:** the extent to which agents have confidence in and abide by the rules of society, including the quality of property rights, the police, and the courts, as well as the risk of crime.
- **Control of Corruption:** the extent to which public power is exercised for private gain, including both petty and grand forms of corruption, as well as elite "capture" of the state.

The WGI does not construct a single governance indicator, but rather ranks countries on each of the six indicators. Looking at the decade 1998-2008, Kaufmann et. al. concluded that while some countries have improved governance on several dimensions, overall there is no general

---

[85] See "Governance Matters 2009" as cited above.

[86] See World Bank, World Development Institute, "Governance Matters 2009" http://info.worldbank.org/governance/wgi/pdf/WBI_GovInd.pdf

trend toward improved governance. Countries that have improved their governance include:

- Voice and Accountability—Niger, Sierra Leone, Serbia;
- Political Stability—Congo, Sierra Leone, Rwanda;
- Government Effectiveness—Serbia, Afghanistan, Rwanda;
- Regulatory Quality—Congo, Georgia and Libya;
- Rule of Law—Liberia, Georgia and Rwanda;
- Control of Corruption—Rwanda, Liberian and Serbia.

Offsetting these gains where deteriorations in a number of other countries, including Zimbabwe, Cote d'Ivoire, Belarus, Eritrea, and Venezuela, while in many other countries there was no trend in either direction.

**Corruption**. By far the biggest challenge to improving governance is controlling corruption. Traditionally, corruption has been defined as "the exercise of official powers against public interest or the abuse of public office for private gain[87]." Kaufmann argues this is too narrowly focused on the public sector, and on strictly illegal acts. He adopts a broader definition, calling corruption "the privatization of public policy"[88]. He argues that private sector actors often influence government policy in ways that are unethical, but may not be illegal, and that corruption can be found within the private sector, as well as the public.

Models of corrupt behavior focus on some form of a principal-agent model[89]. Voters, the principals, elect government officials, the agents, to provide them with services. Supervision of these agents is difficult, however, since day-to-day activities are difficult to monitor. Elected officials may themselves be principals, who hire government officials (agents) to carry out their policies and programs. Officials at all levels,

---

87 Anwar Shah, "Tailoring the Fight against Corruption to Country Circumstances", Chapter 7, in A. Shah, ed., *Performance Accountability and Combating Corruption,* World Bank, Wash. DC, 2007.

88 Kaufmann, Daniel. "Myths and Realities of Governance and Corruption" Chapter 21, *Global Competitiveness Report, 2005-2006,* World Economic Forum. Geneva, October, 2005.

89 Shah, p. 237, has an excellent summary of these models.

whether elected or appointed, engage in corrupt behavior whenever internal controls are slack, when the monetary gains are great, and when the chances of being caught and exposed, and thereby losing an appointed or elected post, are low. Corruption will be high when officials possess high monopoly power and discretion, when there is a lack of transparency in government operations, when the press and civil society are afraid to speak out, or when the electoral system itself is corrupt or dysfunctional.

Whatever the model or definition, corruption itself varies widely between countries, both in kind and in level. A summary listing from Transparency International of its Corruption Perceptions Index (CPI, Table 10.1) shows that the countries with the best perceived performance on corruption (based on surveys within each country) are highly developed countries such as Denmark, New Zealand and Singapore. Those with the worst are such problem cases as Somalia, Haiti and Myanmar. Corruption is not perfectly aligned with per capita income however. Russia, at 147 of 180, is very high in corruption considering it is ranked as a developed country, as are Greece and Italy. Of course, all these rankings are based on "perceptions" from surveys of business people and other experts; there is no objective way to measure corruption. However, the CPI is based on multiple surveys, and some attempt is made to measure the confidence interval of the result.

Table 10.1
2008 CORRUPTION PERCEPTIONS INDEX (selected countries)

| country rank | country | 2008 CPI score | surveys used | confidence range |
|---|---|---|---|---|
| 1 | Denmark | 9,3 | 6 | 9.1 - 9.4 |
| 1 | New Zealand | 9,3 | 6 | 9.2 - 9.5 |
| 1 | Sweden | 9,3 | 6 | 9.2 - 9.4 |
| 4 | Singapore | 9,2 | 9 | 9.0 - 9.3 |
| 5 | Finland | 9,0 | 6 | 8.4 - 9.4 |
| 5 | Switzerland | 9,0 | 6 | 8.7 - 9.2 |
| 9 | Canada | 8,7 | 6 | 8.4 - 9.1 |
| 18 | Japan | 7,3 | 8 | 7.0 - 7.6 |
| 18 | USA | 7,3 | 8 | 6.7 - 7.7 |
| 55 | Italy | 4.8 | 6 | 4.0 - 5.5 |
| 57 | Greece | 4.7 | 6 | 4.2- 5.0 |
| 72 | China | 3,6 | 9 | 3.1 - 4.3 |
| 80 | Brazil | 3,5 | 7 | 3.2 - 4.0 |
| 85 | India | 3,4 | 10 | 3.2 - 3.6 |
| 147 | Russia | 2.1 | 8 | 1.9 - 2.5 |
| 176 | Afghanistan | 1,5 | 4 | 1.1 - 1.6 |
| 177 | Haiti | 1,4 | 4 | 1.1 - 1.7 |
| 178 | Iraq | 1,3 | 4 | 1.1 - 1.6 |
| 178 | Myanmar | 1,3 | 4 | 1.0 - 1.5 |
| 180 | Somalia | 1,0 | 4 | 0.5 - 1.4 |

Source: Transparency International from:
http://www.transparency.org/news_room/in_focus/2008/cpi2008/cpi_2008_table

Corruption itself can be divided roughly into two types: administrative corruption and state capture. These are defined as:

- State Capture is the ability of groups to influence laws, regulations, etc., as a result of illicit and non-transparent actions giving private benefits to public officials. For instance, giving bribes to members of a legislature or executive to pass laws or enact regulations favorable to the bribe giver relative to taxes, subsidies, or monopoly status. Note that "state capture" implies illegal actions aimed at establishing a legal basis for making gains in the future—the state has been "captured" in that certain groups may make money because of the grant of some sort of legal special status, monopoly, tax exemption, or subsidy. In some cases, state capture may take place without an illegal act of bribery up front, such as when groups make large campaign contributions with an implicit understanding of future favorable treatment, or when officials from one ethnic, religious or regional group show favoritism in the allocation of public money, jobs, contracts, etc. to members of their own group.

- <u>Administrative Corruption</u> is the use of payments to public officials to influence the implementation of existing laws, regulations, etc., in such areas as government procurement, taxes, tariffs, and misdirection/ misuses of public funds. Payments include bribes, payments in kind, and/or kickbacks. In this form of "rent seeking" individual government officials are using their powers to discriminate in the implementation of laws and regulations, favoring those who make some sort of payment to them. Shah further distinguishes between "petty corruption" by individual public officials grant favors or divert funds based on personal considerations, and "grand corruption" which constitutes the theft or misuse of large amounts of public resources by powerful elite groups who control the government.

A country can have a high level of administrative corruption, without necessarily having a high level of state capture, and vice versa. The graph below (Fig. 10.1) shows a distribution for "transition" countries (countries formerly part of the Soviet Union and its satellites). Armenia, for instance, appears to be high on administrative corruption but ranks low (relatively) in terms of state capture. Russia, however, scores high in terms of state capture, but only moderate amounts of administrative corruption. Hungary is low on both counts, while Azerbaijan is high on both.

Fig 10.1 Administrative Corruption vs. State Capture in Transition Countries.

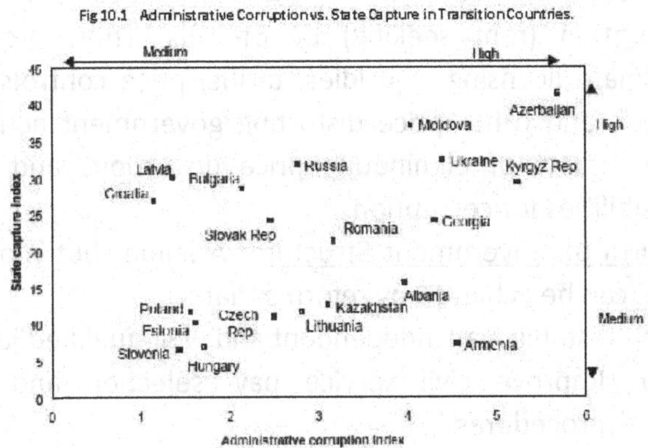


Source: World Bank, Anticorruption in Transition: A Contribution to the Policy Debate ,"Washington D.C., 2000 , p. xviii., based on the EBRD/World Bank BEEPS survey. Used with permission of World Bank.

## Reducing Corruption/ Improving Governance

Governments can take various actions to reduce corruption and improve governance. These basically include steps that eliminate opportunities for "rent seeking" and increase the level of transparency and accountability of public sector operations. While arresting and prosecuting corrupt officials is often necessary, this is only one element in an overall strategy which must focus on eliminating the potential for corruption. In fact, Shah recommends that development practioners avoid using the "C" word (corruption), and rather stress the need for increased accountability, transparency and equity in government operations.[90] Some key measures include:

- Open Political Processes: Having a truly democratic government based on free and fair elections of the legislature and executive gives voters an avenue to dismiss corrupt officials and punish the political parties that tolerate corruption.
- Free Press: An independent media free to investigate and expose public sector actions is an important mechanism bringing transparency to the governance process and for controlling malfeasance. It is most effective, however, when combined with free and fair elections.
- Civil Society Participation: An active civil society can be an important tool for publicizing corruption and questioning government actions.
- Limiting State Involvement: Limiting public sector involvement in the economy means limiting the possibilities for administrative corruption (rent seeking) by officials. Thus, programs that eliminate licensing, subsidies, tariffs, price controls, monopoly power, and other price distorting government actions have a dual impact of eliminating price distortions and eliminating possibilities for corruption.
- Reform of Government Structure: A leaner but more effective state can be achieved by reforms that :
    - Establish an independent and well-qualified judiciary;
    - Improve civil service pay, selection and promotion procedures;

---

90 Shah, p.249.

- o Make procurement procedures open, fair and transparent;
- o Improve auditing and control of public expenditures;
- o Give public open access to records on budget allocations, procurement, promotions, etc.

- Declaration of Assets: Government officials should declare all of their assets before and after serving in the public sector. If assets increase over such a period by more than the public servant's salary, there is a prima facie case that the official has misused his office. If the official understates his assets, he can be prosecuted for misreporting. In either case, the need for the actual proof of a bribe or kickback is reduced.
- Decentralization: It is sometimes suggested that decentralization of government services to localities can reduce corruption. There is no clear evidence on this one way or the other. On the one hand, decentralization can be coupled with greater local control and citizen participation in government, leading to more accountability and transparency. On the other hand, decentralization away from a strong central government with tight financial controls to a weak regional government that is subject to state capture can produce the opposite effect.

All of these reforms presuppose that there is genuine public commitment to reforming the public sector and the elimination of corruption. In many societies, unfortunately, corruption is a social norm and is expected. In countries where officials are grossly underpaid, it may be the only route for their survival. In fact, in extremely corrupt societies, corruption may become a "second-best" alternative for its citizens as well. It is possible that in very corrupt societies no government service could be attained nor a business established or operated without bribes. In this case business people and private citizens may be forced into behavior they find abhorrent as a second-best solution—the alternative is to go out of business and/or starve. In a sense, corruption in these cases is the "grease" that permits the economy to function.[91] One could also argue that corruption is tolerable if it is known and fixed. If the amount of

[91] P-G. Meon and Laurent Will, "Is Corruption an Efficient Grease?", World Development 38,3 (March, 2009), pp. 244-259.

bribe needed for any dealing with the public sector is known in advance, that cost can be figured into a business decision (such as the price set on a contract bid). The presence of bribes is more inhibiting when the exact amount is unknown but fluctuates widely over time for the same transaction. But in either case, corrupt payments to officials is very much a second best solution to a more open and honest system.

In many cases, Governments with poor records on corruption have announced major anti-corruption commissions, studies or reforms, which have been followed by weak or non-existent implementation, or the continuation of special treatment for favored groups or individuals. As Kaufman points out, overall in the last ten years, there has been little evidence of an improvement in the quality of governance in the world, although some countries have made progress in some aspects. However, the focus on issues of governance has only gained credibility in the last ten years, and with the development of better indicators of good governance and corruption. Multilateral and bilateral lenders now routinely raise governance issues in discussions, whereas formerly this issue was considered too political and too sensitive for serious discussion, and not appropriate to a focus on economic development.

How important is good governance? Kaufmann estimates that worldwide corruption at about US $1 trillion, although this is necessarily a very rough estimate, and does not measure the true economic impact (since this may be simply a transfer of profit from private operators to government bureaucrats). In terms of growth Kaufmann[92] estimates that a once standard deviation improvement in governance would raise incomes in the long-run by about two to threefold. In terms of growth, a doubling of output in 30 years would mean an increase in the growth rate by over two percentage points. There is growing awareness that development projects cannot be isolated ("ring fenced") from the overall governance environment. World Bank evaluations clearly show that project performance is lower in countries with high corruption and weak governance.

Major progress has been made in the past decade in raising governance and corruption issues, and bringing the issue out of the "closet". The progress in actually reducing corruption and improving governance, however, has been sporadic with no clear trend yet emerging in either direction.

---

92 Kaufmann, p. 83.

# CHAPTER XI

# POPULATION AND LABOR MARKETS

The power of population is indefinitely greater than the power in the earth to produce subsistence for man.—Thomas Robert Malthus

## I. Population

In the league of "magic bullets" concern over population growth has to rank near the top. Many writers, including such famous people as Barbara Ward and Robert McNamara were convinced that rapid population growth in developing countries would prevent them from ever developing, and the solution therefore was to introduce programs of contraception, or more euphemistically, family planning.

Indeed, the increase in world population over past centuries has been staggering. As shown in Table 11.1, population of the world was about 250 million in 1650, and barely growing. It took about 100 years to double, and a century later it doubled again so that by 1850 the world's population reached 1.2 billion. By 1950, the total had risen to 2.6 billion, and by 1980, 4.4 billion. The world population estimates for 2009 place the total at about 6.8 billion, and experts estimate that it will rise to 9 billion by 2050. Almost all of the population growth since 1950 has occurred in developing countries. Thus, developing countries today represent the majority of the earth's population, and their share is increasing.

**Table 11.1 Trends in World Population**

| Year | Population in millions | Growth Rate (%) |
|---|---|---|
| 1650 | 250 | .04 |
| 1750 | 545 | .29 |
| 1850 | 1176 | .49 |
| 1950 | 2576 | .78 |
| 1980 | 4445 | 1.84 |
| 2000 | 6085 | 1.58 |
| 2009 | 6775 | 1.20 |
| 2050 | 9000 est. | .70 |

Source: World Bank, WDI data bank and UN forecast for 2050.
Growth rates refer to compound growth rate over period

During the 1970s, when population growth was accelerating, few thought there would ever be a leveling off. There was an outcry in the popular and academic press over the population "explosion", and the population meance was seen as a "time bomb" threatening world stability. We now see that since 1980 the population growth rate has declined, as is presently running at about 1.2% per year, much lower than the peak of over 2% per year during the 1960s, and 1.8% between 1950 and 1980. In fact, the period of rapid population growth has also been a period of (generally speaking) rapid growth in the world's average per capita income. The scientific and technological advances of the period since 1850 permitted not only greater productivity, but also advances in medicine and health that reduced death rates and led to the acceleration of population growth.

Is the world in some sense "overpopulated"? The world population density is about 50 persons per square kilometer ($km^2$, 2005). Hong Kong, one of the more densely settled places, has a density of 6348 people per $km^2$. If the world's population were to live atHong Kong's density, they would need only about one million $km^2$, which is less than two percent of the world's habitable surface area[93] of 52 million $km^2$. To further put this in perspective, one million $km^2$ is about the size of Texas and California put together.

Of course, the fundamental limit on population size is access to food and other essentials. However, despite rapid population growth there is no evidence that food has become more scarce. In fact, between 1970-2005 the world's food production index grew faster than world population growth (2.3 vs. 1.6% per annum, see Fig 11.1). In the United States, about

---

93 Surface area of the six habitable continents.

2% of the labor force produces enough food for the entire country, plus enough to export a sizeable amount to the rest of the world[94]. Many successful countries, such as Japan, Switzerland and others exist with high population density and limited domestic food supplies. Among the low income countries, however, the performance has been less satisfactory. In Sub-Saharan Africa, over the same period, food production grew 2.2% per annum, while population grew at 2.8%. Yet, population density in Africa is relatively low (at about 32 people per $km^2$, compared to South Asia's 310 (2005)).

Thus, there is no problem producing enough food for the world's population. The problem is in the unequal distribution of that food, the low purchasing power of poor people and their inability to buy sufficient food, and the resulting malnutrition. Even if Africans cannot produce enough food to feed themselves, with economic development, they could export other goods and services, and import the food needed. The problem, once again, is not food production but overall economic development, or the lack of it.

94 Agricultural labor force in 2004 was 1.8 million or 1.8% of the total labor force. However, many of those in the agricultural labor force are marginal farmers who continue in existence with heavy subsidies from the government. Source: World Resources Institute, Earth Trends data base, available at: http://earthtrends.wri.org/searchable_db/index.php?theme=8&variable_ID=205&action=select_countries.

**Fig 11.1 World Food and Population Growth, 1970-2005**

World:

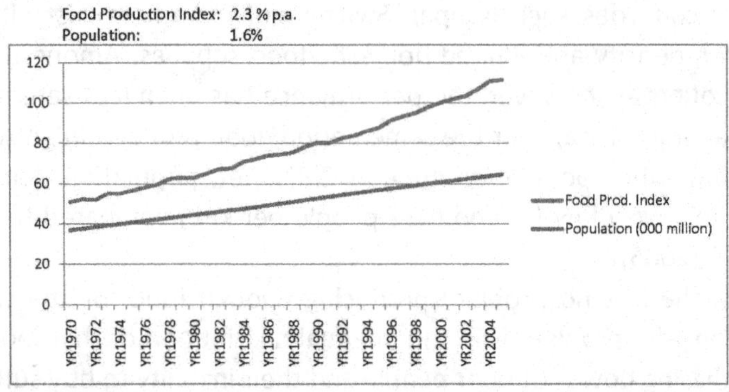


Africa (Sub-Saharan):

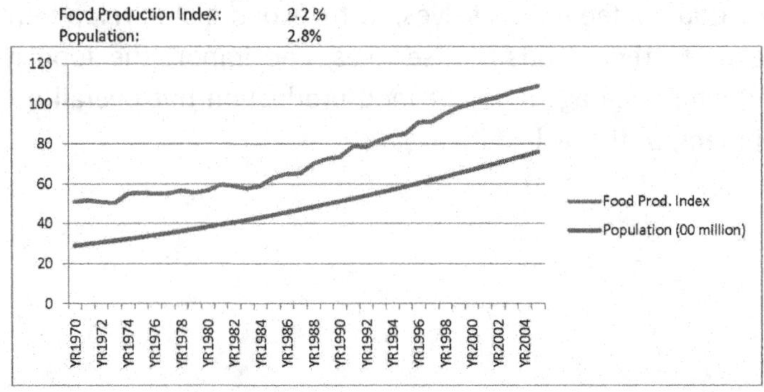


Source: World Bank, WDI data bank. Food Production Index base year 2000

## Demographic Transition

Generally, speaking countries around the world have experienced a "demographic transition", during which population growth first accelerates, then declines. This transition has four stages (see graph):

Stage I: high mortality, high birth rates
Stage II: falling mortality: high birth rates;
Stage III: low mortality and falling birth rates
Stage IV: low mortality and low birth rates.

**Fig 11.2. The Demographic Transition**

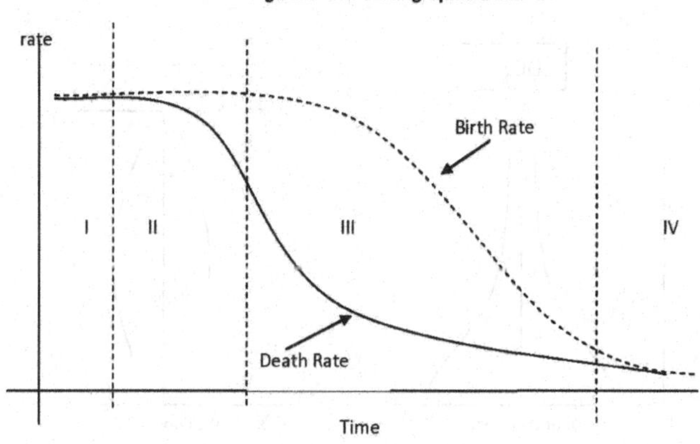


By definition, the growth rate of population is equal to the difference between the crude birth rate and the death rate (assuming zero migration). Thus,improvements in medicine, sanitation, and public health lead to a sudden and unanticipated decline in the death rate, particularly among children. There is a perception lag, in that even rational families may not realize what is happening, and make adjustments only over time as they realize more of their children are surviving to adulthood. The result, measured by the gap between birth rates and death rates in the diagram above, is an acceleration of the population growth rate, followed by a gradual decline, until the country reaches the stage of both low birth and death rates. Even if families adopt a target of only two children per family, population will continue to grow in countries with a high percentage of children in the population (typical of poorer developing countries). Thus, age structures of developing countries differ markedly from the age structures of more developed countries, which have a higher percentage of their populations in the older age brackets (see Fig. 11.3).

Fig. 11.3. Comparative Age Structures, Developed vs. LDC countries

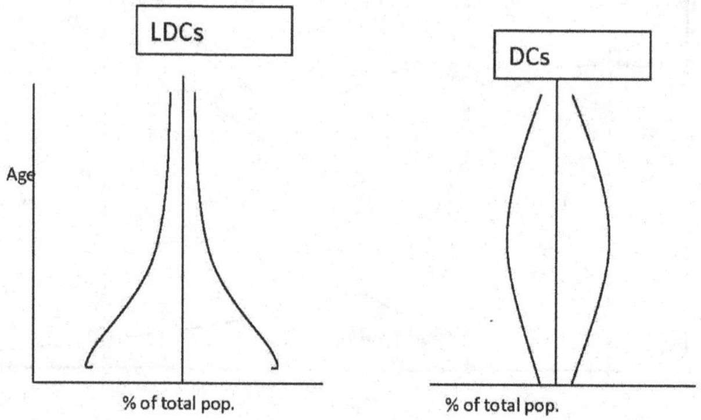

## Malthus vs. Becker

Concerns over population growth is not something that was new to the 20th Century. Thomas Malthus raised the specter of a world doomed to overpopulation back in 1798, with his Essay on the Principle of Population. Malthus felt that historically the passion between the sexes was constant and impossible to mitigate. At the same time, food production productivity increased more slowly. At one point, he argued that population doubled every 25 years, and it thereby continued to double, while food production grew at an arithmetic rate (adding a fixed increment every 25 years). In time, the population would soon outstrip the food supply, rising food prices would mean lower real wages that would fall below subsistence levels, and the result would be poverty, misery and starvation. Malthus had no faith that science could increase food production, or that people could control family size. Interestingly, Malthus' ideas, while they failed to predict human progress, influenced Darwin's ideas that animals would breed out to the point where they reached the limit of the food supply, and would be constantly under pressure for survival, in what Darwin called "the struggle for life".

The problem of the population "pessimists", those that predicted gloom and doom, is that they fail to see people as being able to regulate reproduction. In fact, techniques for regulation or avoidance of conception were well known to the Romans and the people of the Middle Ages. The more modern view, as expressed in the writings of Gary Becker, and the "new household economics", sees humans as capable of making rational choices based on the economic value and cost of children. Becker pioneered the view that children could be considered both a "consumer durable" and a "producer good". As a consumer good, children are part of the household welfare function, generating a stream of benefits along with other goods, or

$$W_H - f(X_j, C),$$

where W equals household welfare, $X_j$ is a vector of all other goods and services, and C are children. The demand for children (C) in household H depends on the price of children ($P_{C)}$), the prices of all other goods ($P_j$), household income (Y), tastes(T), and several unidentified other factors (perhaps tradition, religion, etc), or:

$$C_H = f(P_C, P_j, Y_H, T, \ldots)$$

The "price" of children includes the cost of raising children, including their education, the opportunity cost of the wife not being employed for some time, child care, etc. In societies where women do not work outside the home, and where the education cost for children is low, the overall cost or price of children is itself low. In traditional societies, furthermore, children are a "producer good", that is, they can add directly to a family's income. Thus, the output of a family or household $O_H$, can be viewed as a function of its physical capital, K, including land, the adult labor $L_A$, and child labor $L_c$, or:

$$O_H, = f(K, L_A, L_c).$$

In a rural household, children can start to make productive contribution to the household at an early age, ranging from gathering firewood and water, working in the fields, and even child care. As families migrate to urban areas, these benefits diminish, and it is common to find smaller families among the urban poor than the rural poor. In traditional societies, with low savings and no system of social security for the old, children are a form of "social security". This is particularly true for male children, rather than female, leading to a preference for male children[95].

95 Dasgupta, *op.cit.*, p. 1894

If we assume that half of children will be female, and that the survival rate of children is low, due to high infant and child mortality, people in poor countries would logically plan for a large number of children in order to insure that one or more male children survive to adulthood, and therefore provide a place for elderly parents. Dasgupta quotes a study by May and Hee (1968) which calculates that an Indian couple needed to have 6.3 children in their lifetime to be 95% certain of having at least one surviving son[96].

Thus a rational household is (supposedly) making a careful calculation of the benefits and costs of each additional child, based on the perceived direct utility of having children, and their overall net costs, including opportunity costs and positive income contribution. If, as society advances, jobs for undereducated children become scarce and low paid, while jobs for educated children pay well, there is a growing incentive to have fewer but better educated children. In addition, government programs and even social pressures work to keep children in school longer. In traditional societies with households living as extended families, the cost of child care may be minimal with the presence of older children and grandparents. In modern societies, with more women working outside the home, the cost of paying for child care is a big disincentive to having many children. In fact, the "population problem" of many advanced societies is too few children, not too many. Countries such as France, Italy and Germany have reached a point below the replacement rate, defined as total lifetime births per woman below about 2.1. Some countries have even adopted "pro-natalist" policies designed to encourage and even subsidize having children.

Nevertheless, there is little evidence that the distribution of modern contraceptives (pills, condoms, IUDs) has had a major impact on population control. Experts generally would agree with DasGupta[97] that 70-80% of the decision is influenced by demand factors, and 20% by the supply of contraceptives. Newer methods make birth control easier and more reliable, but they are not responsible for the leveling

---

96 David May and David Heer, "Son Survivorship Motivation and Family Size in India: A Computer Simulation", *Populations Studies* 22 (July, 1968) as cited in Partha Dasgupta, "The Population Problem: Theory and Evidence" *Journal of Economic Literature* 33 (December, 1995) p. 1894.

97 Partha Dasgupta, "The Population Problem: Theory and Evidence", *Journal of Economic Literature* 33(December, 1995).

off of population growth worldwide. The USAID policy (1960s-70s) of "contraceptive inundation" was based on the idea that easy availability of contraceptives would reduce population growth. Reviews of this program have concluded that it was generally a failure.

While the human capital approach of Becker seems to explain things better than the Malthusian gloom theory, it is also true that people are not purely rational. Not all pregnancies are planned, and rational decisions are often discarded in the heat of the moment. In traditional societies particularly, the decision to have or not have children is often not carefully discussed between spouses, but made largely by the man. In fact, the "new thinking" on population and family planning centers much more on female empowerment; giving women voice and access to health care and contraception, combined with better health care for the children that they do have. Discrimination against women is still widespread, particularly in Asia. As Sen[98] points out, there is a clear preference for male over female children in many traditional societies. By his estimate, there are 100 million "missing" women in the world's population, 32 million missing in India alone. While the cause of this is not proven, the hypothesis is that there is a high rate of female infanticide in these societies which explains this gap.

Finally, it should be noted that the household economics approach ignores externalities outside the family. Large families can impose a social cost on society that is not internalized by the family (social costs > private costs). This might be particularly true if a growing population puts increasing pressure on limited natural resources such as forests, pasture or soil. Thus, there may be some legitimate public sector role for encouraging family planning.

## Economic Impact

Is rapid population growth bad for economic development? Most economists have failed to find a clear correlation between high population growth and low economic growth (even though the Solow model suggests that population growth should lead to lower output). As said before, the

---

98 A.K. Sen "More Than 100 Million Women are Missing", *New York Review of Books* 37 (December, 1990).

period of rapid growth of output is coincident with a period of rapid population growth, although the causality can run both ways.

Should developing countries have programs designed to limit population growth? Clearly, in some limited cases there has been "over population" where natural resources are limited. China's policy of strongly discouraging families with more than one child (severe tax penalties on additional children) was a reaction to population pressures on land. China's success in limiting population reflects the strength of government control over its population and the limited avenues for democratic feedback. In other cases, strong coercive programs, such as sterilization programs in India, are seen as contrary to freedom of choice and human rights. India's population continues to grow faster than China's, although economic growth and the spread of female education are having a positive influence on bringing down the rate of population growth. In general, it would seem to make more sense for countries to improve health care, particularly those focusing on child and maternal health, make contraceptive advice freely available without coercion on its use, and make education fully available to the female half of the population. Combining these policies with policies that permit rapid economic growth should eliminate any threat of "over population" for most countries.

## II. Employment

The employment question for LDCs centers around attempting to provide meaningful employment for large numbers of relative unskilled workers. As we have seen, the issue of moving surplus or redundant workers into more highly productive jobs was initially seen as the central problem of economic development. According to the World Bank study "Voices of the Poor", the number one problem identified by the poor is the lack of stable employment and low wages associated with what employment they can find. In general, unemployment is not the main policy issue. Poor people cannot afford to be without work, particularly when they have no savings nor do they have access to any kind of official safety net (unemployment insurance, public welfare, etc.).

Labor markets in developing countries are often segmented three ways; an informal rural market paying market wages determined by supply and demand; an informal urban market paying slightly more than the rural market, but again with wages determined by supply and demand. And finally, an urban formal sector paying higher wages than the informal sector, with these higher wages reflecting either higher mandated minimum wages for the formal sector, and/or additional labor costs and taxes imposed on formal sector employers. While the size of the informal labor market varies from country to country, one study for Peru showed that only one in five private sector workers and one in three wage earners were entitled to receive severance payments, a measure of formality.[99]

**Fig.11.4. Rural and Urban Labor Markets**

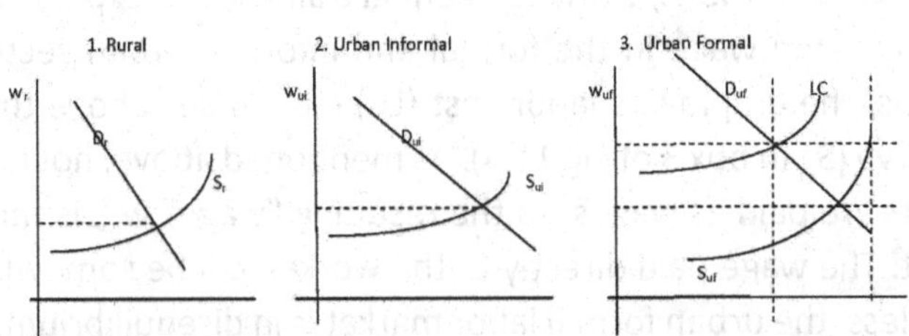


Wages in the informal urban area are roughly equal to those in the rural area, but with a slight premium needed to attract workers from the rural areas. In fact, we know that rural-urban migration may not be permanent, with rural workers coming to urban areas for part of the year, and then returning during harvest and planting seasons. As job prospects improve in urban areas with experience, these workers may eventually settle in urban areas and move their families as well.

Wages in urban formal employment are higher both because labor productivity is higher, and mandated formal sector labor benefits and employment conditions raise labor costs, if not wages. These mandated costs can include minimum wages, vacation days, health care, social security taxes, severance pay, overtime rules and other benefits which may be negotiated under a union contract. Note that some of these are direct benefits, while others (severance pay, social security and other wage taxes) are a cost to the employer that are not received by the

---

99 Donna MacIsaac and Martin Rama (2001), unpublished World Bank study, as cited in I. Gill, C. Montenegro and D. Domeland, *Crafting Labor Policy,* World Bank/Oxford University Press, Wash. DC, 2002.

worker directly as a benefit (but may generate long term benefits). For instance, in Latin America, it is common for workers in the formal sector to receive as much as one month of severance pay for every year worked if they are terminated (Bolivia, Chile, Uruguay), however some countries also impose a maximum equal to one or two years of salary[100]. Guasch estimates that in Latin America, social security and other wage taxes raise labor costs by 22-45%, and that adding non-tax mandated benefits raises this to 45-60%[101]. A study for Argentina[102] found that the wage elasticity of .5, so that a 10% reduction in labor costs would raise employment by 5%, and this seems to be about the average found in other countries in Latin America as well.

Without restrictions, workers of equal training and experience would receive the same wage in the formal and informal urban sectors. With restrictions, the employers labor cost (LC) curve rises above the natural supply curve ($S_{uf}$ in box 3 of Fig 11.4). As mentioned above, not all of these labor costs are paid as wages, so the resulting "wage" $w_{uf}$, is the average labor cost. The wage paid directly to the worker will be somewhat lower. Nevertheless, the urban formal labor market is in disequilibrium, because the supply of workers able and willing to work at the prevailing wage +benefits is greater than the actual demand ($Q_{1-}Q_2$). Workers from the lower paid urban informal sector tend to be ready to move to the formal sector once a job is identified. And so there is a transition, rural informal to urban informal to urban formal. Maloney[103] points out that there is also a fourth transition, where urban formal workers move back to the urban informal sector, often as self-employed in small businesses which are more lucrative than urban formal employment, particularly if they do

---

100 For a detailed listing by country, see: James Heckman and Carmen Pages. "The Cost of Job Security Regulations: Evidence from Latin American Labor Markets", Economia 1(Fall 2000),pp. 109-44, Table A1.

101 The non-tax benefits include paid vacations, mandated benefits, severance liabilities, etc. See J. Luis Guasch, *Labor Market Reform and Job Creation*, World Bank: Washington DC, 1999.

102 C. Pessino, Indermit Gill and Luis Guasch, "Increasing Labor Demand in Argentina" in I. Gill ed., *Crafting Labor Policy*, World Bank/Oxford U. Press, 2002., p.149.

103 William Maloney, "Informality Revisited", *World Bank Policy Research Working Paper* No 2965, January 2003.

not value very highly the likelihood of ever receiving benefits from wage taxes. For instance, if a worker's spouse works in the formal sector, the worker will receive social security benefits via the spouse, and does not need to also work in the formal sector to receive the benefit. In addition, if social security benefits are paid at age 65, and life expectancy is also 65, then it can be expected that about half of the workers will never live long enough to receive benefits. Severance payments are supposed to be paid upon dismissal (a kind of unemployment insurance). However, if the firm goes out of business, there may be no money to pay these benefits. In some countries, such as Colombia, severance payments are placed in a separate fund to avoid this problem.

The basic problem of the dichotomy between formal and informal arises from a government's inability to enforce its own labor and tax laws. In fact, some "formal" sector firms sometimes have both informal and formal workers, that is, some workers are "on the books" receiving mandated benefits, while others are not. This increases firm flexibility during a downturn, since they can release informal workers without paying severance payments. Once workers prove their merit, and are likely to be long-term employees, they can be moved from informal to formal status. Nevertheless, high wage costs still discourage most formal sector firms from taking on additional workers and thus make labor markets inflexible. As a result, there is less employment in the formal sector than would be otherwise, and more workers in the informal sector. A rational policy would be to lower wage taxes and mandated benefits to a more reasonable level, but extend the system to a larger universe, including small firms. At the same time, it would make sense for countries to move away from severance payments to a system of unemployment insurance, as found in the OECD countries, where a worker receives a weekly stipend for a limited period of time provided he/she demonstrates active job search. Very few LDCs have effective unemployment insurance schemes, and many even lack mandated severance payments.

## Safety Nets for the Unemployed

Substantial economic downturns in LDCs (and DCs) often force government to consider programs to reduce unemployment, to provide some sort of "safety net" for those unemployed. Such programs can be useful, but also carry with them the potential for heavy budgetary expenditures, and the creation of a dependent clientele that can be politically active in preventing the repeal of the programs once they are started. The pros and cons of some alternatives are laid out in the paragraphs below:

**Emergency Public Works**. The creation of jobs, mostly in construction, by organizing new projects in the public sector is a classic means of providing more employment. Large scale public works projects, however, take time to design and execute, and might only have an impact on employment well after the immediate crisis is over. Short-term projects, such as community clean-ups, painting schools, cleaning irrigation ditches, etc., might be more of a "make work" type with little long-term benefit. In either case, it is often difficult to create enough projects and jobs to have a meaningful impact on unemployment. Overall cost is high per worker, since the government must pay both the labor costs and the capital costs of the public works. They can also be expensive if the government is forced to pay "average" or "minimum" wages, where minimum wages refer to mandated formal sector minimums. What should be paid is the relevant "market" wage or even less, so that workers have an incentive to return to private sector jobs once they are available. A good example of this approach is the TRABAJAR program in Argentina[104]. On the plus side, these programs provide meaningful work rather than a government dole, and help preserve the self-esteem of the unemployed.

**Free Food.** One simpler and lower cost solution is to provide unemployed with cash or food. Food distribution can take the form of community kitchens, which prepare hot meals for those who walk in. Targeting is usually done informally by locating kitchens in areas of high poverty and/or unemployment. Alternatively, various means can be used to distribute food to the poor/unemployed, again with some form of simple targeting or means test. Food distribution can be linked to public works programs in a 'food-for-work" approach, in order to take advantage of donated food from abroad. Distributing foreign or imported food is often counterproductive except in a severe emergency, since it exacerbates the problems of adequate storage, spoilage and timely distribution. It is far better to purchase local foods, both because they are well aligned with

---

104 J. Jalan and M. Ravallion, "Income Gains to the Poor From Workfare: Estimates from Argentina's Trabajar" Policy Research Working Paper No. 2149, World Bank, Washington DC, July 1999.

traditional diets, as well as because these purchases then help support local agriculture. Even more efficient, in the sense of avoiding expensive food distribution and storage problems, is to issue food coupons or stamps to the unemployed, so they can purchase the quantity and type of food they want, allowing the private sector to cope with the distribution problem, and with a greater reliance on locally produced goods.

**Cash.** If you move to food stamps, then the next logical step is cash. Since food is highly fungible, recipients of food or food stamps can use these in place of using their own money, but then can use their own money to purchase other necessities (utilities, transport, housing, clothes, etc.). There is little evidence that food distribution actually increases food consumption more than a distribution of the equivalent amount of cash. That is, a distribution of $50 worth of food will result in the same amount of food consumed as the distribution of $50 in cash. Of course, the impact of a distribution of cash depends on who gets the money; most programs target such money directly to the dominant woman in the household, not the man, since women are more likely to spend the money on food, medicines, clothes, etc. for the family, particularly the children. Cash programs have evolved from emergency safety nets to conditional cash transfers (CCT), in which cash is given to the family with the requirement that children remain in school and receive public health attention. These programs are often targeted to families with children in secondary school, who are most likely to drop out of school, particularly if there is pressure to earn income for the family[105]. As such, however, CCT are not really safety nets for the unemployed, but a program designed to improve human capital by keeping the children of poor families in school. Ravallion and Wodon[106] have shown that it is not necessary to pay parents the full opportunity cost of a child's labor (I.e. the amount the student would earn if he/she dropped out of school and worked), but rather some smaller fraction of this amount is all that is required (indicating that parents do place some value on this education).

---

105 It is not entirely clear what the impact is of an economic crisis on school attendance. In some cases, since jobs are scarce, a recession will induce students to stay in school.

106 Martin Ravallion and Quentin Wodon, "Does Child Labor Replace Schooling?" *World Bank Policy Research Paper* No 2116 (Washington DC, 1999).

# CHAPTER XII
# INDUSTRY AND TRADE

"Man is an animal that makes bargains: no other animal does this—no dog exchanges bones with another"

—Adam Smith

Industrialization and modernization are often equated. Developing countries in the post-WWII period wanted to rapidly become modern, developed countries; they also wanted to break the colonial era dependence in which they exported agricultural and mineral commodities, and imported manufactures from the developed countries. Despite independence, newly emerging countries found that markets for manufactures in the DCs were closed to imports from LDCs, or had to face a system of high tariffs on manufactured goods and low tariffs on primary products, which tended to perpetuate a kind of post-colonial dependence of LDCs on DC manufactured products.

Indeed, the stylized facts of development indicate that the "normal" pattern is for the share in GDP (and employment) in industry to gradually rise and GDP rises, and for the share of agriculture to decline (see Fig. 12.1). In fact, at higher levels of development (roughly above $20,000) per capita income, the share of industry will decline, as the share of services continues to rise. Thus, the "stylized facts" might look something like:

Fig. 12.1 Stylized Sector GDP Shares by Per Capita Income

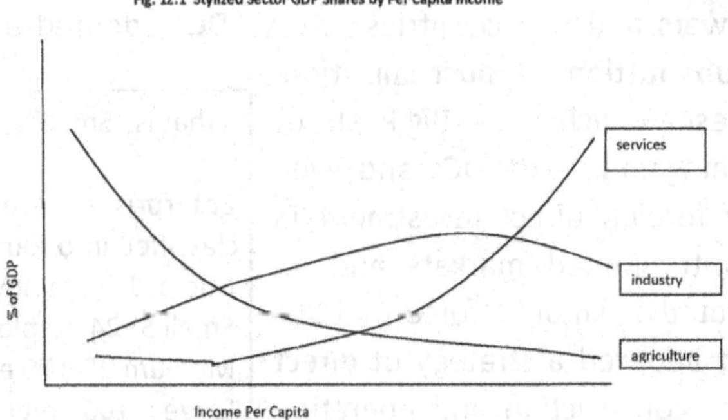


Unfortunately, reality is messier than these stylized facts, and actual income and employment shares vary widely among countries with the same level of the income. Figure 12.2 below shows data on industry share of GDP for a selected sample of countries, rich and poor, for 1970-2006. Clearly, Korea and India follow the pattern of rising industry shares with development, and Korea's shows signs of peaking out. Japan and USA have reached the point of declining industry shares. However, many countries do not follow the pattern, such as Colombia and Kenya. The data for Colombia is distorted because the definition of "industry" includes mining and minerals, and recent oil discoveries have increased industry's share in GDP.

Fig. 12.2 Industry shares for Selected Countries, 1970-2006

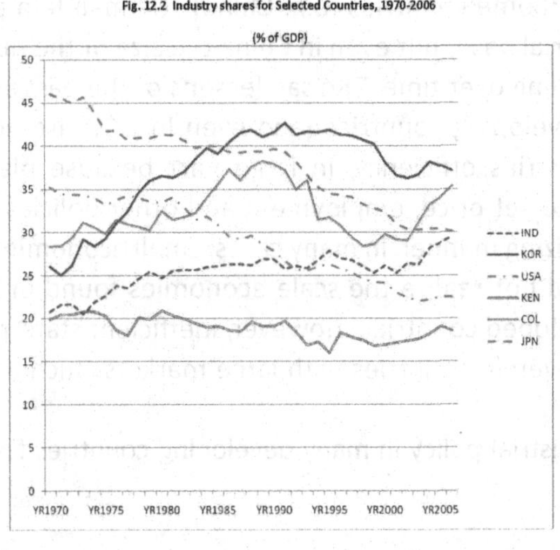


Source: World Bank, WDI Data Bank. IND=India, KOR=Korea, KEN=Kenya, COL=Colombia, JPN=Japan

To overcome their dependence on manufactures from the former colonial powers and rich countries, many LDCs adopted a strategy of **Import Substitution Industrialization.** Given the desire to achieve a "Big Push" or a rapid catching up with the DCs, and given the lack of foreign direct investment in countries with limited markets and an under-educated labor force, LDCs government adopted a strategy of direct public-sector construction and operation of heavy and light manufacturing. A major influence here was the success of the Soviet Union, and many LDCs adopted Soviet-style five year plans, although with a much lower control over the economy and with a much larger private sector. Public sector investments varied by country, but often included such "prestige" projects as steel mills, chemical, textile, and automobile plants. Other, perhaps less prestigious investments, often included plants to produce paint, shoes, pharmaceuticals, as well as supportive infrastructure investments in electric power, telephone, and mining industries, as well as banks and other financial and commercial sector enterprises.

What is "Small"?

Enterprises are generally classified into four groups:
Micro: 1-4 employees
Small 5- 24 employees
Medium 25-100 employees
Large > 100 employees

Most of these large, especially heavy, industries proved to be drains on public resources, as discussed earlier, and were eventually privatized or closed. Today, few LDCs build industries directly in the public sector. Some countries (e.g. China) still maintain a large public sector industrial base, but even in China the size of the public sector in industry is falling over time. The sad lessons of the past are that public sectors in developing countries (and even in DCs) are not capable of running industries efficiency, in large part because plant managers are not free to set price, employment and other policies in a free and profit-maximizing manner. In many cases, small economies with limited markets could not realize the scale economies found in firms located in large, developed countries. However, inefficient state-run industries were found even in countries with large markets, such as China, India and Brazil.

Most industrial policy in many developing countries focused on two approaches:

- Subsidies and assistance for small and medium enterprises (SME); and
- Tariff and non-tariff protection for private entrepreneurs to provide an incentive for domestic production.

## SME Programs.

These programs have been popular in many countries. The initial theory was that SMEs would be more labor intensive than larger manufacturing concerns, and therefore absorb more of the under-employed work force in urban areas. In fact, subsequent research has fairly clearly established that capital-labor ratios in SMEs are about the same as in larger firms. SME programs tended to focus on a variety of mechanisms to help firms, including subsidized credit, technical assistance, and subsidized facilities. Some countries established special industrial parks for SMEs that provided plant facilities and access to technical assistance in one location. Research has also showed that the lack of credit is not the most important constraint for SME development. Rather, it is their shortcomings in management, including both production, personnel and financial management, that contrains their growth and success. While almost all large firms start small (e.g. Microsoft), it is also true that most small firms never become large. In general, SME programs have not proven to be a panacea for creating employment or building the foundation for industrial growth as was once hoped. The transition from small to medium to large is often hampered by excessive government regulations, requiring permits and licenses, which in turn become an opportunity for rent-seeking by government bureaucrats. Small and micro enterprises generally avoid these by remaining in the "informal" sector, that is, they avoid taxes, often do not have the necessary permits and licenses, and usually do not follow mandated labor regulations. However, the extent of regulations themselves impedes the transition to larger scale and participation in the formal sector.

## Tariff Protection

Protection from imports quickly became the major policy tool for LDCs, once it became clear that direct investment was neither efficient nor effective. This protection consisted of two types: protective tariffs and QRs—quantitative restrictions (import licenses, quotas). In general, LDCs adopted tariff schedules that discouraged the importation of finished products. Tariff schedules adopted had roughly the following structure:

- Consumer Goods: High tariffs, esp. on luxury goods
- Food: Low tariffs
- Intermediate Goods: medium tariffs depending on degree of manufacture
- Capital Goods: low tariffs

Low tariffs on capital goods were intended to encourage investment, but they also encouraged capital intensive investments rather than labor intensive ones more suitable to LDC factor endowments. The structure also discriminated against farmers, as it offered no protection for domestic food production. At its extreme, it encouraged marginal investments in operations whose only profit came from importing relatively cheap intermediate goods and making substitute luxury goods. High tariffs on perfume, for instance, encouraged importation of bulk perfume and a manufacturing operation which was little more than a filling and labeling of perfume bottles. Automobile assembly plants were erected that imported car kits c.k.d. (completely knocked down). Unfortunately, to produce the c.k.d kits, car manufacturers produced and assembled an entire car, and then took it apart to put in a box, to be shipped to some developing country for reassembly.

In many cases, countries added non-tariff barriers to restrict imports. This occurred particularly where exchange rates over valued domestic currency, and made imports appear relatively cheap. Unable or unwilling to control the demand for imports by devaluation, countries resorted to import licensing. Licenses to import had to obtained from the Ministry of Trade, and the allocation of licenses became another "rent seeking" opportunity for government officials, and a source of corruption. Most countries have now dropped import licenses, except for dangerous or banned goods, such as firearms, explosives, live plants, etc. for which there is a reason to limit importation. Instead, exchange rates in most countries now reflect more closely market conditions, and non-tariff barriers have been replaced with tariffs, a process sometimes called "tariffication".

The rationale for trade protection often centered around the well-known and legitimate "infant industry" argument first advanced by David Ricardo in the 19th Century. As shown below, a firm whose costs are high now will not be able to compete against imports. However, over time, it might be able to expand its operations, realize scale economies and become more competitive. As shown in Fig 12.3, it would be able to move on its long run average cost curve (LAC1) from a non-competitive situation (point A, above the world price $P_w$) to a position below world costs (B).

In all too many cases, however, these "infants" refused to grow up. Given the high levels of protection, there was little incentive to reduce costs, and in markets with limited scope, their ability to reduce costs to competitive levels was also limited (see LAC2 in Fig. 12.3) Hence, in many cases costs remained high, and protected industries lobbied for continued protection, along with the labor unions whose employees also benefitted. Consumers, who paid for this in terms of overpriced final goods, tended to have no voice in this dialogue.

Fig. 12. 3 Long Run Average Costs over time

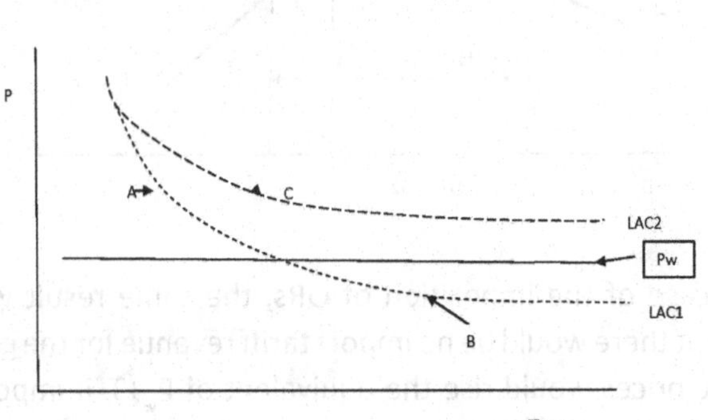


Trade protection results in a net welfare loss to the economy in any case. As shown in the graph, below (Fig. 12.4), the market for a good within the country is met by a combination of domestic production and imports. The demand curve (D) shows that at the world price ($P_w$) demand is met by domestic output of Qd1, and imports of M1. The country can import unlimited supplies at the world price, and only a limited amount of domestic production competes at this price. A tariff is imposed of T, so that the domestic price is now $P_w$+T. At that price, domestic production rises to Qd2, and imports fall to M2. Triangles A and B represent deadweight losses, in that they are loses that are not offset by increases in government revenue or producers surplus. Tariff revenues equal the box C, while F represents the increase in producer surplus. Thus, A is the cost to society of using materials best suited to produce something else, and B is the net loss of consumer surplus. The gross loss of consumer surplus is equal to the sum of the boxes A,B, C and F.

Protection could also be accorded by imposing a QR. Thus, in Fig. 12. 5, imports are limited from M1 to M2, by issuing import licenses. The effect is the same as before, except that there is no increase in government revenue, since licenses are given out free of charge. The domestic price is the one

**Fig. 12. 4 Demand and Supply for a Typical Good, with and without Tariffs**

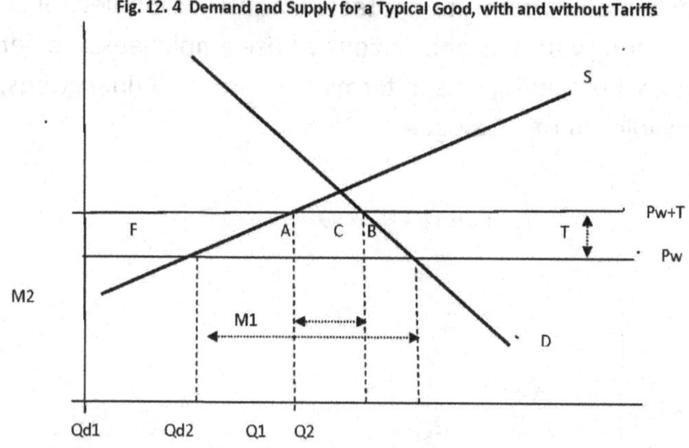


In the case of the imposition of QRs, the same result would come about, except there would be no import tariff revenue for the government, C. Domestic prices would rise the equivalent of $P_w$+T, if import licensing allows only for imports of M2.

Tariffs and QRs can be avoided by smuggling, so that their impact depends on the ability of the government to patrol its borders, and the honesty of the customs service. Not all smuggling involved secret nighttime deliveries. **Technical smuggling** is also common, in which goods are either improperly invoiced (e.g. perfume declared as a medicine), or undervalued (Look, I only paid $1000 for that Mercedes, and I have a (fraudulent) bill to prove it). In this way, goods normally having high tariffs come in at a lower rate, or the total tax collected is on an understated value. Much of technical smuggling happens with the cooperation of customs officials who look the other way or accept false invoices, often for a price.

To combat undervaluation of imports, authorities often resort to specific tariffs, rather than ad valorem tariffs. Specific tariffs arc lcvicd on each unit of imports, regardless of its value (e.g. $1.00 per pound). The disadvantage of specific tariffs is that the effective tariff rate varies with the price of the good, and specific tariffs need to be revised periodically to be kept up to date with inflation and changes in world prices. Most countries have now moved away from specific tariffs for that reason, although they can be used as a "floor" to discourage technical smuggling (e.g. 10% of value <u>or</u> $1.00 per pound, whichever is greater). Governments often exempt non-profit organizations from import tariffs (e.g. schools, health organizations) on the basis that they essential and necessary services for the poor. However, this also can be a loophole in which people form a "non-profit" ostensibly for the purpose of running a charity, but in reality it is a front for importing goods duty-free, and then reselling them.

## Average vs. Effective Rates of Protection

Measuring protection is difficult, since high rates of protection will limit imports, and imports could be limited by QRs even though import duties are low. Thus, a trade weighted calculation of import tariffs will understate the true rate of protection. Nevertheless, the table below shows actual import tariffs collected as a percent of imports, for selected countries (mainly those with data from 1990 on). On this basis we can see that tariff protection was much higher in some countries, and with trade liberalization, has declined significantly. Average tariffs in India have fallen from 42% in 1990 to 8% in 2005, and in Tunisia from 17 to 4% (see Table 12.1)

**Table 12.1. Average Import Duties for Selected Countries**
(% of imports)

| | YR1990 | YR1995 | YR2000 | YR2005 |
|---|---|---|---|---|
| Bahrain | 2.4% | 3.1% | 2.9% | 4.0% |
| Canada | 2.3% | 1.1% | 0.7% | 0.7% |
| China | 5.6% | 2.3% | N/A | 1.9% |
| Costa Rica | 7.6% | 5.8% | 1.8% | 1.6% |
| Cote d'Ivoire | 20.9% | 18.5% | 13.0% | 9.7% |
| Eygpt | 9.7% | 13.0% | N/A | 4.4% |
| Guatemala | 6.1% | 7.5% | 4.2% | 4.4% |
| India | 42.3% | 24.2% | 15.9% | 8.0% |
| Iran | 6.1% | 5.0% | 8.0% | 8.5% |
| Jordan | 7.0% | 5.0% | 8.0% | 8.5% |
| Korea | 6.8% | 3.9% | 2.7% | 2.0% |
| Nepal | 11.9% | 8.8% | 8.4% | 8.6% |
| Nicaragua | 13.4% | 3.7% | 2.5% | 1.9% |
| Pakistan | 25.3% | 21.4% | 11.0% | 9.2% |
| Philippines | 12.0% | 11.6% | 5.3% | 5.0% |
| Sri Lanka | 13.7% | 7.9% | 3.8% | 4.5% |
| Switzerland | 3.7% | 0.7% | 0.6% | 0.5% |
| Tunisia | 16.6% | 16.6% | 6.4% | 3.9% |
| Venezuela | 6.7% | 7.1% | 8.3% | 6.8% |

Source: World Bank, WDI data bank

This is an inaccurate measure of the level of protection for another important reason: it does not balance import duties on inputs against import duties protecting output. Tariff protection protects the value added of an industry, in that it can raise or lower the margin between inputs and outputs. The **effective rate of protection** (ERP) is the comparison of value added at domestic prices, versus the value added that would have been attained if world prices had prevailed. Thus, it can be defined as:

$$ERP = (VA_d - VA_w)/ VA_w$$

Where $VA_d$ is value added at domestic prices and $VA_w$ is valued added at world prices, and the ERP is the percentage increase in value added that arises from the tariff protection. We assume here that $P_d = P_w + T$, that is, the domestic price of goods equals the world price plus the tariff, and there is no price effect of QRs. Then since value added is the difference between output price (P) and the cost of materials(C), we have the full formula for ERP:

$$[(P_d - C_d) - (P_w - C_w)]/ (P_w - C_w) = [(P_d - C_d) / (P_w - C_w)] - 1.0$$

Where $P_d$ is the domestic price of output, $C_d$ is the domestic price of inputs, etc. We assume that all inputs to the manufacturing process are taxed equally, and even if produced domestically, their prices reflect world prices plus the tariff.

To illustrate, take an example with a 25% tariff on products produced in an example industry, no tariffs on inputs. The world price of output is 100, and the world price of inputs is 70 (thus the value added is 30% at world prices). The formula becomes:

$$\frac{(125 - 70) - (100 - 70)}{(100 - 70)} = .83 \text{ or } 83\%.$$

Thus, while the nominal protection of this industry is 25%, the effective protection is 83%.

**Table 12.2 Some Effective Rates of Protection in Developing Countries (average)**

| Country | Year | Primary | Manufacturing | Overall |
|---|---|---|---|---|
| Singapore | 1967 | 5 | 0 | 0 |
| Korea | 1978 | 77 | 5 | 31 |
| Brazil | 1980-81 | -21 | 23 | n/a |
| Colombia | 1979 | 39 | 55 | 44 |
| Philippines | 1980 | 9 | 44 | 36 |
| Chile | 1967 | -7 | 217 | 168 |
| Nigeria | 1980 | -12 | 82 | n/a |

Source: World Bank, *World Development Report 1987*(Oxford U. Press, New York/London, 1987) p. 89

**Table 12.3 Nominal and Effective Rates of Protection in Thailand, Selected sectors, 1984 (%)**

| Sector | Nominal Protection | Effective Protection |
|---|---|---|
| Major Crops | 6.6 | 5.8 |
| Animal Feeds | 1.7 | -2.5 |
| Vegetables & Fruits | 68.3 | 226.0 |
| Basic Chemicals | 11.9 | 20.7 |
| Fertilizer | 3.8 | 1.4 |
| Plastic Wares | 58.3 | 88.3 |
| Tire/Rubber Prod. | 43.0 | 84.4 |
| Glass | 36.6 | 130.5 |
| Fab. Metal Products | 26.3 | 59.7 |
| Electrical Machinery | 18.6 | 27.4 |
| | | |

source: S.Devarajan and C. Sussangkarn (1992), Table 2

The "discovery" of effective rates of protection in the 1960s helped push the dialogue for trade liberalization, pioneered by such economists as Bela Balassa, Gus Ranis, Anne Krueger, and others. As shown in table 12.2, effective rates of protection (ERP) varied widely among countries, and among sectors in the same country. There are also substantial variations between ERP and nominal rates of protection (NRP). In Thailand (1984), the nominal rate of protection for vegetables and fruits was 68%, but the effective protection was 226% (see Table 12.3).[107] Effective rates of protection ranged from a high of 226% to a low of -20%. Negative rates of effective protection can indicate sectors that are actually losing foreign exchange—the value of their product at world prices was less than the cost of imported inputs when valued at world prices, producing negative value added at world prices. High on this list is "transport equipment" which relates to the assembly of cars and trucks from kits, mentioned above. Negative effective protection can also come about when inputs are taxed, but there is no protection on output. In mining, where products are sold at world prices, but capital equipment and other supplies are taxed, is an example of where effective protection can be negative (as in Table 12.2). For instance, in the previous example, suppose there is a 10% tax on imported inputs, but no protective tariff on output, then:

$$\frac{(100-77)-(100-70)}{(100-70)} = -\frac{.07}{.30} = -.23 \text{ or } -23\%$$

The effective rate of protection is -23%, which indicates an industry which is not only not being protected, but being taxed. Negative rates of protection are common for agriculture, where food has no or very low protective tariffs, and inputs are taxed.

Heavy taxes and restrictions on imports create an anti-export bias. In simple terms, reducing demand for imports means a country can maintain a more appreciated exchange rate, and avoid devaluation. In fact, many restrictions on imports, particularly QRs, were invoked just for that reason. To illustrate, consider the market for foreign exchange, in which demand comes from imports and supply comes from exports. The price of foreign

---

107 S. Devarajan and C. Sussangkarn, "Effective Rates of Proection when Domestic and Foreign Goods are Imperfect Substitutes", *Review of Economics and Statistics* 74 (Nov. 1992), pp.701-711.

exchange is the number of local currency units (LC) needed to purchase one unit of foreign exchange ($). It is assumed here that exchange rates are flexible, and respond to the demand and supply of foreign exchange coming only from commodity trade. Imposing a tariff or QR on imports reduces the demand for foreign exchange (see fig 12.5), shifting the demand curve to the left, causing the exchange rate to appreciate, and the quantity of exports to fall. Thus, a tax on imports becomes a tax on exports (Likewise, a tax on exports is implicitly a tax on imports, since it will cause a shortage of foreign exchange, and a devaluation of the exchange rate).

**Fig. 12.5 A Tax on Imports is a Tax on Exports**

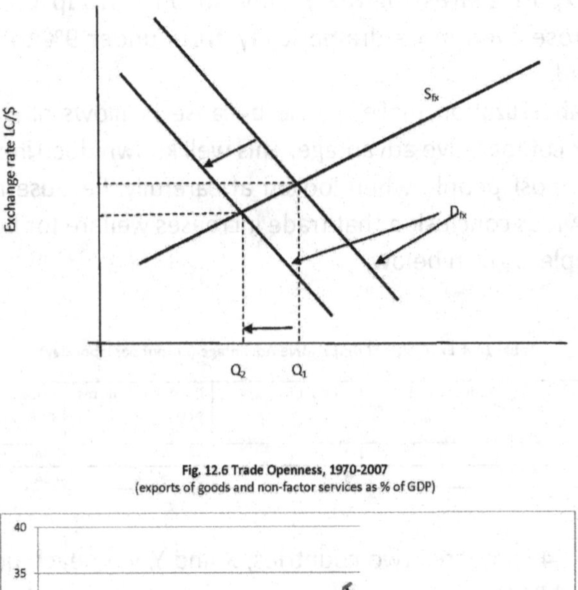

Exchange rate LC/$

$S_{fx}$

$D_{fx}$

$Q_2$ $Q_1$

**Fig. 12.6 Trade Openness, 1970-2007**
**(exports of goods and non-factor services as % of GDP)**

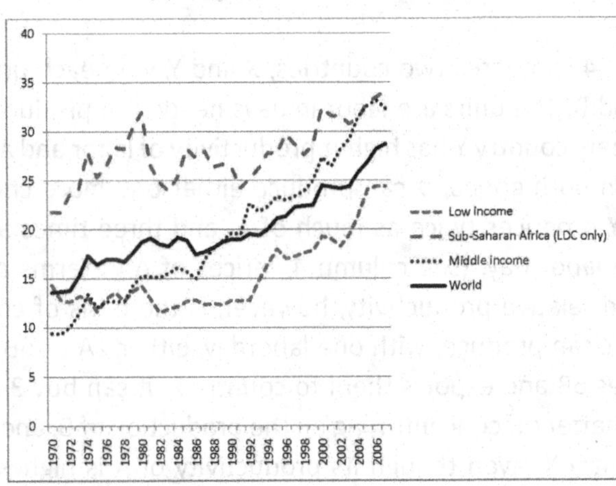


Source: World Bank, WDI data base.

The need for trade liberalization and openness in general became particularly evident during the 1980s debt crisis, when over-borrowing from banks and a shortage of foreign exchange earnings led to defaults and rescheduling of debt by developing countries, and the imposition (as a *quid pro quo*) of reforms by the IMF and World Bank that liberalized trade regimes and reduced tariffs. At the same time, many LDC officials began to recognize the disadvantages of heavy protection, and began to push for more open policies. As a result, the degree of openness of developing countries, and the world in general, has increased dramatically since 1980 (see Fig. 12.6). The ratio of exports to GDP in the world has increased from 14% in 1970 to 28% in 2007. Export shares for the middle income group of developing countries rose even more dramatically, from under 9% to 32% in the same period.

Trade liberalization makes sense because it allows all countries to follow their comparative advantage. This well known doctrine still seems to surprise most people when looked at carefully, because it comes to the non-obvious conclusion that trade increases welfare for both sides. A quick example is given below.

**Table 12.4 Example of Comparative Advantage (output per labor day)**

| | Product A | Product B | Price of A in terms of B | Price of B in terms of A |
|---|---|---|---|---|
| Country X | 1 | 2 | 2B | .5A |
| Country Y | 2 | 6 | 3B | .3A |

Table 12.4 compares two countries, X and Y, who each produce two goods, A and B. The units are labor in days needed to produce one unit. As can be seen, country Y has higher productivity of labor and an absolute advantage in both goods; it can produce either one more cheaply than country X. Y produces twice as much of A, and three times as much of B, with one labor day. (see column 4 "prices of A in terms of B"). The difference in relative productivity, however, is the basis of comparative advantage. Y can produce, with one laborday, either 2A or 6B. However, if it produces 6B and exports them to country X, it can buy 3 units of A. Hence, it is better off concentrating on the production of B, and importing A from country X, even though its productivity of A is higher. Likewise, if X uses its one labor day to produce A, and sells it to country Y, it can

purchase 3 units of B (compared to its internal ability of producing 2 units of B). Thus, trade gives Y more A, and X more B, than without trade.

Graphically, this can be illustrated using the production possibility curve for A and B in country Y (see Fig. 12.7). Normally, without trade, Y will produce at point a, which is where the production possibilities curve is tangent to the highest indifference curve. Any other combination of A and B would result in a lower level of welfare. However, with trade, country Y can produce more of B and trade to reach a higher indifference curve. The possibility of this rests with the concept that relative prices when trading are different that domestic relative prices (as shown by the two price lines). By exporting some of B, country Y can now import more of A than it could have before as in the example above). It moves to point C on indifference curve $I_2$. In this graphic example, it winds up with a lot more A, and slightly less B. However, it could be possible to end up with both more A and more B, depending on the shapes of the curves.

Fig.12.7 How Trade Allows Movement to Higher Indifference Curve

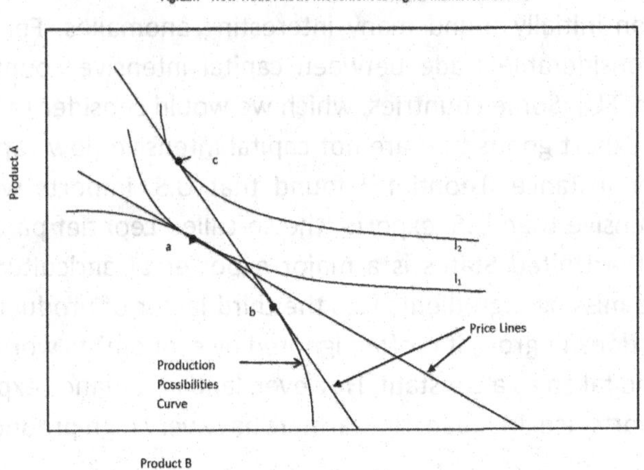


Not all import restrictions occur in LDCs. Many developing countries subsidize agriculture, which reduces the ability of LDCs to compete in developed country markets. In some case, certain kinds of products are limited by quotas (bananas until recently in the EU, sugar in the US). Ironically, trade policy has been biased against agriculture in LDCs, but has promoted agriculture in developed countries, working against natural comparative advantage. Agricultural subsidies and distortions are significant. It is estimated that the elimination of all quotas, tariffs and subsidies to agriculture in developed countries would add $100 billion annually to the GDP of LDCs[108]. Support to agriculture in developed countries is estimated to have averaged $273 billion per year[109]. It has been calculated that the average cow in Europe receives $2.70 per day in subsidies, and in Japan, $8.00 per day. In the United States, 20,000 cotton farmers collectively share subsidies of $10 million per day[110].

## Hecksher-Olin Thesis

But what determines a country's comparative advantage? The famous Hecksher-Olin thesis simply states that countries with a relative surplus of labor will export labor intensive goods, and those with a relative abundance of capital will export capital intensive goods. The thesis rests on a simplistic two-factor (capital and labor), two-commodity (labor intensive, capital intensive), two-country world. Studies of trade composition initially found many interesting anomalies. For instance, there is considerable trade between capital intensive countries (e.g. U.S., Japan, EU). Some countries, which we would consider to be capital intensive, export goods that are not capital intensive (low capital/labor ratios). For instance, Leontief[111] found that U.S. imports were more capital intensive than U.S. exports (the so-called Leontief paradox). For instance, the United States is a major exporter of agricultural goods. One of the missing ingredients was the third factor of production, land. Since land doesn't grow, it is often ignored by economists worried about growth, and taken as a constant. However, land abundance explains why the US exports rice. In Japan, rice farmers have very high productivity per

---

108 World Bank, *Global Economic Prospects 2002* (World Bank, Washington DC, 2001), p. 167.

109 World Bank, *World Development Report 2008*, (World Bank/Oxford Univ. Press, Washington DC, 2007), p. 7.

110 Devinder Sharma at: http://www.stwr.org/imf-world-bank-trade/farm-subsidies-the-report-card.html

111 Wassily Leontieff, "Domestic Production and Foreign Trade The American Capital Experience Reconsidered", Proceedings of the American Philosophical Association 97(September, 1953), pp. 332-349.

hectare, but on small, inefficient farms. Rice farms in the United States are large, with lower output per hectare, but with greater use of capital equipment, and much higher productivity per unit of labor input.

The real world is made up of multiple commodities, and with factors of differing quality. The United States both produces cars and imports cars, because some people prefer European or Japanese cars. Likewise, the U.S. exports wine and imports wine. Wine is not a homogenous commodity. Many countries, such as in Latin America, are somewhere between a labor-surplus country (such as India) and a capital rich country (such as Japan). Countries in Latin America have a hard time competing with China for labor intensive industries, but can compete for those industries requiring a somewhat higher level of education. In agriculture, Latin American has a seasonal advantage for the exports of flowers and fresh vegetables, since in the northern hemisphere winter is the southern hemisphere summer.

Comparative advantage can also change over time (dynamic comparative advantage). As real wages rise with growth, labor intensive manufacturing industries become unprofitable and migrate to new locations. Hence, we have seen in recent decades the manufacture of clothing, shoes, and textiles migrate from Japan and Korea to places like China, India and Bangladesh. In reality, comparative advantage is based on the inequality of factor endowments, which in turn generates flows that tend to equalize these differences. The logical result of Hecksher-Olin trade will be **factor price equalization.** If capital intensive countries import labor intensive goods, the demand for labor intensive goods tends to increase the demand for labor in labor surplus economies, and decrease demand for labor in capital intensive countries. This in turn will increase the demand for capital in labor surplus countries, and capital will flow from high capital to low capital economies (assuming there are no restrictions on capital movement). Factor price equalization can also occur through the movement of labor, a much more common phenomenon in the last decade than before.

Hecksher-Olin trade may also help explain answer of why countries continue to grow and do not reach a Solow steady state. Increased demand from trade for capital intensive goods means the possibility of postponement of the effect of diminishing returns to capital.[112]

---

112 For a fuller critique of Hecksher-Ohlin, see Edward Leamer. "The Hecksher-Olin Model in Theory and Practice", *Princeton Studies in International Finance* 77 (February, 1995).

## Openness and Growth

There are many critics of trade liberalization and "globalization", or the tendency for greater inter-connectedness in the world. There is a common perception that trade openness benefits only one side of the equation (although it is never very clear which side that is). In general, attempts to define the elements of growth usually find that some measure of openness to be correlated with growth, although not always. The problem is on how one measures "openness". The standard measure is (M+X)/GDP, that is imports plus exports divided by GDP. However, these ratios tend to be higher in small economies, and higher in economies dominated by mineral exports. Such high ratios may prevail even though an economy is characterized by high tariffs, QRs, and distorted exchange rates. Likewise, the level of trade distortions is difficult to judge. For instance, if high tariffs really limit imports, then tariff collections will be low if tariff rates are high. Hence, a measure of "tariff collections/ imports" will not measure the restrictiveness of the tariff system. The same problem arises with measuring the impact of QRs.

One of the most thorough studies of this question was done by Sebastian Edwards[113]. His study looks at the growth of TFP (total factor productivity), which means the growth of the economy after allowing for growth of capital and labor, or the Solow residual. He regresses TFP growth against various measures of openness and trade distortions, as wells as initial GDP, and a human capital variable. The results are shown in table 12.5. As expected, the measures of openness are positively related to growth, and 2 out of 3 are significant at the 95% level. Likewise, the measures of trade distortions are negatively related to growth. Of the six measures of trade distortions, however, only the black market premium (BLACK), the Heritage Foundation index (HERITAGE), and collected trade taxes ratio (CTR) are significant. Following other studies, Edwards finds that the human capital measure is positively related to TFP growth in all cases, and the level of GDP is negative (indicating conditional convergence), and in almost all cases at the 95% level of confidence. While the trade measures are important, Edwards notes that the initial level of GDP and

113 S. Edwards, "Openness, Productivity and Growth: What Do We Really Know"?" *Economic Journal* 108 (March, 1998). Pp. 383-398, also published as NBER Working Paper 5978, March 1997.

the human capital variable are relatively more important in explaining TFP growth. In fact, without the human capital and trade openness measures, the initial level of GDP would not be significant, indicating that the hypothesis of absolute convergence can be rejected.

**Table 12.5 Edward's TFP Regressions with Various Trade Openness Measures**

| Openness Measure | GDP65 | Human65 | Trade Orientation | $R^2$ | N |
|---|---|---|---|---|---|
| OPEN | -0.011<br>(-2.41) | 0.005<br>(3.27) | .094E-2<br>(2.12) | 0.24 | 51 |
| WDR | -.013<br>(-2.53) | .004<br>(2.17) | .075E-2<br>(3.57) | 0.45 | 32 |
| LEAMER | -.005<br>(-.90) | .003<br>(1.94) | 0.41E-2<br>(1.03) | 0.23 | 44 |
| BLACK | -0.008<br>(-2.43) | 0.003<br>(2.53) | -0.022<br>(-3.59) | 0.28 | 75 |
| TARIFF | -0.10<br>(-2.69) | 0.003<br>(2.99) | -0.045<br>(-2.77) | 0.24 | 67 |
| HERITAGE- | 0.007<br>(-2.81) | 0.002<br>(2.58) | -0.58E-2<br>(-4.56) | 0.42 | 58 |
| WOLF | -.009<br>(-1.91) | 0.004<br>(2.83) | 0.35E-4<br>(0.27) | 0.14 | 53 |

Source: Sebastian Edwards, "Openness, Productivity and Growth: What Do We Really Know?", *Economic Journal* 108 (May, 1998), p. 692. Used with kind permission of Wiley Publications.
Notes: Each row corresponds to a TFP growth regression using weighted least squares and using a different openness indicator in each equation. The indicator is identified in column one, and the coefficients given in column four. The numbers in parentheses are t-statistics.
Indices of Openness:
OPEN = Sachs/Warner Index of Openness WDR = World Development Report index of openness
LEAMER = Leamer's Index of openness
Indices of Distortions:
BLACK = average black market exchange rate premium TARIFF = average import tariff
HERITAGE = Heritage Foundation Index of trade distortions WOLF = Index of trade distortions by H. Wolf
QR = average coverage of quantitative restrictions on imports CTR= trade taxes collected as ratio to trade
Results for QR and CTR are not shown above since coefficients are not significant at the 95% level.

## If Trade Is So Good, Why Is There So Much Opposition?

If both sides benefit from trade, why is there so much vocal opposition to trade openness and globalization? Here are some possibilities:

- Differential Impact: The benefits from trade tend to be spread over the general population, but the impact of trade liberalization is likely to impact some specific industries quite severely. It does not help the furniture workers in North Carolina to know that trade liberalization will eliminate their jobs, but help increase the demand for workers to make computers in California.
- A corollary of this is that capital, once invested, is not flexible. You cannot make computers with machines designed to make shoes.
- Likewise, while everyone benefits from lower prices for shirts, shoes and clothing from imports, this benefit might seem

microscopic if your job has been eliminated in these industries, and you have no income to buy shirts, shoes, etc.

- Political Power: An industry, particularly a large one with sizeable profits, has substantial political power and is able to influence government policy to prevent liberalization, and often can ally itself with the labor unions in its industry to appeal for greater protection and/or fight against further trade opening.
- Xenophobia: People fear being dependent on foreigners for key products, such a food, steel, cars, etc. and/or see their national image damaged when these industries close down.

Is opposition to trade liberalization irrational? It is from an economic sense, but may not be if your welfare function includes things other than pure economics, such as national pride. In addition, to those directly affected it may make perfect sense. Economists need to take into account these social/political motives to the opposition to liberalization programs and include such things as job retraining and transition assistance for affected industries. Another alternative is to phase in reforms over time, so that entrepreneurs have time to adjust, and do not make investments in industries that will not survive. However, many would argue that a time-phased reform program can provide time for opposition forces to organize, oppose the reform, and defeat it.

## WTO and Regional Trade Arrangements

In theory, a country is better off liberalizing trade even if partner countries do not, provided that it maintains a flexible exchange rate. In practice, countries generally see trade concessions as necessary in order to extract concessions from trade partners. Thus, they see it as a kind of prisoner's dilemma, with unilateral trade liberalization being the worst outcome, but with multilateral trade concessions being the best outcome. Hence, the past 50 years have seen a series of multilateral trade negotiations resulting in concessions toward openness on all sides, first via the GATT (General Agreement on Tariffs and Trade) and after 1995 through the GATT's successor, the World Trade Organization (WTO). Regional trade groupings have also negotiated regional free trade areas, such as NAFTA (United States, Mexico, Canada), CAFTA (Central America

+ U.S), LAFTA (Latin America), AFTA (ASEAN-South Asia), and the EU (European Community). Arrangements that include similar countries, such as LAFTA and AFTA, often have limited possibilities for trade, as opposed to arrangements such as NAFTA and CAFTA that include both developed and LDCs, or the EU, which creates a large market among rich countries. In addition, several countries have negotiated bilateral trade agreements, often out of frustration with the slow pace of multilateral and regional progress. Bilateral, and even regional, arrangements however can be counterproductive in terms of world welfare. The issue is **trade creation** versus **trade diversion**. Suppose Brazil buys shoes from India, a low cost supplier, but levies a 35% tariff on shoes. Suppose also that it negotiates a free trade agreement with Peru, the result of which is that shoe manufacturers in Peru can now sell shoes in Brazil, since they do not have to pay the 35% tariff, even though their production costs are higher than India's. Trade in shoes has been diverted from India, a low cost producer, to Peru a high (or at least higher) cost producer. The world is worse off, in that capital and labor are not being used to their best advantage.

In a multi-lateral framework, if Brazil negotiates tariff concessions with Peru, it has to extend these to other countries, the so called **Most Favored Nation** (MFN) treatment. This was part of the GATT agreement signed in 1947. However, regional and bilateral arrangements are undertaken outside of the MFN framework. Under GATT/WTO countries also agree to not give subsidies to exporters, not to "dump" goods at prices below costs, phase out general production subsidies (e.g. agriculture), and not to impose quotas and non-tariff barriers that act like tariffs. Despite much progress, agricultural subsidies and some important quota restrictions remain. Negotiations within the WTO are particularly focused now on liberalizing trade in services, protection of intellectual property rights, and reducing agricultural subsidies. While the GATT was a low profile organization that few people outside of trade/economics professionals had ever heard about, the creation of the WTO in 1995 seems to have created a lightning rod for anti-globalization protesters. In reality, the WTO is a forum for countries to come together and agree on trade concessions, and a mechanism to ensure that such agreements are enforced.

## Annex: Understanding the Balance of Payments

The net impact of trade and capital flows is summarized in a table on the balance of payments (BoP), which refers to international transactions. There are many ways of presenting the balance of payments, but generally all follow the same principles.

Fundamentally, the BoP consists of three broad accounts, the current account, the capital account, and changes in reserves. The three accounts must be in balance overall, so that:

(1) CURBAL + CAPBAL + RES = 0

Where CURBAL is the balance on current account, CAPBAL is the balance on capital account, and RES is the use of reserves, which includes net disbursements from the IMF (the IMF insists that it provides reserves, not capital for financing imports). If reserves are increased, RES is a negative.

The current account is composed trade in goods (exports and imports), trade in non-factor services (transport, tourism, professional fees), factor payments (interest, wages, profits) and official and private transfers. It is defined as:

X = Exports of goods, f.o.b.
M = Imports of Goods, c.i.f.
X-M = TB = trade balance
NFS = Non Factor Services, net (transportation, tourism, professional fees, etc.)
NFY = Net Factor Payments (interest, dividends, wages, profits)
OT = official transfers net (includes aid grants)
PT = private transfers, net (includes workers remittances)

(2) CURBAL = TB+NFS+NFY+OT+PT

The capital account contains capital inflows which finance the current account. The capital account is defined as the sum of medium and long term borrowings (less repayments of principal), direct foreign investment, short term capital flows, and errors and omissions. Thus:

MLT, net = Disbursements of private and official medium and long term loans, less amortization
DFI, net = foreign direct investment flows, less repatriated capital
ST, net = short term capital (loans with less than one year maturity)
E&O = Errors and Omissions

(3) CAPBAL = MLT+DFI +ST+E&O

Thus, the current account balance is offset by the capital account balance and reserve movements, so that

(4) CURBAL = CAPBAL+RES

Since the current balance will normally be in deficit, and therefore negative, a negative negative makes CURBAL positive in the equation above. In some cases, errors and omissions are included with reserves as a balancing item; here we put it in the capital account.

Most transactions involve two entries: Normally, one in the current account on one side, and the capital account, or changes in reserves, on the other. However, it is possible that both entries would be one just one side; i.e. current account or capital account.

Here are some examples for a country named "Euphoria" whose balance of payments is shown below in Table 12.6, both in its original preliminary form, and after revisions reflecting these transactions.

1. A manufacturer exports $10 million of shoes. Exports rise by $10 million, and reserves go up by the same amount. An increase in reserves shows as a negative, similar to a capital outflow, but in this case the outflow is into the coffers of the Central Bank. Since the original position showed a use of reserves, this use of reserves goes down.
2. An aid agency provides a loan for $50 million to finance equipment imports. This year, the country uses $12 million to import electric power equipment. Imports rise by $12 million, as does disbursements of loans, MLT. A rise in imports increases the deficit of the CURBAL by $12 million, covered by an increase of

$12 million in the CAPBAL. Note that if this aid came as a grant, the $12 million would be recorded in the current account as an official transfer, offsetting the $12 million in imports, and the current account would not change. In either case, the remaining $38 million commitment has no effect on this year's balance of payments.

3. An American corporation invests $20 million to construct a new factory in Euphoria. It imports equipment of $10 million and uses $10 million for local construction costs. Direct foreign investment (in the capital account) increases by $20 million; imports (equipment) go up by $10 million and reserves go up by $10 million (since the corporation converts dollars to local currency via the Central Bank—depositing dollars and receiving local currency equivalent to pay for local construction costs).
4. The country pays the World Bank $5 million in interest payments on past loans, and $8 million for repayment of principal on these loans. Factor payments (interest) rise by $5 million, disbursements of loans MLT show a negative $8 million. The country's reserves go down by $13 million.
5. I send a gift of a car worth $30,000 to my brother in Euphoria. Imports rise by $30K. If the customs documents show it to be a gift, then it will be recorded as $30 million under private transfers. If not, then the amount could simply go into errors and omissions. Both import and private transfer are in the current account; errors and omissions are in the capital account.

**Table 12.6 Country Euphoria: Balance of Payments with Revisions**

| Item | Preliminary | Revisions (cumulative) | | | | | Revised BoP |
|---|---|---|---|---|---|---|---|
| | | 1 | 2 | 3 | 4 | 5 | |
| **Current Account** | | | | | | | |
| Exports, fob | 1528 | 10 | | | | | 1538 |
| Imports, cif | -3112 | | -12 | -10 | | -30 | -3164 |
| Trade Balance | -1584 | | | | | | -1626 |
| Non-factor services, net | -155 | | | | | | -155 |
| Receipts | 312 | | | | | | 312 |
| Payments | - 467 | | | | | | -467 |
| Factor Payments, net | -100 | | | | | | -105 |
| Receipts | 50 | | | | | | 50 |
| Payments | -150 | | | | -5 | | -155 |
| Official Transfers, net | 689 | | | | | | 689 |
| Private Transfers, net | 444 | | | | | 30 | 474 |
| Current Account balance | -706 | -696 | -708 | -718 | -723 | -723 | -723 |
| | | | | | | | |
| **Capital Account** | | | | | | | |
| Official capital flows, MLT, net | 455 | | 12 | | -8 | | 459 |
| Private capital flows, MLT, net | 123 | | | | | | 123 |
| Direct Foreign Investment | 56 | | | 20 | | | 76 |
| Short Term Capital Flows | 23 | | | | | | 23 |
| Errors and Omissions | -11 | | | | | | -11 |
| Capital Account Balance | 646 | 646 | 658 | 678 | 670 | 670 | 670 |
| | | | | | | | |
| Overall Balance | -60 | -50 | -50 | -40 | -53 | -53 | -53 |
| Financed by: Use of reserves (excl. IMF) | 60 | 50 | 50 | 40 | 53 | 53 | 53 |
| Change in IMF position | 0 | | | | | | 0 |

## An Important Point on the Transfer of Resources:

Real resources can be transferred to developing countries only by their having an increase in imports, which is financed by the disbursements of official aid. If aid comes as a grant, there is no major impact on the balance of payments. However, if aid comes as a loan, it is recorded in the capital account. Therefore, there needs to be a deficit in the current account that has to be financed. Financing deficits with long-term concessional aid flows is not necessarily dangerous, provided the economy and exports grow sufficiently to meet future debt service obligations. In fact, advising LDCs to eliminate their current account deficit would be tantamount to telling them to stop accepting aid inflows in the form of loans. Massive short term borrowings to finance a current account deficit, of course, would be dangerous as it would lead to unsustainable debt service burden in the near future.

# CHAPTER XIII

# THE MACRO-ECONOMICS OF DEVELOPMENT: EXCHANGE RATES, INFLATION, SAVINGS

"By a continuing process of inflation, governments can confiscate, secretly and unobserved, an important part of the wealth of their citizens."

—John Maynard Keynes

## Exchange Rates and Development

The exchange rate is a critical factor in determining trade outcomes. The original goal of the post WW-II world was to establish a system of fixed exchange rates, supported by assistance from the International Monetary Fund, which would supply reserves to ease temporary problems, or provide counsel on how the need to devalue to a new or more appropriate exchange rate. This created a role for the IMF to advise on general macro-economic policies, but particularly those such as inflation, which had an adverse impact on the nominal fixed exchange rate, or taxes on exports which limited foreign exchange earnings. In general, LDCs tended to have overvalued exchange rates because they were reluctant to undertake the painful process of devaluation, and because the exchange rate itself became a symbol of national value (e.g. devaluation makes our currency worthless).

In the modern era of flexible or floating exchange rates, the role of the IMF continues as an advisor on macro-management and exchange rates, and few countries adhere to a rigid fixed rate. It provides large amounts of short-term resources to countries facing difficult transitions from the effects of various economic crises, and its approval of a program of support provides a stamp of approval that assures other lenders that a country has a sound macro-economic program. It also has been a major voice in removing trade and exchange rate restrictions. As more and more countries adopt a "Washington Consensus"—type reforms (constrained budget deficits, liberalized trade, limited monetary expansion), the role of the IMF has been more limited and less necessary.[114] However, the interplay between exchange rates, inflation, interest rates and growth remains critical.

In the previous chapter, we have seen how comparative advantage works out so that each country gains from trade, even if one does not have an absolute advantage in any one product. The example there was done in labor units, not currency. What is the role of the exchange rate in determining the balance of trade?

The doctrine of comparative advantage is really about comparative costs of production, reflecting unequal factor endowments. In practice how does comparative advantage get translated into price signals that generate trade along comparative advantage lines? Imagine another example of two countries, named Mexico and the US, trading only two commodities, shirts and computers.

**Table 13.1 Example of Trade and Exchange Rate Interaction**
(costs of production in local currency, Mexico and US
x- rate= exchange rate, Mexican pesos per US $)

| | **x-rate= 1:1** (P/$) | **Shirts** | **Computers** | |
|---|---|---|---|---|
| Period I | Mexico | 10.00 | 5,000 | |
| | United States | 5.00 | 1,000 | |
| Period II | **x-rate = 2.5:1** (P/$) | | | |
| | Mexico | $ 4.00 | $ 2,000 | Prices in US $ |
| | United States | $ 5.00 | $ 1,000 | |
| | **x-rate= 2.5:1** (P/$) | | | Prices in Mexican Pesos (P) |
| | Mexico | P 10.00 | P 5,000 | |
| | United States | P 12.50 | P 2,500 | |

Initially, there is no reason to trade because at an exchange rate of 1:1, the United States can produce both shirts and computers more cheaply than Mexico (first two lines of Table 13.1). However, given the

114 It is interesting to note the revived role of the IMF in the weaker Euro zone countries where the option of currency devaluation is not available (Ireland, Greece).

ability to trade, residents of Mexico will quickly start trying to acquire goods from United States, because they are cheaper. To do this, they need US dollars, since people in the US will not accept Mexican pesos as payment. The result is a bidding war for dollars, which drives up the exchange rate, which is effectively a devaluation of Mexico's currency in terms of the US dollar. In the fictitious example in Table 13.1, an exchange rate of 2.5:1 produces an equilibrium where shirts are relatively cheaper in Mexico, and computers are relatively cheaper in the US. The result will be a trade; Americans will buy Mexican shirts and sell American computers to Mexico. The 2.5 exchange rate is only an example; the exact rate will depend on the volume of trade in each commodity, plus all other factors that affect the supply and demand of foreign exchange (transfers, factor payments, capital flows, etc.). The final result, however, will be an equilibrium where the exchange rate balances the supply and demand for foreign exchange (see fig. 13.1). This example is very simple, and abstracts from the complexities of multi-product and multi-country trade in the real world. The main point is that there is an equilibrium exchange rate that balances supply and demand, and reflects comparative cost differentials. In a sense, the exchange rate turns comparative advantage into an absolute advantage.

**Fig 13.1 Demand and Supply of Foreign Exchange in Me co**
(demand for FX comes from Import demand, supply of FX comes from exports)

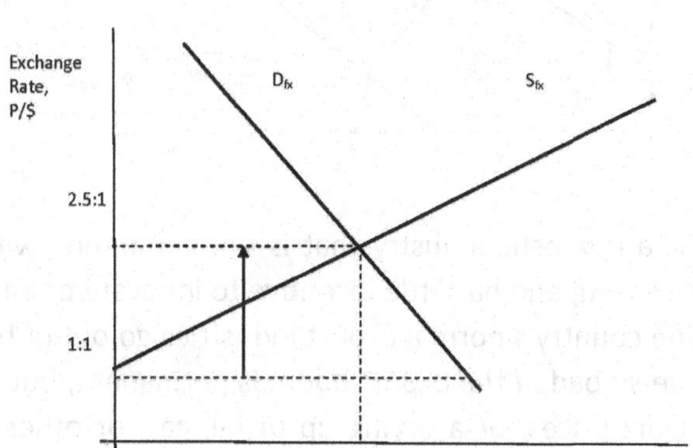

## Dutch Disease—too Much of a Good Thing

Equilibrium exchange rates can be distorted by a number of factors. One common problem is the sudden rise in export earnings, coming from, for instance, a sudden discover of oil or mineral deposits generating large export revenues. This is often called "Dutch Disease ", because of the impact of major natural gas exports on the economy of the Netherlands in the 1960s. The problem is one that large foreign exchange earnings cause an appreciation of the exchange rate, making survival difficult for other export industries. As shown in 13.2, the initial position is in balance, with domestic industries producing export goods to match import demand. In stage II, we add a large export from an oil discovery, which causes the exchange rate to appreciate. The appreciation is so extensive, that oil exports cover all import demand, and there is no incentive for domestic production for world markets. Domestic producers focus on "non-tradables", mostly local services, construction, and local foods not sold on world markets.

Fig. 13. 2 Impact of "Dutch Disease" on Country X
(XR = exchange rate, units of X currency per $)

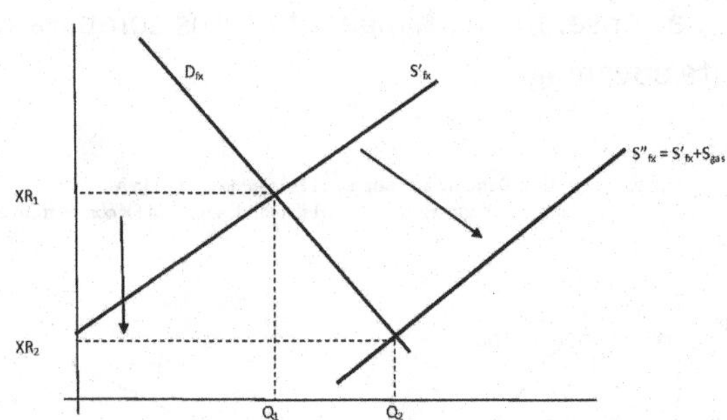


The result is a domestic industry that is not competing with other producers of the world, and has little incentive to innovate or adopt new technologies. The country's normal export industries go out of business. This might not be so bad, if the export boom is permanent, but few are. A decline in export prices, or a drying up of oil, gas, or other mineral resources, could lead to the need to make painful adjustments back to the initial position. Recognizing that export booms might be temporary, countries are often wise to put a lid on exchange rate appreciation. This can be done by taxes on the booming sector, or Central Bank purchases of foreign exchange to build reserves. The latter policy, however, expands the money supply, so additional steps have to be taken to prevent an inflationary impact, through tighter monetary policy.

The effect can be generalized to countries which have abundant natural resources, not just boom in commodity prices or sudden discoveries. Ironically, richly endowed countries like Nigeria, Philippines, and Brazil have not done nearly so well in terms of economic development as countries with limited natural resources, such as Korea, Japan, and Singapore. Jeffery Sachs and Andrew Warner did a careful analysis of growth experiences, introducing a variable for the share of natural resource exports to GDP. Again, using multiple regression panel data techniques, they found that countries with higher levels of natural resource exports in 1970 tended to grow more slowly in the subsequent 1970-1990 period. This relationship was found to be true even after controlling for many variables that were found to be important for growth in other studies (such as Barro's).[115]

## Real Exchange Rates

Any nominal exchange rate can be affected by the combination of inflation in the local economy, as well as inflation in other countries. Higher prices in the outside world mean that a country's exports are more attractive, to the extent production costs are determined by non-tradable items, such as labor. The effect is the same as a devaluation of the domestic currency. If there is equilibrium in the foreign exchange market at 2.5:1 (as in Table 13.1), but nominal prices in the US suddenly double, there will be a huge demand for the now cheap goods of Mexico which have not changed in price. If exchange rates are free to move, the real exchange rate will be restored, but the nominal exchange rate will have doubled (thus maintaining the real exchange rate). The formula for the real exchange rate, RER, is given as (where NER is the nominal exchange rate):

$$RER = NER\ (P_t/P_n)$$

[115] Jeffery Sachs and Andrew Warner, "Natural Resource Abundance and Economic Growth",Harvard University, Cambridge MA, November, 1997. Available at: http://www.cid.harvard.edu/ciddata/warner_files/natresf5.pdf

where $P_t$ is the price index of tradables, and $P_n$ is a price index of non-tradables. In practice, it is impossible to calculate prices of a country's tradables and non-tradables, so economists substitute the domestic price index for the price of non-tradables, and the US CPI for the prices of tradables (on the assumption that the RER is being calculated with reference to the U.S. dollar). So we have (where uscpi is the consumer price index for US and xcpi for country x):

$$RER = NER\ (P_{uscpi}/P_{xcpi})$$

When prices rise abroad, the amount of foreign goods one can buy with a unit of domestic currency declines, so the exchange rate devalues, and RER rises. Conversely, domestic inflation, by raising domestic prices, causes exchange rate appreciation. Exports will suffer because their production costs are rising, while foreign goods will be more attractive as imports. Movements by $P_t$ and $P_n$ can be offset by changes in the nominal exchange rate. It is not entirely clear what the RER is measuring or shows. In countries with managed exchange rates, it can indicate that the authorities are not allowing the nominal rate to devalue in line with relative inflation, causing an appreciation of the real rate. In a country with flexible exchange rates, it is not clear what it means. For instance, we know that RERs tend to appreciate over time as countries develop, so while it may be an indicator of a domestic imbalance, it is not absolute proof.

## Macro Management

In an open economy, changes in external trade and capital flows impact on the money supply, inflation and adjustment. The reason for this is that an imbalance in the balance of payments is resolved by reserve movements. As mentioned above, this results in a change in the money supply. Exporters turn in foreign exchange earnings to the Central Bank (directly or through dealers and commercial banks) and get domestic currency equivalent. The Central Bank in turn sells foreign exchange to importers for domestic currency, thus producing a return flow of domestic currency and no net change in the money supply. Likewise with capital inflows and outflows, but for the sake of simplicity, we will ignore these. Then, the growth of the money supply ($M_t$) in period t, is a function of that part of the government deficit which is financed by the Central Bank, $G_{def}$ plus the gap between exports and imports (X-M), or:

$$M_t = G_{def} + (X\text{-}M) + M_{t\text{-}1}.$$

The price level is assumed to be a function of the size of the money supply, GDP, and the velocity of money (v), or:

$$P = v(M_t)/GDP$$

In a purely open economy, imbalances in the balance of payments tend to be self correcting. A splurge in exports will increase the money supply, causing inflation, which in turn causes an appreciation of the real exchange rate. The appreciation of the rate reduces exports and increases imports, thus restoring the balance at a new price level and with new nominal and real exchange rates.

The problem is the system may not work smoothly in both directions. A surge in imports would result in a smaller money supply, and a deflation of domestic prices, and a devaluation of the real exchange rate. Exports would rise and imports fall. However, this would mean a decline in the prices of non-tradables, particularly wages. As Keynes pointed out many years ago, nominal wages tend to be sticky downwards; that is, workers, especially unions, resist reductions in nominal wages. The result could be unemployment, and a decline in output, rather than the restoration of a new equilibrium at full employment. The easier way to reduce real wages is with inflation, but that creates more problems.

## Inflation

The main challenge in macro-management is the control of inflation. Governments find it easier to use deficit financing of the budget rather than raising taxes. Some increase annually in the money supply is needed in a growing economy, and some of the deficit can be financed by borrowing from the private sector, which tend to be somewhat less inflationary. Some writers see inflation as good for growth, in that it helps maintain demand and full employment. Early writers on development saw inflation as a convenient tax on savings, one that could be a mechanism for the transfer of resources from banks to the coffers of the government, and be used for the famous "big push". In Latin America, inflation was used to reduce real wages. Government would give large nominal wage increases, but then permit inflation to erode real wages back to some more competitive level. The problem was that unions soon saw what was happening, and the result was larger and larger demands for nominal wage increases, and spiraling inflation that soon became uncontrollable. Some of the worse cases were Bolivia, where inflation reached 12,000% in 1985, and Nicaragua, with inflation of over 13,000% in 1988.[116]

In an era of fixed exchange rates, inflation was the main culprit leading to exchange rate misalignment. IMF missions dialogued with countries about how to control budget deficits and to implement monetary policy to prevent inflation from undermining the nominal exchange rate. If all else failed, then the IMF would suggest (demand?) a devaluation, but devaluations were traumatic affairs, and could lead to speculation against the exchange rate, capital flight, and inflation.

While countries have mostly adopted flexible exchange rate systems (managed float, free float, etc.), the IMF continues to serve as a macro-economic watchdog preaching the evils of inflation and the need for macro stability. But what is the evidence of the impact of inflation on growth? Fig. 13.3 shows a scatter diagram of inflation rates on GDP growth rates, taken from the work by Bruno and Easterly[117].

---

[116] Based on data from World Bank, WDI, for annual change in GDP deflator.

[117] Michael Bruno and William Easterly, "Inflation Crises and Long-Run Growth", Journal of Monetary Economics 41 (February, 1998), pp. 3-26.

Fig. 13.3 Inflation and Growth

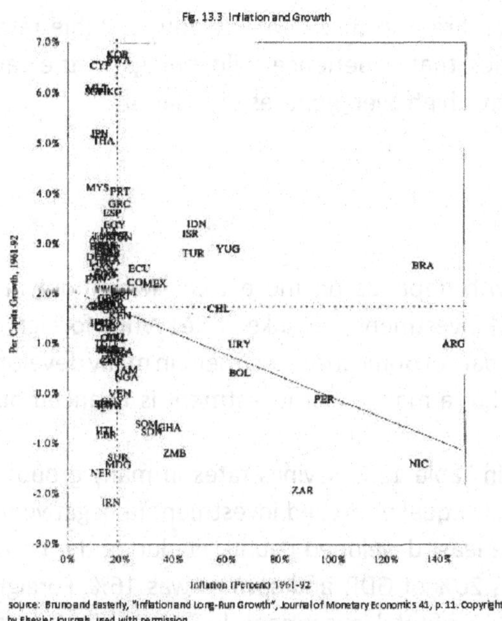


Source: Bruno and Easterly, "Inflation and Long-Run Growth", Journal of Monetary Economics 41, p. 11. Copyright by Elsevier Journals, used with permission

What Fig 13.3 shows is that most countries have an inflation rate of about 10-20%. There is a definite negative association between inflation and growth; more inflation, less growth. However, these correlations are heavily influenced by a few outliers such as Zaire, Nicaragua, Peru, Brazil and Argentina, all with average rates of inflation of over 100% per year during a 30 year period (1961-92). In fact, Bruno and Easterly's research showed that there was no correlation between inflation and growth if countries with inflation over 40% per annum were dropped from the sample. Defining an inflation crisis as a time of inflation over 40%, they also found that while pre-crisis conditions often led to a decline in growth, there was surprisingly strong recover afterwards. In fact, there was some evidence that growth might be higher in the post-crisis period than in the pre-crisis period. Thus, their research cuts both ways. There seems to be nothing gained from reducing inflation if it is already below 40%. However, it is also true that there is no evidence that policies that promote stabilization reduce growth.

One reason why inflation may have no effect on growth is the ability of key actors in the economy (producers, consumers) to adjust to inflation, if it is steady and predictable. It is the wild swings in inflation that are costly because they unexpected. However, it is also true that countries with low average inflation are also those with relatively stable rates of inflation; that is, countries that experience wild swings in the rate of inflation typically also have high average rates of inflation.

## Savings

While growth depends on more than investment, it remains true that capital and investment play a key role. While foreign capital inflows provide a good part of domestic investment in many developing countries, it is also true that a majority of investment is financed out of domestic savings.

As shown in Table 13.2, savings rates in many groups of developing countries actually equal or exceed investment (a negative means a capital outflow). In the least developed countries, during the period 1995-2004, investment was 20% of GDP, and savings was 16%. Foreign capital flows financed only 20% of total investment. In Europe and Central Asia, foreign capital financed only about 5% of investment, and about 10% in South Asia.

**Table 13.2 Savings and Investment Rates**
Average 1995-2004
(% of GDP)

| Group | S/Y | I/Y | Resource gap |
|---|---|---|---|
| East Asia/Pacific+ | 35.9 | 32.9 | -3.0 |
| Europe/Central Asia | 21.2 | 22.6 | 1.4 |
| South Asia | 35.9 | 32.9 | 3.0 |
| Sub-Saharan Africa | 16.2 | 18.3 | 2.1 |
| Middle East/N. Africa | 26.5 | 23.8 | -2.7 |
| | | | |
| Low Income | 22.8 | 22.8 | 0.0 |
| Lower Middle Income | 28.8 | 27.6 | -1.2 |
| Upper Middle Income | 22.1 | 21.7 | -.4 |
| High Income | 20.9 | 21.2 | .3 |
| | | | |
| Least Developed | 16.1 | 20.0 | 3.9 |
| Source: calculated from World Bank, WDI data bank. | | | |

Total savings available for investment is the sum of domestic savings $S_d$ plus foreign capital flows, F, which is essentially a transfer of foreign savings. In an open economy, investment equals savings plus the foreign capital inflow, or:

$$I = S_d + F$$

While domestic savings can be divided into public savings ($S_g$), and private savings($S_p$):

$$S_d = S_g + S_p$$

Public savings is simply the difference between government revenue and government current consumption expenditure. If government savings are inadequate, the gap is filled by borrowings from the private sector or foreign borrowing. Private saving is composed of savings of households and of corporations. In reality, most governments generate little savings, particularly in low income countries, and a large part of investment expenditures are financed by foreign aid or domestic borrowing. In very poor countries, the government investment program is almost dictated by the kinds of foreign assistance available, and while the government nominally has an investment plan, in reality it is the sum of the projects approved by foreign donors.

In national income accounting, we know that:

$$Y = C + I - M + X;$$

Where Y is GDP, C is consumption, I is investment, M are imports and X are exports. This can be rewritten as:

$$I = Y - C + M - X.$$

Since Y - C equals domestic savings, we get the following:

$$I = S + M - X,$$

Where M - X is the current account balance, and therefore:

$$S = I - (M - X).$$

In constructing national income accounts, it is relatively easy to obtain estimates of imports and exports, because foreign trade is monitored at the border and by the Central Bank. Investment can usually be estimated by a combination of imports of capital equipment and an estimate of construction activity. Total GDP is estimated from surveys on the output side of agriculture, industry, government, etc. This means that any estimate of S is a residual, it is not estimated directly but by subtracting from GDP the estimates of the other parts. As a residual, estimates of savings include a true measure of savings, plus errors in the estimates of all the other variables. For this reason, measures of savings from the national income accounts have to be treated skeptically.

As can be seen from Table 13.2, low income countries tend to have lower savings rates, compared to middle income and high income countries. However, the relationship is far from exact, as indicated by Fig. 13.4, which shows a scatter diagram of per capita gross national income and gross savings rates. While the trend line shows a positive relationship with income, the correlation is low and there are many countries far off the line. Variations in savings rates also parallel variations in investment rates, and factors affecting investment also affect savings. Countries with high savings, and high investment, do not necessarily grow faster, because growth depends on the quality of investment, as well as other factors, as we have seen in the previous chapters.

Fig. 13.4 **Savings Rates and Gross National Per Capita Income, 2006**

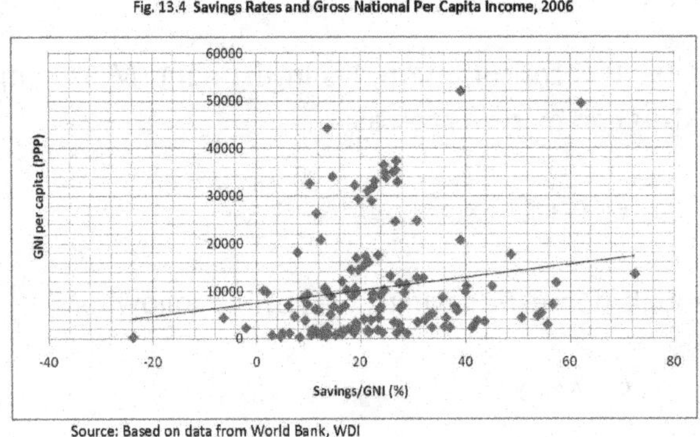


Source: Based on data from World Bank, WDI

There are many motives for savings. People save as a hedge against loss of income, and/or because they recognize that their income is variable or seasonal (such as in farming). People save against the time when they will be too old to work. There is a life cycle element to savings: young people are often net dissavers, borrowing in the early years of their lives. They become net savers during their productive middle years, and then net dissavers in later years (see Fig 13.5). Savings can be discouraged if there are no safe facilities for holding money without losing their value.

Hence, many poor people in developing countries lack access to banks, or distrust banks, and put their savings into tangible assets, such as gold jewelry, or hide cash in their houses. Even bank deposits can be risky, if a country's financial sector is unregulated, and bank failures are common. Savings can be eroded in years of high inflation, when interest rates fall below the rate of inflation (negative real interest rates).

## The Financial Sector

A good financial sector can move money from savers to investors, and do it efficiently. A weak or underdeveloped financial sector, faced with many risks and uncertainties, can result in low interest rates on savings and high interest rates for loans (high spreads). Thus, financial sector development is an important aspect of overall development, and more developed countries tend to have more developed financial sectors, with more sophisticated institutions (including not only banks, but insurance companies, stock exchanges, investment bankers, etc.). Measuring financial sector development is not easy. One common measure is simply the ratio of the money supply to GDP, on the idea that development brings more people into the money economy. This is a very gross measure, and it is not clear what it is measuring. It is also not clear what concept of "money" should be used; $M_1$, which is cash and demand deposits, $M_2$ which is $M_1$ plus savings and small time deposits, or $M_3$, defined as $M_2$ plus large time deposits. However, we also know that the ratio of money to GDP can vary between countries, based on such factors as the use of credit cards (not counted as money), or the desire to hoard cash at home or in bank vaults. Financial development can actually reduce the motivation to save. Easy access to credit reduces the need to save as a precaution against lost income. In the United States, private savings rates have dropped to extremely low levels, about 1-2% of GDP in 2008 (although rising during the recent economic crisis).

The Government itself can affect private savings. David Ricardo argued that an increase in public savings would result in an equivalent reduction in private savings. This is called **Ricardian Equivalence.** Stanley Please, a former World Bank economist, argued that raising taxes often resulted in lower savings, since Governments often used tax revenue to finance current consumption, while the reduction in taxpayer income resulted in their reducing saving (as well as consumption). This phenomenon is known as the **Please Effect.** Furthermore, if people save to cover old age insecurity, a Government financed social security system will reduce the incentive for private savings. If the Government system is "pay as you go" (meaning no net savings in the system), then the overall effect could be less total savings in the economy.

**Fig 13.5 Life Cycle Savings**
( Saving % of Income, typical Household)

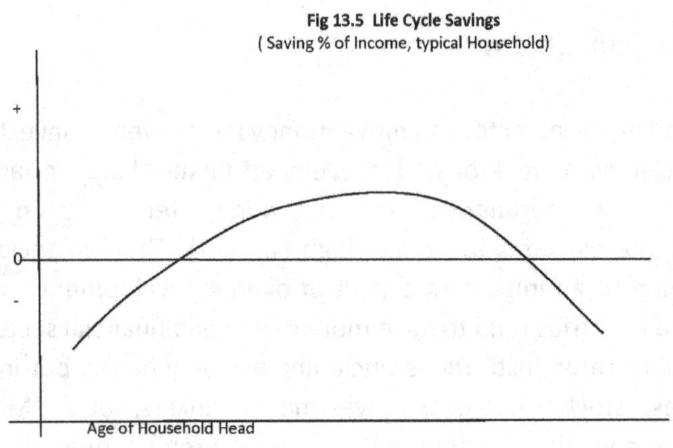


In theory, the interest rate on savings should also be a factor in determining the rate of savings. A person has to trade off between present consumption ($C_0$) and future consumption ($C_t$), but future consumption will be greater since it includes the interest earned on savings. Future consumption in period t will equal savings in the present (year 0), plus return on savings (r) compounded, or:

$$C_t = S_0 (1 + r)^t$$

But the present value of $C_t$, $PVC_t$, will depend on how much value present consumption has over future consumption. The consumer will discount future consumption by some discount rate, d, which reflects his or her rate of time preference. Thus,

$$PVC_t = C_t / (1 + d)^t$$

Thus if $PVC_t > C_0$ then a person would save, and if $PVC_t < C_0$, person would consume. The question boils down to whether or not d is greater than, or less than, the rate of interest r, on savings. In fact, in most countries, developed and developing, the interest rate is only weakly a factor in determining savings. In LDCs, many people lack access to reliable financial instruments that they can count on to earn a promised return. In this case, the $C_t = S_0 (1 + r)^t$ should be rewritten to include a risk factor that the anticipated savings may not be there in the future.

Savings can also depend on the growth of income. If households consider increases in income to be temporary, they may save these increases, as a precaution against an eventual decline. Households may consider some income to be "permanent" and some "transitory". In a period of rapid growth, they may not immediately recognize that income increases are permanent, and their consumption may rise more slowly than income. By the same token, a decline in income may result in dissaving—maintaining past consumption levels by using past saving or borrowing. Thus, saving may be positively related to the rate of growth.

Sebastian Edwards[118] has examined why savings rates differ across countries, and what determines savings. He uses instrumental variables in order to separate out the cause and effect of savings on such things as growth of GDP. His regression results for developing countries are shown in table 13.3.

**Table 13.3 Edwards: Determinants of Private Savings**
instrumental variables, panel data

| | | Results for LDC group | | |
|---|---|---|---|---|
| | coefficient. | t-statistic | coeff. | t-statistic |
| Age Dependency | -.281 | (-2.684) | -.056 | (-1.206) |
| Urban | -.087 | (-1.086) | -.120 | ( 3.229) |
| Government Savings | -.650 | (-2.645) | -.359 | ( 3.483) |
| Social Security | -.563 | (-4.400) | -.116 | (-1.531) |
| Growth Per Capita | .877 | (2.835) | .521 | ( 2.805) |
| GDP per Capita | - | - | 1.10E-03 | ( 2.152) |
| Money/GDP | .652 | (3.286) | .289 | ( 3.490) |
| Real Interest Rate | - | - | -.038 | (-1.104) |
| Current Account | .564 | (1.846) | .625 | (2.785) |
| Inflation | .671 | (1.020) | -- | -- |
| Political Instability | -1.720 | (3.361) | -- | -- |
| | $R^2$=.401 | n=90 | $R^2$=.605 | n=100 |

Source: Sebastian Edwards, "Why Are Savings Rates So Different Across Countries"? NBER Working Paper No. 5097, April 1995, Table 2. Copyright 1995 by Sebastian Edwards.

118 Sebastian Edwards, "Why Are Savings Rates So Different Across Countries"? NBER Working Paper No. 5097, (April, 1995)

Edwards' findings are as follows:

- per capita growth is one of the most important determinants or both private and public savings, reinforcing the permanent income hypothesis;
- savings is higher in countries with lower dependency ratios;
- public savings, and the operation of a social security system, tend to lower private savings (but less than a one-to-one fashion);
- savings do not respond to the level of real interest rates;
- financial sector development is correlated with higher levels of saving;
- political instability tends to reduce private savings, and
- greater use of foreign savings (larger current account deficit) tends to reduce private savings (but again, not on a one-to-one basis).

Savings seems to be a two way street: higher savings finances investment, which promotes growth, but growth itself generates more savings. This may explain how countries continue to grow and avoid the Solow "steady state", and is a direct link to the idea of endogenous growth. Interestingly, inflation does not seem to have a material influence on savings rates. However, borrowing from abroad tends to discourage or replace private savings. Thus, the impact of savings in terms of increasing investment is more muted, and the impact of foreign aid in terms of promoting growth is undercut. However, the role of foreign assistance in promoting growth and development is more complex, and we turn to this topic in the next chapter.

## Financial Sector and Savings

In theory, a well developed an efficient financial sector can facilitate investment by channeling savings to investors by accepting deposits and making loans. The financial sector is broader than just banks, but includes finance corporations, micro-credit groups, insurance companies, the stock market, and other non-bank financial intermediaries.

Entrepreneurs the world over, including developed countries, always complain about the high cost and/or lack of availability of credit. But the fact is that people who complain about a lack of credit are often poor risks in terms of making repayments. Initial development efforts in most LDCs started with government not only building industries but also establishing one or more commercial banks, and one or more development banks designed to make longer term loans for industry and agriculture (typically one bank for each sector). In addition, private banks were "directed" to make a certain percentage of their lending in rural areas and/or in agriculture, and/or for small scale establishments. In many cases, ceilings were placed on the interest rates that could be charged, as well.

Many of the development banks were established with assistance and advice from the World Bank. The sad experience of these development banks is that eventually they almost all went bankrupt. Why? In part because lending decisions were politically determined rather than being based on careful financial/economic analysis. However, even when this was not the case, government officials running banks were often not capable of determining who was a good credit risk, and who was not. In addition, the public often had the attitude that since this was a government institution, repayment was not necessary, and government officials were reluctant to foreclose on private sector operators, particularly if these operators were politically well connected.

But private bankers in developing countries often had some of the same problems, particularly when forced to make loans in sectors and to people with which they lacked familiarity and/or lacked adequate collateral to back up the loan. This problem is labeled as one of *asymmetric information*. The borrower knows very well his capacity to repay the loan, but the lender does not. One side has more information than the other, and is another classic case of market failure. If lenders had perfect information, they would target loans to good credit risks, thus making more credit available to those that need and can use it. Without perfect information, lending falls short of what is socially optimum. In many countries, directed lending and interest rate controls proved very costly to private banks, ultimately leading to financial crises, and bankruptcies. With the structural reforms pushed in the 1980s, most of these practices were done away with, and most of the government run development banks were closed.

In parallel to the labor market, there is a duality to the financial market in most LDCs. There is a formal credit market run largely by commercial banks, which offers shorter term loans to large businesses that are able to offer collateral (e.g. a lien on real estate, machinery, etc.). Then there is an extensive informal market, particularly in rural areas, that offers short term loans usually at very high interest rates, often without any collateral requirements. Lenders in this market overcome the asymmetric information problem because they only lend to people they know in their immediate community. They know from experience who is capable and trustworthy, and who is not. The informal market consists of various operators, including village money lenders, pawnshops, and agricultural suppliers and processors who advance seed and fertilizer on credit (often requiring that the farmer sell his harvest to him/her, from which is deducted the initial loan, plus interest). Short term credit is often used to bridge the gap between the time when food supplies held by farmers run out, and new crops are harvested, and may run only 2-3 months. Interest rates, however, may be as high as 100-300%, when calculated on an annual basis.

Many commentators rail against "exorbitant" interest rates and "exploitative" money lenders, calling for government intervention and/or control. From an economist standpoint, this raises some interesting questions. If interest rates charged are truly exorbitant, then money lenders must be making huge profits. If money lenders are making huge profits, then this should attract others to enter this business which seems so lucrative, increase the supply of funds available, and drive down interest rates. Why does this not happen? There are two possible answers:

1. The costs of lending are high, the repayment rate to money lenders is not all that great, and given the amount of capital at stake, their returns or their overall profit level is not attractive for further entry. In addition, village money lenders face problems of *systemic risk*, as well as *idiosyncratic risk*. While the money lender can handle the failure of one farmer who does not repay (idiosyncratic risk), they will be bankrupt if the village endures a drought, flood, etc. which causes all crops to fail and all farmers cannot repay. Thus to survive, they must make large profits in good times to be able to have reserves against periodic systemic crises.
2. There are barriers to entry that outsiders have a difficult time overcoming. The chief one being that the money lender knows his people; the outsider does not. A new money lender will

typically lend to those people that the traditional money lender has rejected (for good reasons). Again, information is asymmetric. In addition, there can be social barriers to entry; people may not want to borrow money from an "outsider" particularly if that person is from and different ethnic or religious group.

Economic research has not yet conclusively confirmed the answer to this problem, and there are few studies of the economics of informal money lenders. A study of money lenders in the Sind region of Pakistan by Irfan Aleem[119] offers some interesting insights. Aleem finds that in the village used for his study, entry by money lenders was possible, and indeed new money lenders appeared during the study. He found that the implicit interest rates charged reflected their costs of operating in this risky market, including costs for screening lenders, pursuing delinquent loans, overhead, and the cost of capital, suggesting that lender's charges were equal to their average cost of lending. While this conclusion may not be valid in all parts of the world, it does suggest that informal credit markets are relatively efficient and not exploitative, given the risks and the costs faced by the money lenders[120].

## The Micro-Finance Revolution

Against this background, we have the growth of micro-finance. Pioneered by such people as Muhammed Yunnus[121] (Grameen Bank) in Bangladesh, various micro-finance organizations have been successful in making very small loans without collateral at moderate interest

119 Irfan Aleem, "Imperfect Information, Screening, and the Costs of Informal Lending: A Study of a Rural Credit Market in Pakistan", *World Bank Economic Review* 4(3), pp. 329-349.

120 Evidence from Bangladesh shows that in areas where micro-credit programs are effective, the result is higher interest rates by informal lenders, presumably because micro-credit operations are taking away the better credit risks. See Debdulal Mallick, "Microfinance and Moneylender Interest Rate: Evidence from Bangladesh" MPRA Paper No. 17800 (May, 2009). Available online at: http://mpra.ub.uni-muenchen.de/17800/

121 Yunnus and Grameen Bank won the Nobel Peace Prize in 2006.

rates. How do they do it? The model used by Grameen is based on group responsibility. Small groups of neighbors are organized, and they determine who will receive credit. Furthermore, the group accepts responsibility for repayment, pressuring the recipient in case she/he falls behind in payments. The failure to repay by one person means the other members of the group are not eligible for a loan. Typically, these are very small loans made to women to make small investments (cows, cell phones, sewing machines), with which they can earn extra money. Women have a much better record of repayment, and profits earned by them are more likely to be invested in the family (better food, school supplies, health care). For Grameen, 98% of loan recipients are women, but the ratio is somewhat lower for other groups, indicating that not all men are bad risks.

While many of these organizations are NGOs[122], it is clear that the sector is composed of a variety of similar organizations, including not-for-profit banks, government banks, and community self-help organizations, as well as NGOs.[123] While micro-credit organizations point to their high repayment rates, the fact remains that making small loans is very costly. Most NGO microcredit organizations are not financially self sufficient. Cull et. al. estimate that NGOs subsidize every loan by $233, and even then have only a 3% return on equity. The more commercially oriented institutions (microbanks) are more likely to be self sufficient, but generally make larger loans which are more profitable. Most NGOs are receiving grants and or capital funds from donors at zero or very low interest rates, which is the source of the subsidy. The average interest rate for NGOs is about 27%; for microbanks about 13%.[124]

When it comes to "magic bullets", microcredit is right up there with the best of them, and has several "messianic" advocates. It undoubtedly has had a substantial impact on many poor people, and it particularly liberating for women as a means of improving their earning power, and thereby their worth and independence. However, it is not the miracle

---

122 NGO = Non Government Organization. This is a misnomer; these are really non-profit organizations, but the term NGO is commonly used.

123 Robert Cull, Asli Demirguc-Kunt and Jonathan Murdock, "Microfinance Meets the Market" *Journal of Economic Perspectives* 23 (Winter 2009), pp.167-192.

124 Cull et. al., Op. cit.

that will end poverty or accelerate overall growth, and it does illustrate that making very small loans to poor people is costly even with group responsibility. Many NGOs, in fact, try to hide the fact that their operations continue to be subsidized (esp. Grameen). Nevertheless, it is an extremely useful activity that helps bring poor people into the modern economy, and provide a way for them to move up the economic ladder to a better standard of living.

# CHAPTER XIV

# ECONOMIC ASSISTANCE FOR DEVELOPMENT

*Foreign aid is neither a failure nor a panacea. It is, instead, an important tool of American policy that can serve the interests of the United States and the world if wisely administered.*

—Lee H. Hamilton

Before World War II, governmental international economic assistance was directed to the development of a nation's colonies, so that they could better function as suppliers of raw materials. Such assistance included the development of infrastructure, justice and government administration, and other basic services. Colonies paid for these services from taxes on their exports, either implicitly or explicitly, but many colonial powers complained nevertheless that colonies were often a losing proposition. In addition, independent countries (such as in Latin America) borrowed from private capital markets to finance infrastructure and industrialization, and some private capital flowed to less developed countries via foreign direct investment. Foreign assistance, as we know it today, did not exist.

In the post WW-II era, foreign assistance to former colonies and other independent developing countries came into full bloom[125]. The Bretton Woods conference in 1944 sought to establish the framework of international economic relations in the post war era. It included the establishment of the International Monetary Fund, which was designed to support a system of stable exchange rates based on gold, and the

[125] The term foreign aid can mean cover both military and economic assistance. References in this chapter to aid refer only to economic assistance.

International Bank for Reconstruction and Development (World Bank), which was designed to assist in the reconstruction of Europe and, later, the development of the newly emerging developing countries. The advent of the "Cold War" (post 1947), and the difficulties of organizing the World Bank, gave birth to the famous "Marshall Plan" under which the United States pledged massive amounts of money (up to 3% of its GDP) for the reconstruction of Europe. The motivation of the Marshall Plan was mainly to prevent Western European countries from falling under the Communist Bloc. Whatever its motivation, it did succeed in providing a major assist to the rebuilding and restoration of the economies of Western Europe. The very success of the Marshall Plan, however, led to the belief that similar amounts of aid to LDCs would have a similar rapid impact, financing a "big push" toward industrialization and modernization.

Aid giving, however, then and now has always combined a mixture of motives and objectives. These include:

- Political—a desire to win friends to a certain political persuasion, support friends and allies, and/ or induce support internationally (e.g. votes in the UN);
- Cultural Ties—a desire to maintain ties with former colonies and those with a similar cultural or linguistic background. Most aid from ex-colonial powers went to former colonies.
- Export Market Development—development of markets for the donor country's producers (achieved in many cases by "tying" aid procurement to donor country providers);
- Surplus Disposal—dispose of surplus agricultural products by gifting them to LDCs (often with a negative impact on domestic agriculture in recipient countries, discouraging local production);
- Peace—provide for development so as to achieve a community of countries living in peace, without instability that could spill over to the donor countries in the form of terrorism, immigration, etc.;
- Altruism—a genuine desire to eradicate poverty, promote economic growth, and close the gap between rich and poor countries, without any ulterior motive;
- Emergency Humanitarian—linked to the altruism objective, but a more immediate and short term responses to natural disasters (earthquake, flood, drought, war, etc.), not longer term development;

- Environment—help reduce negative impact on global public goods by limiting damage to shared resources (mainly aid and water). This would include assistance to reduce CFC emissions, curtail fishing of endangered species, limit deforestation, etc.

The United States was the prime provider in the early days of foreign assistance, but as European countries rebuilt, they also launched programs of foreign assistance. The U.S. encouraged other countries to develop programs, as part of "burden sharing", and was instrumental in the formation of the OECD (Organization for European Cooperation and Development) and its DAC (Development Assistance Committee). The DAC, in turn, developed a recommended target of economic assistance of 1% of GDP, which was later refined into a target of .7% of GDP in terms of concessionary assistance (ODA or Official Development Assistance). In fact, few countries have achieved this ODA target, and the U.S. performance (.18% in 2008) is one of the lowest (see Table 14.1). The average for the DAC countries in that same year was .30%, about half of the agreed target. However, because the U.S. has one of the largest economies, the total amount of U.S. aid, at about $26 billion in 2008, was still the largest among DAC members. To put U.S. assistance in perspective, one must remember that U.S. military spending was $495 billion in FY08, and US sales of cigarettes in 2005 were $75 billion. It is estimated that about half of US economic assistance in 2004-2006 went to just two countries: Iraq and Afghanistan.

**Table 14.1: Official Development Assistance, 2008**

| Country | Amount ($ millions) | ODA/GNI |
|---|---|---|
| Canada | 4.7 | .32 |
| Denmark | 2.8 | .82 |
| Germany | 13.9 | .38 |
| Japan | 9.4 | .18 |
| Netherlands | 7.0 | .80 |
| United Kingdom | 11.4 | .43 |
| United States | 26.0 | .18 |
| Total, DAC | 119.8 | .30 |
| Memo: US Defense spending, 2008 $494.8 billion (excluding spending on Iraq, Afghanistan) | | |

Source: OECD/DAC

As shown below (Fig.14.1), there is an upward trend in ODA in recent years, rising from a low of .22% in 2000 to .31% in 2008. As part of the Monterrey Accords reached in 2004 at the Monterrey Summit, the OECD countries agreed to increase ODA by $50 billion by 2010, of which $25 billion would go to Africa. This would raise the ODA performance to .35% by 2010, but recent allocations to not seem to be on pace to reach that target. A peak of .33% was reached in 2005, but much of this consisted of one-time debt relief.

**Fig 14.1 Trends in ODA, DAC Member Countries 1990-2008**

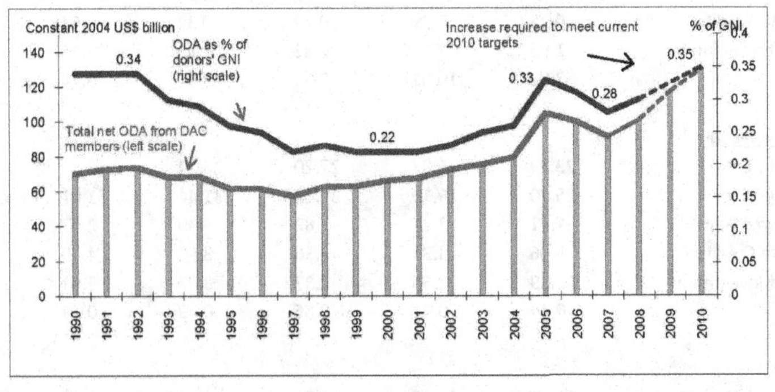


Source: World Bank, Global Monitoring Report, 2009, p.115, and the supplied data link in the Annex. Based on OECD data; figures for 2008 are preliminary, 2009 and 2010 are projections

Even so, ODA does not account for the dominant share of capital flows to many developing countries. ODA flows to middle income developing countries in 2008 (see Table 14.2) were only .3% of recipient country GDP, compared to 3.5% for private direct investment, and 3.3 % for private credits. In low income countries, ODA is more significant, equal to 9% of GDP in 2008 (thus financing about 60% of the resource gap). Country groups average individual country data, and can be misleading. For instance, China has a huge surplus of savings over investment, and an average savings rate of 50%. It does rely on private investment and private credits, but very little ODA, and is a net exporter of capital to the rest of the world. This helps explain why the aggregate total for middle income countries shows a surplus. Kenya, however, is more typical of developing countries. It has a total resource gap (Investment minus savings) of 14%, but over half of that is financed by transfers from abroad (private and official). Net ODA flows are equal to 4.5% of

GDP, and private flows about 3%. India is similar to Kenya, except that transfers and ODA are less important, and private direct investment and private credits constitute the bulk of the capital inflow. ODA represents only .17% of India's GDP.

**Table 14.2 Resource Gaps and Net Financial Flows, 2000-2008**
(% of GDP)

| Low Income | 2000 | 2004 | 2005 | 2006 | 2007 | 2008 |
|---|---|---|---|---|---|---|
| Investment | 19.39 | 20.63 | 22.25 | 22.57 | 23.84 | 24.38 |
| Savings | 10.77 | 10.40 | 10.10 | 10.75 | 10.83 | 9.33 |
| Resource Gap | 8.62 | 10.23 | 12.14 | 11.82 | 13.01 | 15.05 |
| Private Credits | 0.15 | 0.39 | 0.29 | 0.32 | 0.64 | 0.29 |
| Direct Investment | 1.65 | 2.54 | 2.32 | 2.65 | 4.15 | 3.97 |
| ODA | 7.03 | 10.51 | 9.59 | 9.41 | 9.44 | 9.26 |
| | | | | | | |
| Middle Income | | | | | | |
| Investment | 23.99 | 26.93 | 27.20 | 28.14 | 28.54 | 29.05 |
| Savings | 25.70 | 29.19 | 30.02 | 31.44 | 31.01 | 30.02 |
| Resource Gap | -1.71 | -2.27 | -2.82 | -3.30 | -2.47 | -0.97 |
| Private Credits | 3.06 | 3.31 | 3.56 | 3.56 | 4.19 | 3.22 |
| Direct Investment | 2.59 | 2.55 | 2.87 | 3.02 | 3.61 | 3.48 |
| ODA | 0.44 | 0.44 | 0.66 | 0.49 | 0.34 | 0.32 |
| | | | | | | |
| China | | | | | | |
| Investment | 35.12 | 43.26 | 43.61 | 43.64 | 41.73 | 42.55 |
| Savings | 37.53 | 45.81 | 49.14 | 51.33 | 50.50 | 50.24 |
| Resource Gap | -2.41 | -2.55 | -5.53 | -7.69 | -8.77 | -7.70 |
| Net Current Transfers | 0.53 | 1.19 | 1.12 | 1.07 | 1.10 | 1.01 |
| Private Credits | 0.92 | 1.12 | 1.20 | 0.84 | 0.96 | 0.76 |
| Direct Investment | 0.87 | 0.29 | 0.11 | 0.23 | 2.69 | 0.31 |
| ODA | 0.14 | 0.09 | 0.08 | 0.05 | 0.04 | 0.03 |
| | | | | | | |
| Kenya | | | | | | |
| Investment | 17.41 | 17.09 | 16.91 | 17.95 | 19.06 | 19.16 |
| Savings | 7.28 | 10.83 | 9.45 | 8.06 | 8.01 | 5.10 |
| Resource Gap | 10.13 | 6.26 | 7.46 | 9.89 | 11.05 | 14.06 |
| Net Current Transfers | 6.77 | 6.23 | 6.69 | 7.94 | 7.77 | 7.70 |
| Private Credits | 0.67 | 0.26 | 0.15 | 0.00 | 0.00 | 0.02 |
| Direct Investment | 0.78 | 0.80 | 0.91 | 2.14 | 2.04 | 3.39 |
| ODA | 4.01 | 4.09 | 4.02 | 4.19 | 4.88 | 4.48 |
| | | | | | | |
| India | | | | | | |
| Investment | 24.16 | 32.48 | 34.30 | 36.00 | 37.58 | 35.59 |
| Savings | 23.24 | 30.72 | 31.56 | 32.95 | 33.52 | 30.16 |
| Resource Gap | 0.92 | 1.76 | 2.74 | 3.05 | 4.06 | 5.44 |
| Net Current Transfers | 2.79 | 2.85 | 2.93 | 3.14 | 3.38 | 3.63 |
| Private Credits | 1.59 | 1.77 | 1.86 | 3.03 | 4.83 | 2.67 |

## Aid Modalities

Aid can be provided as a grant, or as a loan. Obviously, a loan is not a favorable as receiving assistance as a grant, since interest and principal must be paid. In practice, ODA loans have "concessional" terms, in that the interest rates are below market, so there is an implicit subsidy. Nevertheless it is difficult to compare ODA from different donors when each donor provides assistance on different terms. This can be overcome by converting loans into their grant equivalents. By discounting loan repayments by some discount rate, one can calculate how much the loan is a "gift". As long as the interest rate is below the discount rate, the NPV of the repayments will be less than the face value of the orginial loan. This gap is the grant element in the loan (see annex for detailed example). In general, only loans with at least a 25% grant element count as concessionary loans. To qualify as ODA, the purpose of the loan/grant must be for development purposes. Thus, concessionary financing for military expenditures does not count as part of ODA.

Originally, aid was provided largely as grants, but then shifted to low interest loans to give the appearance of being businesslike and not a form of international "welfare". High debt service in poor countries, however, eventually led to the need for the rescheduling and eventual forgiveness of debt repayments. At present there is a general move back to putting aid, particularly to the poorest countries, on a grant basis.

In general, aid flows take roughly five forms:

- Physical Projects: Financing for specific development projects, such as roads, schools, health programs, power supply, etc. For large projects, aid money is often disbursed directly to foreign suppliers under international competitive bidding. For smaller projects, involving local costs, loan money may be converted to local currency and used to hire local contractors, or reimburse government expenditures.
- Technical Assistance: These may be labeled "projects", but generally finance expert advice, often foreign advisors, in order to carry out or implement reforms in various sectors, including agriculture, education, health, infrastructure, etc. Technical assistance flows are often financed by grants, and can also be

part of larger physical projects as described above. The impact of TA projects are often not as easy to identify.

- Program Aid: Program assistance provides quick disburseing foreign exchange in return for agreement on a series of reforms, or in return for making progress on an agreed reform program. These would include the "structural reform loans/credits" of the World Bank, now called "development policy operations".
- Food Aid: Food aid is simliar to program aid, but it arrives in the form of commodities which may either be distributed within the country through government or non-profit orgainzations, or be sold for local currency and the proceeds used to finance an agreed set of development activities. Food aid can also include non-food items such as cotton and tobacco.
- Debt Relief: Debt relief involves the forgiveness of debt service obligations on past loans, and may be also tied to agreed set of reforms or development expenditures. By counting aid as loan, and then counting the debt relief of that loan, donors get to count the same money twice.

## Fungibility

Debate on the utility of various aid forms goes on, with fads coming and going. Initially, most aid was in the form of projects or technical assistance (TA). Physical projects have the attribute of having a physcial presense, so that donors can see clearly what was financed and report back to their constitutuents. Years of project funding however revealed that many projects failed to reach their objectives because of what might be called "the policy environment." What was needed, for instance, was not more schools but reform of the education system. Having a wonderful project which was "ring fenced" from the rest of what was going on in the sector gave a misleading impression of success. To really achieve success, one had to look at the broader issues.

In addiiton, aid is **fungible.** If a donor finances a good project, it can free up resources that the government can use to finance a less productive project. Suppose a government has two projects on its agenda, a hospital and a racetrack. Each costs $2 million, but the government has only $2 million available in its development budget. If a donor provides $2 million for the hospital, then the government can spend its $2 million on the racetrack. The donor is proud of financing the hospital, which it can show off to its constituents at home. However, the reality is that its money, at the margin, financed the racetrack. Fungibility happens when both donor and recipient agree on the relative priorities. It is possible that the number one priority for the recipient is the racetrack, while the top priority for the donor is the hospital, so that not funding the hospital by the donor would still result in the racetrack being built and no hospital. Empirically, studies show that fungibility exists, but it is less than 100%.[126] The general conclusion here is that there needs to be a meeting of the minds between donor and government over what are the priorities overall in the government budget, and to lift one's eyes above these Potemkin-like ring-fenced projects to the broader picture. Clearly, it is not productive to provide good projects to a country which is wasting its own money on racetracks, large defense expenditures, or nuclear processing plants.

Moving from project to program support, however, presents different problems. Govenments may agree to reforms principally to obtain free resources, and not be geninuely committed to reform. They may use the excuse that these reforms were forced on them by the IFIs[127] and abandon them at the first sign of popular discontent. The best examples of these kinds of policy-based loans happened where govenrments already agree on the need for reform, and call in the multilateral organizations to provide advice and technical assistance based on experience in other countries on the details of the modalities. In this case, the question arises: why does the country need to borrow money to carry out these reforms? If the reforms are good, they could be carried out with a small amount of TA money, rather than a large policy based loan. The answer here is unclear, but recipients like to see that they are receiving financial support of the IFIs to show that they have their support for their program. The IFIs, for their part, fund their operations from the interest on loans, and so cannot provide a great deal of free TA without also making a lending operation.

---

126 William Easterly, "Can the West Save Africa?" Journal of Economic Literature 47 (June 2009), pp. 397.

127 IFIs = International Financial Institutions, including World Bank, IMF, and regional development banks, such as the Inter-American Development Bank, Asian Development Bank, and African Development Bank.

However, the large amounts of money involved (sometimes in the hundreds of millions dollars) can serve as a disincentive to carrying out structural reforms. The money from these loans obviates the need for immediate reform, since it (temporarily) solves the problem of a shortfall in the government's budget. Government officials are often trying to strike a bargain of what is the minimum they have to do to get the loan; the IFI staff want to have the strongest program possible to make it seem the program is worth financing. IFIs are criticized for being too harsh in their push for reforms, ignoring for instance, the impact on the poor, or being being too doctrinaire in their requirements. At the same time, they are also criicized for being too lax, not enforcing agreed policy conditions, and not holding up money until reforms are complete. IMF programs, particularly, were supposed to be emergency support combined with structural measures designed to prevent further problems, but in many countries the IMF was involved for 10-20 years with a series of programs, many of which would end in failure, and be followed by new agreements and new promises for reform. Likewise, World Bank structural adjustment lending, or policy based lending, has a very mixed record, and no clear correlation with higher growth.[128] Perhaps structural reforms take time to have an impact, but the record of repeated loans/credits with the same conditions suggests that governments were not serious about reforms, and the Bank was not serious about withholding money until the reforms were accomplished.

## Aid Effectiveness

The basic question is this: does aid work? Does it really help countries develop and raise their growth rates? The problem with this question is that it assumes that the goal of all aid is to promote economic development and growth. As we have seen earlier, there are multiple goals in aid: building alliances, developing exports, dumping agricultural surpluses, humanitarian relief, etc., many of which have little or nothing to do with development and growth.

In the simple classic version, aid was designed to break the "low level equilibrium trap" of low income leading to low savings and low invesment.

---

128 See Easterly, p. 420-429.

In other words, finanical flows, F, supplemented domestic savings, S, so that there would be higher investment I,a larger capital stock, and therefore, given a fixed ICOR (k), and higher output, as in;

$$I = S + F$$

$dY = I/k;$ where dY is the increment to GDP.

In fact, most regressions find only a weak link between capital inflows and growth, or no relation at all. For instance a simple cross country regression of I on F shows the following relationship for a sample of developing countries in 2007[129]:

$$I/GDP = 24.70 + .180\ CURDEF$$

(2.60) adj. $R^2 = .057$ n = 95

This simple regression suggests that for every dollar of increase in the current account deficit, F, investment goes up by only $.18. Edwards' regressions for savings indicates a somewhat higher coefficient—about .56. Clearly, capital inflows are not raising investment on a one-to-one basis. Rather, a good part of capital inflow goes to consumption. However, given the composition of aid, and its purposes this is not surprising. In addition, F excludes official grants, but includes all capital inflows net of repayments, including short term capital and direct foreign investment, so this finding relates to total capital flows, rather than the effectiveness of aid itself.

A direct measure of aid effectiveness is to regress ODA (grants and loans) as a share of GDP to growth of real per capita income. The simple scatter and corrleation is shown below (Fig. 14.2) from an article written in 2005 by Doucouliagos and Paldam[130]. There is no correlation, and the estimated coefficient is not significant. The authors review 97 ariticles in the aid effectiveness literature, most off which come to equally pessimistic conclusions. The authors' review of studies of the effect of aid on savings and investment concluded that about 30% of aid leads to a rise

[129] Author's regression using WDI data bank, developing countries, 2007.

[130] H. Doucouliagos, H. and M. Paldam," The Aid Effectiveness Literature: The Sad Result of 40 Years of Research", *Journal of Economic Surveys* 23 (July 2009), pp. 433-461.

in investment, the remaining 70% to an increase in public consumption. At best, the authors conclude that perhaps 40 years of giving aid has raised the standard of living of the average LDC citizen by 20%, ignoring the fact that the correlation is not significant.

Fig. 14.2: Simple Relationship Between Aid and Growth

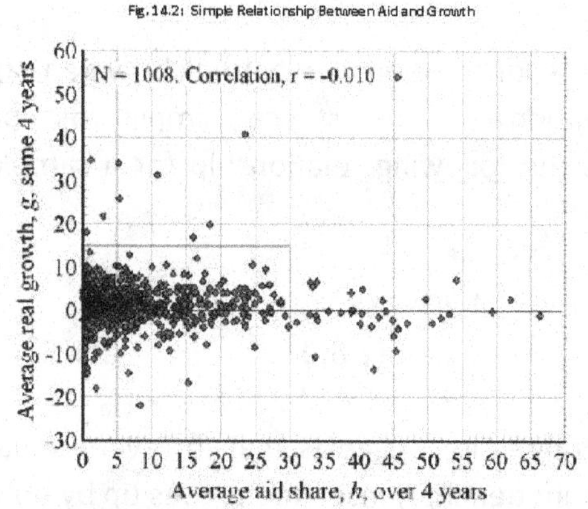


Source: Doucouliagos, H. and M. Paldam," The Aid Effectiveness Literature: The Sad Result of 40 Years of Research", *Journal of Economic Surveys* 23 (July 2009), pp. 433-461. Based on data from World Bank, WDI. Graph compares ODA to GNI over a four year period to the growth of GNI per capita over the same period. Graph copyright by Wiley-Blackwell publishers, used with permission.

The difficulty of finding a relationship between aid and growth is a result, in part, in the nature of aid. Some of it (humanitarian, political) is not really meant to promote growth. Aid goes to countries in trouble; countries doing well receive less aid and move into private capital markets for financing. Hence, lower aid levels can be associated with more rapid growth. However, if donors give support to countries with good prospects for growth (picking winners), and ignore the basket cases, then there could be a positive association between aid and growth that does not reflect a causal relationship. In addition, much of aid is aimed at promoting things which while developmental, are not considered investment: education and medical supplies, training, technical advice, food, maintenance, etc. Finally, much of aid given has a long term impact. For instance, aid that improves education and health today will improve growth (hopefully) over the long term, not just in the year the aid is received. Food aid is unlikely to result in any increase in growth, or investment. Given the nature and multiple objectives of aid, it is no wonder that it is difficult to find a correlation with growth.

Some attempt has been made to categorize aid into different types. A study done at the Center for Global Development[131] divided aid flows into humanitarian, short-term development and long-term development flows. Looking just at the second or "short-term" group, they found significant positive association with growth ($1 of short term aid would raise the present value of income by $1.64). However, these findings were disputed by a following study done by IMF staff, who found that the regressions were not robust, and small changes produced wildly different results.[132]

The most significant "breakthrough" in aid effectiveness research was the work of Burnside and Dollar[133]. Running multiple regressions explaining per capita growth, they also concluded there was no correlation with aid/GDP. However, when they combined the aid variable with a variable measuring good economic management, there was a significant correlation. This work had a significant influence on many donors, including the World Bank, suggesting that aid be focused on countries with good policies. The Bank's study "Assessing Aid: What Works, What Doesn't and Why" gave a big play to these results. Unfortunately, subsequent research by Easterly and others has shown that the results are not robust when the sample size, the number of years, the definition of aid, and number of control variables are changed.[134] Nevertheless, the findings of Burnside and Dollar launched a number of aid intiatives by multilateral and bilateral donors to link aid to "performance", including the US government's Millennium Challenge Account. Here, disbursements

---

131 M. Clemens, S. Radelet and R. Bhavnani, "Counting Chickens When they Hatch: The Short Term Effect of aid on growth", Working Paper No. 44, Center for Global Development Dec. 2, 2004

132 R. G. Rajan and A. Subramanian, "Aid and Growth What Does the Cross Country Evidence Really Show?", IMF Working Paper WP/05/127, June 2005.

133 Craig Burnside and David Dollar, "Aid, Policies and Growth", *American Economic Review* 90 (September, 2000), pp. 847-68. See also World Bank, *Assessing Aid: What Works, What Doesn't and Why* (World Bank: Washington DC, 1998).

134 William Easterly, Ross Levine, and David Roodman, "Aid, Policies and Growth: Comment", *American Economic Review* 94 (June, 2004), pp. 774-780.

of essentially non-project aid are linked to the attainment of a number of agreed targets on economic and social progress.

## Micro vs. Macro Evidence

There is a "micro-macro paradox" in aid: micro studies seem to show many aid interventions are successful, while the macro evidence shows little overall impact. It may be that macro approaches to aid effectiveness are too blunt to find the relationship. We know that IFI projected rates of return on projects are, at their intial stages, quiet high. But we also know that *ex post*, rates of return do not measure up. The famous "Wapenhans Report" (World Bank) [135] on project performance found that only 74% of World Bank projects could be considered successful (i.e. *ex post* rates of return over 10%), and the rate of success in Africa was a disappointing 59%. Many factors influencing project outcomes include an inappropriate policy environment, changes in external factors (weather, world prices), inappropriate project design, and failures by government authorities to carry out the project in the way intended. In fact, one of the big problems with project aid is the assumption that recipient government can and will provide the requisite funding for recurrent costs and maintenance. Poor countries are replete with aid projects (hospitals, schools, roads) which are either not operating because the government cannot afford staff costs, or are deteriorated prematurely due to lack of maintenance. Hence, optimistic rates of return on aid projects *ex ante* are misleading.

Good evaluations point to many cases where aid has been effective, although good evaluation work is often hard to find. Much evaluation by the World Bank and others is antedotal and desriptive, based on a new team reviewing the work of their collegaues. Good evaluations should be based on the comparison of a "treatment" group with a "control" group, where the first group receives some sort of aid intervention, and is compared to a similar group without the intervention. Despite these methodologies being well known, precious little randomized controlled evaluations (RE)are done by donor agencies. As a World Bank handbook

---

[135] *Effective Implementation: Key to Development Impact: Report of the World Bank's Portfolio Task Force*, (The Wapenhans Report), World Bank, Washington DC, October 1992.

states: "Despite the billions of dollars spent on development assistance each year, there is still little known about the actual impact of projects on the poor"[136].

REs are not without their own problems. The world if full of instances where pilot projects on a small scale failed miserably when an attempt to "scale up" to a national level. Pilot projects often are placed in areas where they are bound to succeed, and receive heavy inputs of supervision and management supplied by the donor or an NGO. When scaled up, implementation often falls short because the government lacks the kind of management and supervision skills needed. It is often difficult to define a control group. For instance, within a village, it is impossible, for humanitarian reasons, to give a medical attention to a randomized selection to see if they live longer than those in the non-treatment group. Choosing different villages is one solution, but people can travel from one village to another in order to receive the treatment, thus destroying the purity of the control group. Doing interventions on a regional or state basis (one region receives, one does not), opens up problems of the influence of other factors on the outcome (weather, culture, etc.). Nevetheless, there is a crying need for more and better evaluations of aid projects.

## Private Aid Efforts

On of the biggest changes in aid relationships in the past twenty years (in my opinion), is the growing role of private aid efforts, especially non-profit organizations or non-government organizations (NGOs).[137] In 2007, the total amount of aid from private groups to developing countries was estimated by the OECD to have been $19 billion, and this probably underestimates their contributions since they often use voluntary labor, or pay below market wages (compared to donor aid agencies and IFIs). The

---

136 Judith L. Baker, *Evaluating the Impact of Development Projects on Poverty: A Handbook for Practioners*, World Bank, Washington DC, 2000., p. vi.

137 NGO is a misnomer, since one could say that General Motors is a non-government organization. NGOs are really non-profits: organizations formed for social or economic purposes and not for making profits for the organizers, often using voluntary or semi-voluntary workers (below market wages).

OECD figure may be a gross underestimate. The Hudson Institute estimates flows from private groups at $37 billion[138] just from the U.S. (this includes private foundations, corporations, educational institutions, religious organizations, and private and voluntary organizations). Furthermore, they have been useful in promoting a kind of "people-to-people" relationship between organizations in OECD countries, particularly churches and schools, and partner organizations in LDCs. This has a great education value for taxpayers in these countries, affording them an opportunity become acquainted with developing country issues, at the same time giving them a way of providing assistance directly without paying the overhead of official aid programs.

## Conclusion

Foreign assistance has been helpful to development, but by no means the most critical factor explaining success and failure of efforts to attain high rates of growth. As Lee Hamilton said (see quote above), there are no easy answers, and no magic bullets. Perhaps the biggest contribution of aid agencies like the World Bank, IMF and bilateral agencies is the research and advice they can give on what works, and what does hinders growth and development efforts. This may be much more important that the amounts they lend or give, and the returns on those investments. Ultimately, it is the policies and actions of the government themselves, not the aid donors, that will determine success.

But it is also true that aid professionals and development economists alike have to be humble in terms of what kinds of advice is given, and the effectiveness of proposals. There are few universal prescriptions that will work in all countries and all cultures; each country is unique and facing different constraints, politically, economically and socially. In the last 50 years, has been a great learning experience for development economists, but there is still much more to learn.

[138] As quoted in World Bank, Global Monitoring Report, 2009, p. 123.

## Annex
## Grant Elements
## A Note and Example

A grant of any type is a pure gift. There is no obligation to repay interest or principle. A loan, on the other hand, implies an obligation to pay interest and principle. Loans that are given but with a lower than market, or "concessional", interest rate function as if they were partly a grant. The level of the concessional interest rate and the length of the loan, as well as the grace period between granting and the beginning of repayments, will determine the amount of the gift, or the grant element.

The grant element is calculated by discounting the total repayments, and comparing the net present value (NPV) of the repayments to the original or face value of the loan. If a loan had a 6% interest rate, and we discounted the repayments at 6%, there would be no grant element as the discounting would be offset exactly by the interest payments.

Grant Element = (Loan Amount - NPV Repayments)/ Loan Amount, or

= 1-(NPV repayments/ Loan Amount)

Typically, grant elements are usually calculated using a 10% grant element. Loans with more than 25% grant element are considered "concessional" lending, or development assistance. Here are two examples:

Example A:

Loan amount: $1200 million, interest rate 3%, repayment scheduled over 4 years after a two year grace period. The loan is made on Dec 31 of year 0. Interest and principle are paid at the end of the year, and interest is calculated for every year on the unpaid balance outstanding during of the year.

| Table 14.3. Grant Element Calculation – Example A | | | | | | | |
|---|---|---|---|---|---|---|---|
| Year | 0 | 1 | 2 | 3 | 4 | 5 | 6 |
| Outstanding, beginning of year | | 1200 | 1200 | 1200 | 900 | 600 | 300 |
| Repayment of principle | | 0 | 0 | 300 | 300 | 300 | 300 |
| Interest | | 36 | 36 | 36 | 27 | 18 | 9 |
| Total Repayment | | 36 | 36 | 336 | 327 | 318 | 309 |
| Discount | 1.00 | 1.10 | 1.21 | 1.33 | 1.46 | 1.61 | 1.77 |
| NPV | | 33 | 30 | 253 | 224 | 198 | 175 |
| Sum NPV | 913 | | | | | | |

Grant Element = 1 - (913/1200) = 1 - .76 = .24 or 24%

Example B:

The loan is the same as before, except that it is repaid in a lump sum at the end of year 6.

| Table 14.4 Grant Element Calculation – Example B | | | | | | | |
|---|---|---|---|---|---|---|---|
| Year | 0 | 1 | 2 | 3 | 4 | 5 | 6 |
| Outstanding, beginning of year | | 1200 | 1200 | 1200 | 1200 | 1200 | 1200 |
| Repayment of principle | | 0 | 0 | 0 | 0 | 0 | 1200 |
| Interest | | 36 | 36 | 36 | 36 | 36 | 36 |
| Total Repayment | | 36 | 36 | 36 | 36 | 36 | 1236 |
| Discount | 1.00 | 1.10 | 1.21 | 1.33 | 1.46 | 1.61 | 1.77 |
| NPV | | 33 | 30 | 27 | 25 | 22 | 698 |
| Sum NPV | 835 | | | | | | |

Grant Element = 1 - (835/1200) = 1 - .70 = .30 = 30%

**Note: Example A is not a concessional loan (grant element below 25%) but Example B is concessional**

# AUTHOR INDEX

# SUBJECT INDEX